LANGUAGE SHIFT

Social Determinants of Linguistic Change in Bilingual Austria

This is a volume in

Language, Thought, and Culture: Advances in the Study of Cognition

A complete list of titles in this series appears at the end of this volume.

LANGUAGE SHIFT

Social Determinants of Linguistic Change in Bilingual Austria

SUSAN GAL

Department of Anthropology
Rutgers University
New Brunswick, New Jersey

ACADEMIC PRESS   New York   San Francisco   London

A Subsidiary of Harcourt Brace Jovanovich, Publishers

COPYRIGHT © 1979, BY ACADEMIC PRESS, INC.
ALL RIGHTS RESERVED.
NO PART OF THIS PUBLICATION MAY BE REPRODUCED OR
TRANSMITTED IN ANY FORM OR BY ANY MEANS, ELECTRONIC
OR MECHANICAL, INCLUDING PHOTOCOPY, RECORDING, OR ANY
INFORMATION STORAGE AND RETRIEVAL SYSTEM, WITHOUT
PERMISSION IN WRITING FROM THE PUBLISHER.

ACADEMIC PRESS, INC.
111 Fifth Avenue, New York, New York 10003

United Kingdom Edition published by
ACADEMIC PRESS, INC. (LONDON) LTD.
24/28 Oval Road, London NW1 7DX

Library of Congress Cataloging in Publication Data

Gal, Susan.
  Language shift.

  (Language, thought, and culture)
  Bibliography: p.
  1. Bilingualism--Austria--Oberwart. 2. Language
and languages--Variation. 3. Oberwart, Austria--
Languages. 4. German language--Social aspects.
5. Hungarian language--Social aspects. I. Title. Series
P115.5.02G3   301.2'1   78-23330
ISBN 0-12-273750-4

PRINTED IN THE UNITED STATES OF AMERICA

79 80 81 82 83 84   9 8 7 6 5 4 3 2 1

TO MY MOTHER AND FATHER

Contents

3

Styles of Hungarian and German 65

4

Synchronic Variation in Language Choice 97

5

Social Networks 131

6

The Process of Language Shift 153

Appendix 1

Language Usage Interview 177

Appendix 2

Language Choice, Peasantness, and Social Network 183

Preface

From a linguistic point of view, the most important thing happening in bilingual Oberwart (Felsőőr) today is a change in patterns of language choice. The widespread variation in language use that I encountered when I arrived in 1974, reflected a language shift in progress. An ethnography of speaking in this community could hardly follow the traditional synchronic format: instead, I concentrated on describing the historically situated process of change.

The mechanism of linguistic change has been of central concern in recent sociolinguistic studies of phonology and syntax. I found that language shift closely resembles these other kinds of linguistic change. However, in the case of language shift, it was necessary to consider not only change in the social distribution of old and new variants—styles as well as languages—but also changes in their expressive function. As I got to know bilingual speakers in Oberwart, it became increasingly apparent that changes in their language choices derived from changes in how they wanted to present themselves in interaction. And these changes in turn could be traced to socioeconomic developments that had occurred in Oberwart and in Central Europe during the past several decades. In studying language shift, I was studying the impact of large-scale historical processes on the minute details of intimate verbal interaction and of individuals' linguistic expression of their own identities. The macroscopic and the microscopic levels of analysis dovetailed.

I wish to thank Paul Kay and John J. Gumperz for their advice and encouragement while I was in the field and for their assistance and discussion in the preparation of this book. My thanks are due as well to E. A. Hammel and Susan Ervin-Tripp for their thoughtful criticism.

The year of field research reported here was supported by an N.I.M.H. Anthropology Traineeship, which is gratefully acknowledged. I would also like to acknowledge the aid of Béla C. Maday of the University of Virginia, Dr. Samu Imre of the Linguistic Institute of the Hungarian Academy of Sciences, Dr. Tamás Hofer of the Ethnographic Museum in Budapest, and Prof. Dr. Károly Gaál and Prof. Dr. Peter Wiesinger of the University of Vienna.

For their interest and warm friendship in Oberwart I would like to express my appreciation to Dr. Ladislaus Triber, Mrs. Edit Gyenge, Dr. Imre Gyenge, and, most of all, to the many others, particularly in the Felszeg, who took the time to talk to me. To ensure their privacy, I have not used the Oberwarters' actual names, but I hope that they will recognize, in what I have written, a part of their experience.

William Lockwood, Micaela diLeonardo, Yvonne Lockwood, and Michael Sozan all contributed to this book through numerous discussions and suggestions over several years. My uncle, the late Paul Gal was, through his interest, a source of moral support and, by his example, a source of inspiration.

Above all, my thanks are due to Sam Hamburg, for musical accompaniment.

LANGUAGE SHIFT

Social Determinants of Linguistic Change in Bilingual Austria

1

The Problem

The use of two or more languages within one community is the rule rather than the exception in the world today. While on every continent there are groups that have been bilingual for centuries and are remaining so, there are always others in transition: bilingual towns, villages, or neighborhoods in which the habitual use of one language is being replaced by the habitual use of another. These communities are experiencing language shift (Weinreich 1953:68). Historical accounts make it clear that language shift has occurred repeatedly in all parts of the world and language censuses show that it continues to happen. Over the past 300 years, villages of Breton speakers in France, of Welsh speakers in Great Britain, and of Slovenian speakers in Austria have shifted to using only the national languages of those countries. In the urban centers of Papua New Guinea, tribal languages have been receding for several generations in favor of English and the former trade language, Tok Pisin. African cities have experienced very similar changes. And in many parts of North America the grandchildren of immigrants, although they may retain some competence in their parents' language, use English exclusively. Yet, although language shift is geographically and historically widespread, there have been no ethnographic descriptions of it and, despite a large literature on the subject, the process by which it occurs is not understood.[1]

The town of Oberwart (Felsőőr) in eastern Austria, is one in which, after 400 years of Hungarian–German bilingualism, German is starting to replace Hungarian in business, in the local inn and at home in everyday interaction. My aims are to provide an ethnography of this transformation and to account for the way in which language shift happens by viewing it as an instance of socially motivated linguistic change.

Most writing about language shift, especially in Europe, has focused on its probable social causes and correlates. Scholars guided by an early nineteenth century conception, which equated a people's language with their culture and nationality, naturally found communitywide bilingualism an anomaly and therefore paid attention to it as a problem in its own right. At the same time, European political debates about the proper treatment, status and identity of ethnic minorities have, for at least 200 years, been framed in linguistic terms (Deutsch 1942; Hymes 1968). Therefore, depending on the ideological commitment and nationality of the scholar and the political climate of the time, bilingualism in a community could be taken as indication of a variety of sociopolitical problems. It could provide evidence of the community's mixed ethnic loyalties and thus of a threat to the ideal of an ethnically homogeneous nation state. Alternatively, bilingualism could signal the need for cultural revival and political independence for the endangered linguistic–ethnic minority. In Europe, language shift has been taken as a sign of linguistic and cultural assimilation to a national majority and therefore has specific political implications. At least partly because of this, the most important conceptual distinction has been between stable bilingual communities, which "maintain" both languages, and unstable ones in which shift and therefore assimilation occurs (Fishman 1968). This distinction and the related emphasis on discovering the social causes of shift rightly have special political importance. However, research motivated by these questions has failed to show how language shift happens.

The search for the causes of language shift has been unsuccessful first

---

[1] Some recent historical reports of language shift in Europe include: Timm (1973) on Breton; Wenger (1977) on Welsh; Wall (1969) on Irish (cf. also Hechter 1975:164–207); and Brudner (1972) on Slovenian. Harmaan (1975) provides a useful statistical overview of current multilingualism in Europe and the case of "imperial languages" in Europe replacing indigenous ones is discussed by Brosnahan (1963). In addition, the following will provide some indication of language shift in other parts of the world: language shift in New Guinea is reported by Sankoff (1976); in Africa by Tabournet–Keller (1968), and Cooper and Horvath (1973) among many others; some of the North American immigrant cases have been surveyed most recently by Fishman (1965, 1966) and Lieberson (1970), while Miller (1971) has described one of the many American Indian examples.

because the distinction between stable and unstable bilingual communities is less useful than some conception of the *process* by which stability and shift occur. The distinction itself depends, in many cases, on the duration of observation: Communities undergoing shift continue to use both languages for several generations (Weinreich 1953:68–72) and even formerly stable bilingual communities such as Oberwart, may abandon one language in the course of social change.

Second, although it is possible to list the broad social circumstances in which various cases of language shift have occurred, it has proved considerably harder to isolate a specific set of factors whose presence allows one to predict a language shift. For instance, military conquest, changes of national boundaries, formation of nation–states and nationalist ideologies can all create ethnic–linguistic minorities, which, lacking political and economic power and a nationalist ideology of their own, often experience language shift. The migration of formerly isolated groups to cities or countries where a different language is spoken, and the emergence of a new standard language in former colonies have also been occasions for shift toward the majority, or national, language. However, in similar circumstances shift sometimes does not happen. The correlations observed so far have not led to a systematic understanding of the conditions under which language shift occurs. While generalizations about the macrosociological causes of shift offer industrialization, urbanization, loss of isolation, loss of national self-consciousness, loss of group loyalty, and several others as essential factors, each of these fails to account for large numbers of cases and many are too broadly defined and inclusive to be of value at all. For example, "group loyalty" is not always present when bilingualism is maintained, although it has often continued to exist without language maintenance (Fishman 1964). But, in my view it is not, as some have suggested, a larger or a more complex combination of factors which will yield a satisfactory solution. Instead, the process of language shift should be seen within a broader framework of expressively and symbolically used linguistic variation.

What is of interest to know is not whether industrialization, for instance, is correlated with language shift, but rather: By what intervening processes does industrialization, or any other social change, effect changes in the uses to which speakers put their languages in everyday interactions? How does the social change affect the communicative economy of the group? How does it change the evaluations of languages and the social statuses and meanings associated with them? How does it affect the communicative strategies of speakers so that individuals are motivated to change their choice of language in different contexts of social interaction—to reallocate their linguistic resources radically so that eventually they abandon one of their languages altogether?

An account that answers these questions would start with an ethnography of speaking and take seriously the sociolinguistic notion that, far from being anomolous, bilingual communities are salient instances of a universal phenomenon: the multiplicity and functional distinctness of linguistic varieties in speech communities. It is within such a framework that language shift can be explained as a special instance of linguistic change.

The distinguishing characteristics of sociolinguistic analysis are the focus on linguistic diversity—the several possible ways of expressing what is referentially "the same thing"—and the aim of demonstrating how, if at all, the apparent redundancy serves the social and communicative purposes of speakers. The emphasis on variation and on language as a tool of social interaction stands in contrast to the direction taken by structural linguistics and especially transformational grammar. In an effort to discover cognitive universals, structural linguistics has viewed language as a system removed both from its speakers and from the uses to which speakers put it (Lyons 1971:50). While recognizing the existence of regional and social variants at all levels of grammar, structural linguistics nevertheless considered variation itself to be theoretically uninteresting. Since the goal was to discover the abstract organization of constant features, it was advantageous to emphasize the analysis of a system defined as ideally constant, homogeneous and shared equally by all speakers (Chomsky 1965:3, cf. de Saussure 1959:11–13). The significance and structure of variation, whether in phonology, in syntax, or in communitywide bilingualism was recognized when the notion of language as a disembodied system was supplemented by the study of language as it is used by speakers of differing identities within particular contexts. It is this functional view of language that has helped to clarify the relationship between synchronic and diachronic analysis: The systematic and socially motivated nature of linguistic variation provides part of the solution to the problem of how language change happens.

The hypothesis that linguistic change has its source in synchronic heterogeneity in the speech community (Weinreich, Labov, and Herzog 1968) is now supported by empirical work on phonological change (e.g., Labov 1963, 1965), syntactic change (e.g., Bickerton 1975; Sankoff 1977) and lexical semantic change (Dougherty 1977; Kay 1975). It is clear that, contrary to earlier conceptions, linguistic change is neither so slow nor so fast as to be unobservable. It develops from two sorts of synchronic variation: differences in the speech of one speaker as the social context changes, and differences between speakers when the context remains the same. This latter is closely related to social diversity. New forms that eventually replace older forms can first be located as synchronic variants in the speech of emically demarcated subgroups within the community. Differences between speakers occur in part because linguistic features can assume social significance, symbolizing the statuses and values of the subgroups with which they are associated. They can therefore be used by speakers in impression management. It is the redistribution of such synchronic variants to new linguistic contexts, to different social contexts, and to new sets of speakers that results in linguistic change over time. Further, language change is usually complicated by the fact that new generations of speakers and new immigrants into the community reinterpret the association between social groups and variants and between evaluations and variants. This affects their own strategies of linguistic impression management and, therefore, further influences the course of language change.

Many studies of linguistic variation and change, even when they include the social correlates of variation, have naturally enough focused on the way in which the change is embedded in linguistic structures: the order and nature of linguistic environments to which it spreads; the influence of the change on the rest of the related linguistic system, and on how that system should be conceptualized (e.g., Chen 1972; Carden 1973; Wang 1969). Relatively less emphasis has generally been placed on the social processes responsible for the reallocation of linguistic variants to new speakers and new social contexts. At the same time, ethnographies of speaking, which are primarily concerned with just such rules relating linguistic variants to particular types of speakers and environments, have paid little attention to change. This in spite of early descriptions of language use in monolingual as well as bilingual communities showing that the kinds of variation underlying linguistic change occur at this level of structure as well (e.g., Ferguson 1964). For instance, situational variation in the language use of one person is demonstrated by Rubin (1968) when she shows that, although a Paraguayan speaker in a legal or government setting would choose Spanish, that same speaker at home among family members would use Guaraní. In addition, both Rubin and Albert (1972) describe differences between speakers of different statuses in their patterns of choice within a single context. Albert notes that in Burundi, situations requiring elaborate rhetoric of herders are precisely those in which peasants must use halting "plain speech." However, while variation in language use continues to be reported, (e.g., Irvine 1974; Keenan 1974), recent ethnographies of speaking have remained largely synchronic. As a result, although it is now widely recognized that rules of speaking are subject to change (cf. most recently Bauman and Scherzer 1974:11), very few studies have focused on how and when this happens.

Just as bilingualism is a clear instance of diversity in ways of speaking, so language shift is a salient case of changing patterns of speaking. Hence, change in patterns of speaking can be approached by considering changes in bilingual use. At the same time, a solution to the narrowly conceived problem of how stable bilingual communities come to experience language shift is possible if the question is integrated with what is known about the general process of linguistic change and the symbolic use of linguistic variation. Because in a study of language shift the variants of interest are entire languages in the community's repertoire, the linguistic embedding problem is simplified. But, since explanation of shift requires one to specify the links between social changes and linguistic changes, the issues that emerge as crucial are just the ones neglected by many studies of linguistic change: the social processes by which variants are redistributed across speakers, and the new social meanings these variants convey in conversation as change is occurring.

If diachronic change in language choice arises from synchronic variation—or, put differently, if synchronic variation is viewed as a moment in the process of change—then the social determinants of change must be sought in the social correlates of synchronic diversity. There is no doubt that both intraindividual and interindividual diversity can have social correlates, but how these are to be measured is subject to debate (Gumperz 1972). How their effects on speech are to be conceptualized influences the way in which change is explained.

CONTEXT AND LINGUISTIC VARIATION

No individual speaks the same way at all times. In fact, variation in the speech of a single person can occur at any level of linguistic structure, often involving choices among "referentially equivalent" forms in phonology, syntax and lexical items. But the variation is systematic. Because the choice of a variant in one part of an utterance limits the speaker in choices made later, in other parts, it is possible to divide the speech of even monolingual speakers into varieties: co-occurring sets of alternates. A speaker's choice between varieties, whether these constitute styles, dialects, or languages, is also systematic. It is usually related to some aspect of the social context. This means that the communicative competence which enables people to speak in a socially appropriate and interpretable way includes implicit knowledge not only about the rules that distinguish between grammatical, less grammatical, and ungrammatical utterances, but also knowledge of when to use the varieties in their linguistic repertoire. The cultural knowledge underlying appropriate language use includes, first of all, rules for speaking in explicitly defined speech events such as, for instance, litigation for the Yakan (Frake 1972) or greetings in most social groups. The presence of participants with particular role–relationships assembled for a given purpose in a certain setting, constrains speech and makes one set of linguistic variants more expected and appropriate than any others (Fishman 1971). What the recognized speech events of a community are, when and how one event changes into another, can be determined through ethnography (Hymes 1962, 1972). Typically, the co-presence of a set of situational components defines an event and allows one to predict the participants' choice of linguistic variety. At the same time, the linguistic choices they hear allow knowing participants to discern what event is occurring. In all communities some speech events are highly structured in this way, with linguistic forms closely tied to explicitly defined social contexts. Often these are situations in which ritual or political activities are accomplished (Bloch 1975). However, in no community is all of verbal interaction so rigidly constrained.

In the more flexible, and implicitly structured situations that constitute most of everyday life, intraspeaker variation also occurs, but it is not so directly linked to changes in social context; nor are such changes in context always simple to define. Two approaches to this problem have been proposed. They differ fundamentally in their view of the nature of human communication and are descended from opposing social theoretical traditions. The contrast between them will clarify why only the second of these, and its corresponding method, is useful in the analysis of language shift.

The first view posits the existence of a casual variety of speech which is the most "natural" for a given community, as well as a continuum of formality on which the whole range of variants in the community's repertoire can be ranked. The most natural or casual speech is that used in informal situations, when people are not being recorded by a linguist; when they are involved in the substance of interaction, and are paying least attention to their speech. This "vernacular" speech (Labov 1970) is held to have special significance for linguistic analysis because it is not under conscious control and is therefore the most systematic. Progressively more distant from casual speech are the formal varieties in the production of which more and more attention is paid to speech. The formal varieties are easily accessible to recording because the taped interview is, in western industrial societies, a common formal speech event. But casual speech is elusive and hard to document. The acts of observation and recording set up a formal situation that draws attention to speech, and in which formality must be peeled away to reveal the vernacular.

It is implicit in this view that people normally pay little attention to their speech because of a variety of diversions such as involvement in the content of interaction or in emotional stress. However, in the absence of such diversions people have the chance to attend to their speech and can therefore produce formal, careful varieties. But if, in producing this careful speech, they are again distracted by stress or by involvement in the event, they will relapse, forget to audio-monitor themselves, and once again use casual speech. Therefore, to encourage use of casual speech in an otherwise formal setting, the theory suggests that investigators should create an emotionally absorbing situation, get the speaker involved in content, or set up some other diversion. This, for instance, was one interpretation of what occurred in Labov's classic Lower East Side interviews in which informants produced casual speech when they were asked to tell stories about life-endangering events they had experienced. It has also been suggested that another source of similarly good sociolinguistic data is radio and television interviews at the scene of disasters. In such interviews speakers are too strongly under the influence of the event to monitor their speech (Labov 1970:48). Speech at disasters is comparable to emotional narratives in interviews because the use of the vernacular is linked to loss of control and lack of self-consciousness, which, in this view, can result as much from extreme stress as from normal involvement in casual interaction with intimates.

The rejection of this approach to language use rests on a number of considerations. First, the link between formal speech and monitoring may well be spurious. Although some people monitor to produce what they consider formal or correct speech, others are most self-conscious when trying to be colloquial (Wolfson 1976). Further, the focus on studying casual speech results in the neglect of communicative skills that enable speakers to pick the variety appropriate to the social context, whether or not the context is formal. In the search for the most natural style, speakers' many communicative abilities appear as obstacles to be circumvented rather than as subjects of investigation.

More fundamentally, if the move from formal to informal speech, whether in an interview or in everyday life, is accomplished by diverting speakers' attention away from their speech, then people's choice of linguistic varieties is motivated neither by the impression they want to convey about themselves nor by the interactional and rhetorical effects they want their words to accomplish. In fact, this view of language use, like the tradition in social theory from which it derives, does not address the question of how speakers impute intentionality to each other (Ryan 1973:8) and so neglects the socially patterned expressive and rhetorical uses of language. It assumes instead that one can directly link the form of speech to private states within the individual (Mills 1940:109). A consequence of such an assumption is the confusion of speech that results from overwhelming emotion and consequent lack of control, as at a disaster, with the conventionalized symbolic use of speech variants to artfully convey such intended impressions as personal involvement in narratives or everyday interaction. By conflating these two phenomena, the audio-monitoring view of language use stands in opposition to the tradition emphasizing the symbolic and expressive uses of language (e.g., Burke 1935; Jakobson 1960; Mead 1934) on which the second and contrasting analysis of language use relies.

This alternative view holds that, casual or not, speech that is felt by speakers to be appropriate to a situation must be considered natural in that context. It provides important evidence of speakers' competence to interact in culturally acceptable and meaningful ways. Linguistic variants, in this view, are means available to speakers for encoding various kinds of social information not directly or necessarily related to formality. To understand why varieties gain connotations such as formality, Gumperz (1970) has suggested that in most socially diverse communities speakers distinguish between (a) varieties used with and by people identified by the speaker as his or her in-group, and (b) varieties used with and by out-group members. The varieties usually used in these two ways come to symbolize in-group and out-group values and activities. Further, if the in-group and out-group are themselves perceived to be ranked with respect to each other in power, wealth, and prestige, as is usually the case in stratified societies, the variants associated with the higher-ranked group are identified as prestigious by all groups, while others are stigmatized. It is the forms felt to be prestigious that appear in formal contexts. That is, the connotations of linguistic varieties as formal or informal are derivative of the more basic dichotomy they represent, one that may well be a universal characteristic of social interaction: solidarity versus power (Brown and Gilman 1960).

The association of linguistic varieties with social groups and their activities means that in most activities one variety will be normal, culturally expected and, therefore, unmarked, whereas other varieties will be heard as unusual. Although speakers most often satisfy each others' expectations in linguistic choice, they sometimes do not. Instead they use variants in an unexpected, marked way, in contexts where another variety would be more usual. For instance, monolingual speakers sometimes insert stylistically informal narratives or asides in otherwise formal interviews; bilingual speakers engage in conversational language switching (Gumperz 1976a), using utterances from both of their languages in situations where only one of the languages is normal. Such unexpected or marked choices have also been described for address terms and personal pronouns (Ervin–Tripp 1972; Geoghegan 1971).

Rather than thinking that these unexpected choices are the results of lapses in attention or audio-monitoring, listeners interpret them as indicators of speakers' momentary attitudes, communicative intents and emotions. And, because listeners ordinarily take such linguistic choices to be meaningful, it becomes the investigator's task to analyze how participants derive meaning from each others' marked linguistic choices. When a linguistic variety is used in its usual context, it identifies the situation but remains largely unnoticed. However, when it is used in an unexpected way it is foregrounded. The connotations of the usual context are then juxtaposed to the current context. Re-interpretation of the unusual choice in the light of the on-going interaction then yields a wide variety of contextual meanings derived from the basic dichotomy represented by the linguistic varieties: inclusion (we, in-group) and exclusion (they, out-group) (Gumperz 1970:10). For instance, if the relationship between two prerevolutionary upper-class Russian speakers is defined by them as relatively distant, the use of the polite second person pronoun would be usual and expected in conversations between them. Then, depending on the nature of their relationship and the immediate content of talk, a switch by one speaker from the polite form to the marked familiar pronoun can momentarily change or emphasize a different aspect of their relationship. It can convey new intimacy under certain circumstances and, in other cases, anger, insult, or sudden emotionality (Friedrich 1972).

In the use of linguistic varieties, unexpected choices are rarely met by a lack of understanding; rather, they are open to *mis*understanding (Garfinkel 1967). This is because, with regard to choice of variants just as in other aspects of conversation, listeners use their own knowledge of linguistic norms and exceptions to try to create sensible interpretations in which the combination of the choice, however unusual, within the context, can be understood as an expression of the speaker's intent, attitude, personality, or social background (cf. Sacks 1972; Sudnow 1972). At the same time, from the point of view of speakers, marked choices do not directly depend on such observable contextual features as the setting or participants of the event, but rather on the speakers' use of the linguistic expectations associated with that and other contexts. As a result, although unmarked choices can often be predicted by participants and investigators through knowledge of how the community associates linguistic varieties with groups and activities, the occurence of marked choices cannot be predicted. They can only be interpreted after they occur. To understand the contextual meaning of marked choices as well as the process by which listeners decipher them, one can utilize the interpretive abilities of the participants—both their reactions during the interactions and their judgements on listening to tapes of interactions afterward.

In contrast to the audio-monitoring view of language use, the distinction between the expressive functions of marked and unmarked choices is particularly useful in the study of language shift because it highlights the facts that need to be explained: the change in expectations about which language is normal for which kinds of activities in the community. However, notice that in illustrating this expressive view of language use it was possible to draw on examples as diverse as style choice, pronoun choice and language choice. Indeed, the generality of the formulation is one of its advantages because it allows for a unified analysis of many kinds of variation and their uses. Within this framework, style-shifting and language choice are functionally very similar because the same sort of context or communicative intent that would lead a monolingual to move from a colloquial to a formal style also would induce a bilingual to switch from one language to another (Gumperz 1969:435). However, this equation of style-shifting with language choice obscures differences between monolingual and bilingual communities that cannot be overlooked when the object of study is the process by which one changes into the other.

In bilingual, unlike monolingual communities, speakers can choose not only among the languages available to them but also among styles of each language. Marked and unmarked choices are possible with styles as well as languages. This is because, contrary to the tacit assumption of internal linguistic homogeneity that has guided most studies of bilingualism, the languages themselves are often internally heterogeneous and include styles or dialects demarcated by covariation rules (Gumperz and Wilson 1971; Ma and Herasimchuk 1971). That is, bilingual repertoires, in addition to their own special characteristics, contain some of the features of monolingual ones. For instance, although they have relatively rigid co-occurrence rules separating the languages, they also have more flexible covariation rules, which, just as in monolingual repertoires, distinguish styles within each language. Whereas it is relatively easy for the linguist to separate, for analytical purposes, the languages in a bilingual community, the stylistic differences within each language are more difficult to specify, as they are in monolingual communities. Finally, it is common for natives of bilingual communities to distinguish and label their languages on the basis of salient features and to be able to accurately report at least some of their own usage patterns. In addition, they recognize that the languages provide symbolic representations of subgroups and activities within the community. But there remain stylistic differences that, in bilingual as in monolingual repertoires, are more difficult for speakers to discuss, and, although they too are evaluated and carry social connotations, these tend to be further from awareness (Tucker and Lambert 1969).

The presence of both kinds of variation within one community's repertoire brings into question their functional equivalence. When both style-shifting and language choice are simultaneously available, they are not usually used in the same way. As I will later suggest, they serve complementary functions. Further, during language shift, there is variation *between* speakers within the community both in patterns of language choice and in the distribution of these functions.

VARIATION BETWEEN SPEAKERS

Like other kinds of cultural knowledge, the rules for the use of linguistic varieties are not necessarily shared, even by people who are in close contact with each other in a single village, neighborhood or club (Sankoff 1971; Wallace 1961). Despite the heterogeneity in speech and in language use that characterizes all communities (Gumperz 1968), the idea of a speech community remains useful. Although not always sharing rules for linguistic behavior, and not geographically or socially isolated, speakers can be considered co-members to the extent that, because of frequent and significant interaction together, they are able to communicate with each other in ways not readily understandable to outsiders (Agar 1973:130). Members have the background knowledge necessary to interpret each others' variable behavior. For example, just as the difference in the speech of one person in different situations allows the initiated listener to gain information about the social context and the speaker's attitudes or intentions, so the systematic variation between speakers within the same context provides information about aspects of the speaker's social identity.

There are a variety of ways in which an investigator can relate differences in speakers' linguistic behavior to differences in their social identities. The most common has been to correlate conventional macro-sociological measures such as social class, ethnic background or sex with the occurrence of speech features in controlled contexts (e.g., Cedergren 1973; Labov 1964; Sankoff and Cedergren 1971; Shuy *et al.* 1967; Trudgill 1972). This also can be done for patterns of language choice and can provide a precise description of the distribution of linguistic resources with respect to, say, class and ethnicity, at a particular time. However, it is not clear how the social measures themselves should be defined. What theory of social class for instance should be used, or must class itself be replaced by some other construct (Sankoff and Laberge

1978). More importantly, whatever the social measures, correlations in themselves reveal little about the processes that bring about, maintain, or change these correlations. They do not explain why, in a particular community, one set of social measures correlates well with speech differences while another does not. In short, correlations do not show how changes in macrosociological factors come to affect language choice. To link the two, and to explain language shift, one has to show how factors such as class, education, or sex enter into speakers' cognitive strategies, their linguistic choices during interaction. It is systematic changes in such choices that result in language shift and, over time, in a change in the correlations.

One hypothesis for explaining this link is often implicit in correlational studies. It is based on the understanding that linguistic varieties are evaluated by speakers as prestigious or stigmatized on the basis of the social groups with which they are associated. Further, speech is an important part of a speaker's linguistic presentation of self (Goffman 1959:12, 1967). In a given context people can, to a large extent, sound like those with whom they claim group or social category membership, those with whom they identify. This was the process described in Labov's study of Martha's Vineyard, where individuals who felt able to claim and maintain their status as natives of the island adopted increasingly centalized vowels (1963). But to the extent that Vineyarders abandoned the claim to stay on the island and earn a living there, and failed to feel allegiance to native values, they also stopped centralizing and used standard forms.

When the status claimed by a speaker in using a linguistic form is highly valued, as Vineyarder is in Martha's Vineyard, then the individual is claiming high prestige along with group membership. A more complicated situation emerges when the social category and the markers of membership in it are defined negatively or even stigmatized by those who do not claim membership. The use of many linguistic varieties, for instance, TexMex, Black English, r-less speech in New York, Chamar or Sweeper dialects in parts of India, and local Hungarian in Oberwart, all have the effect of claiming membership in a stigmatized minority. They therefore claim low prestige for the speaker, at least in the eyes of those who do not use these forms, and sometimes even for those who do. Yet, regardless of stigmatization, people continue to use these varieties, at least in in-group contexts. For minority speakers, these varieties symbolize not only group solidarity but also positive values associated with the group, including, for instance, feelings of sincerity, toughness or reliability (Gumperz 1964). In addition, such forms sometimes function to restrict use of group resources and information to those who can validate their claim to group membership by using the low-prestige linguistic form (Brudner 1972). It is this role of linguistic differences, either as emblems of group membership (Barth 1969), or as symbols of group values, that has been emphasized most in studies of interspeaker linguistic variability.

Yet, other evidence indicates that in some communities individuals who clearly belong in different socially significant categories do not present themselves differently in speech. Elsewhere there are important linguistic differences between individuals who, according to most indicators— standard sociological measures as well as local emic ones—should agree in their linguistic presentation of self. These apparent exceptions support the view that a speaker's qualification as a member of a particular social group or category is not itself enough to explain that person's use of a linguistic form symbolic of the group. Instead, each of these exceptions directs attention to the networks of informal social interaction in which speakers are enmeshed and through which, by pressures and inducements, participants impose linguistic norms on each other.

Two studies have isolated the influence of social networks from other influences on language use and thus illustrate the effect of social networks most clearly. In the village of Khalapur, India, a culturally important ritual distinction backed by behavioral prohibitions separates high and middle castes. Yet Gumperz (1958) found no linguistic differences between high and middle castes in the village. In the case of these castes, informal friendship contacts and children's play groups cut across caste lines. Whenever such play groups existed no linguistic differences were found between castes; where friendship contacts remained exclusively within a caste, as in the case of several untouchable groups, linguistic differences did exist. The pattern of speakers' informal contacts exerted greater influence on their speech than the caste to which they belonged.

The far-reaching effect of an interacting group on the speech of its members is best documented in Labov's studies of Black English in New York City's Harlem (1973). Out of hundreds of boys living in the same neighborhood within blocks of each other, all of the same socioeconomic class, age, and ethnic group, those who were isolated individuals ("lames") differed significantly in their speech from those who were regular members of peer-group street gangs. Adolescents and preadolescents who belonged to gangs spoke a different version of Black English than "lames." In explaining this difference Labov noted the vast number of interactions among gang members in which "[T]he group exerts its control over the vernacular in a supervision so close that a single slip may be condemned and remembered for years [p. 83]."

In short, while the conventionally recognized social categories that speech forms symbolize—such as class and ethnicity—are undoubtedly important to speakers in choosing the way they will manage their linguistic presentation of self in a particular situation, the social network of which they are a part can be equally important. There is a correspondence between social network studies and the present analysis of language use: both are concerned with characterizing the process by which macrosociological changes eventuate in changed decisions during the everyday interactions of individuals. The usefulness of network analysis in explaining linguistic diversity stems from the fact that speech is social activity. Norms of language use are, therefore, also partly social. Just as the differences in people's social networks can account for the process by which differences arise in their norms and expectations regarding, for instance, sex roles (Bott 1971), they also can be used to help explain differences in linguistic expectations. And just as the strategic use of resources to reach culturally defined goals is both constrained and made possible by a person's social network (Mitchell 1971), it is likely that the comparable use of language to claim or attain a social status (Frake 1964) can also be influenced by the nature of the speaker's social network.

The effects of certain kinds of network contacts in generating speech differences was recognized by traditional dialectology in studies of the effects of trade routes on the spread of linguistic innovations. Studies of speech differences since then have implicitly relied on what has recently been called a person-centered definition of network (Barnes 1974): all of the social contacts an individual has with others in face-to-face interaction. For instance, Bloomfield (1933:46–47) argued for the importance of frequency of contact in determining speech similarities by suggesting that the more interactions there are between two people, the more similar their speech would be. However, it has become clear that the nature of the relationship between speakers, the social identity of the contacts and the purpose of the interaction are at least as important as frequency of contact in influencing speech. Some kinds of contacts do not result in linguistic similarities, although they might be quite frequent, whereas others, for instance the informal peer-group interaction in the Khalapur and Harlem studies, appear to have a primary role in shaping patterns of language behavior in many communities (cf. also Wolfram 1972).

Social networks do not influence language use directly, but rather by shaping people's goals and their means of action. Particularly relevant here are the effects of networks on the social categories with which speakers aim to identify themselves. Social networks influence people's communicative strategies when such identification is expressed through speech. In turn, the power of social networks to constrain linguistic presentation of self depends on the fact that social contacts associate certain linguistic choices with particular social categories. Hence, when the differences between the social networks of two speakers exert differential constraints and inducements regarding self-identification, differences between those speakers in language use can be brought about and maintained.

The relationship between social networks, identity and communicative strategies was illustrated by Blom and Gumperz (1972) in their study of language use in a Norwegian village. They compared the use of dialect and standard varieties between two sets of speakers by tape recording informal discussions in each of two naturally occurring groups of friends. The two discussion groups provided a contrast in types of social networks. In the first group, the social relations of all the participants were limited to contacts with other locals. The participants in the second discussion group also identified themselves as locals, but the content of their networks was quite different. Since they were college students home for the summer, they had important social relationships outside, as well as within the village. Participants in both sessions were competent in standard and in local dialect and they agreed that only the dialect was appropriate for local informal discussions, such as those being taped. The dialect symbolized their unanimously felt solidarity and pride in local identity; the standard represented the outside world and national culture. The speakers whose social contacts were limited to locals did indeed limit their choice to the dialect, in accordance with stated ideals. But those who also had significant nonlocal contacts engaged in unexpected, marked choices as well by using utterances with standard features during the informal discussions. They did this when allusion to their extralocal ties with the intellectual world and to their status as students could be used to add credibility and emphasis to their statements. Because social statuses and values were culturally associated with the linguistic varieties, speakers were able to accomplish rhetorical effects by alluding to their social status through their linguistic choices. Not all speakers could use the standard in this way; speakers' social networks affected the range of values and statuses they could symbolize in speech, and so differences between speakers in social networks were reflected in differences of language use.

To understand the social aspects of synchronic linguistic heterogeneity, it is necessary to describe the social processes that maintain it. Two such processes, working together, have been suggested here: linguistic presentation of self and the constraints placed on it by speakers' social networks. The effect of these processes is particularly clear in the case of Oberwart's language shift. The social changes that have occurred in Oberwart in the last century and that coincide with the occurrence of language shift include the growth and diversification of the city as well as a recent period of unprecedented prosperity and economic expansion in Austria. Both have drawn Oberwart's young people away from traditional peasant agriculture and into industrial work. However, the effect of these changes on strategies for language use in particular situations was felt only indirectly, when they caused a change in Oberwarters' evaluations of their languages and in the processes maintaining older patterns of language choice. Specifically, language shift began when German gained prestige because choice of it, as opposed to Hungarian, came to symbolize the speaker's claim to worker rather than peasant status. Speakers started to present themselves as workers and not peasants in everyday conversations as their social networks changed, weakening previous constraints to claim only peasant identity in speech. In sum, it is through their effects on the shape of social networks, on the statuses speakers want to claim, and on the cultural association between linguistic varieties and social groups that macrosociological factors can influence the language choices of speakers in everyday interactions.

LANGUAGE SHIFT AS LINGUISTIC CHANGE

Given these social determinants of language shift, the process of shift, once it starts, is very much the same as other kinds of linguistic change. It consists of the socially motivated redistribution of synchronic variants to different speakers and different social environments. In Oberwart 20 years ago there were young-adult speakers who, during informal exchanges with acquaintances of their own age, used only Hungarian, while other Oberwarters of the same generation used only German under the same circumstances. In recent years, all young adults have begun to use only German in such situations. Hungarian is similarly not used by the present generation of young adults in many other social contexts where, for previous generations, it was appropriate and common. Since historical records reveal that the present pattern used by older speakers is in fact an older pattern, it is possible to reconstruct the process of change in patterns of language choice by taking age-correlated differences in synchronic patterns as a surrogate for repeated sampling in real time. The resulting reconstruction of change shows that the two languages of Oberwart have been reallocated, Hungarian to a narrower and German to a wider range of speakers and of social environments. Moreover, the use of German has spread through the community in a systematic way that closely resembles the spread of other kinds of linguistic change. It has proceeded simultaneously along two dimensions of variation. Change has come about not only because German is used by categories of speakers who have never used it before, but also because it is now used in social situations for which it was previously inappropriate.

In addition, perhaps the most important aspect of language shift, one it shares with other kinds of linguistic change, is that as innovations spread, the new form is never immediately categorical on either dimension of variation. Rather, alternation between the old and the new form—in the case of Oberwart between Hungarian and German—is characteristic of change in progress. No generation of speakers switched categorically from Hungarian to German in all situations, although each generation since 1900 has used German in more and more situations. Similarly, in no situation is categorical use of German appropriate for a particular generation, unless previous generations have used both German and Hungarian in that social context. In language shift, as in linguistic change generally, the new form first occurs variably for each new set of speakers in each new situation in which it is used (Bailey 1970:178, 1974). The fact that alternation of new and old variants is a characteristic of language change has implications for the way the structure of change is to be described for an entire sample of speakers, as well as for the way in which variation and change are related to the communicative strategies of the individuals involved in change. From the point of view of interacting speakers, the alternation between old and new variants in a single context can carry social meaning and can provide a way for them to express communicative intents. For the linguist trying to characterize the language behavior of a community, such variation provides a problem in linguistic description. It is this latter aspect of change that has received most attention. The issue is whether the variability apparent during language change is best represented by implicational scales or with variable rules.

Variable rules, although they resemble the notation of generative grammar, were first developed to display the quantitative results of speech community studies (Labov 1969). They specify the differential effect of linguistic and social environments in determining the frequency of some linguistic variants at the expense of others within a sample of speakers. Because they deal with frequencies, variable rules can indicate not just that two forms are in alternation, but also which form is used relatively more by whom and in which environments. However, in both well-known versions of variable rules (Cedergren and Sankoff 1974), no interaction is allowed between the social and linguistic constraints operating within a rule. Yet, in all the studies of linguistic change reported to date, systematic interaction between linguistic and social constraints is a characteristic of the process, so that change simultaneously involves both new linguistic environments and new sets of speakers. Consequently, variable rules as currently formulated appear to be unsuitable for the description of linguistic change (Kay 1978).

In contrast, implicational scales graphically suggest waves of change and can show the interaction of linguistic and social constraints. Typically in scale analysis the "lects" that particular speakers exemplify are ordered along some social dimension and the linguistic environments are also ordered. Consequently, when arrayed as functions of each other, the linguistic variants produced by each speaker in each linguistic environment form an implicational or Guttman scale. Bickerton's (1973) analysis of the alternation between two forms of a complementizer in the Guyanese creole continuum provides a good example. He showed that over the course of about 100 years the new variant, which at first occurred only in a limited linguistic environment and in the speech of a few high-status speakers, was successively generalized to more linguistic environments, being initially variable in each new environment, while spreading to speakers of lower and lower socioeconomic status. In Oberwart's language shift there is a similar interaction of two dimensions of variation, but the use of the new form spreads to new *social*—not linguistic—contexts as it spreads to new sets of speakers.

Implicational scales have been criticized as tools of linguistic analysis, because they can only be applied when political, geographic and social factors affect language in such a way that "all changes, innovations etc. emanate from one end of [a] linear configuration (Sankoff 1974:42)." However, it is also true that, as in the case of language use in Oberwart, the existence of implicational relations between environments and speakers provides good reason to look for unidirectional social factors to account for the pattern. And, in defense of implicational analysis, it has been noted that scales, in contrast to variable rules, allow for the matching of a linguistic continuum to a sociological continuum. Hence, one need not divide informants into groups if there is little ethnographic or historical reason to sharply segment continously varying social differences (Fasold 1970). This consideration is important in analyzing language shift in Oberwart because the social distinction most relevant to the linguistic change is that between peasants and workers. Although Oberwarters think of these as contrasting statuses, most speakers are actually some combination of the two. Not only does people's commitment to peasant agriculture vary continuously, but differences in degree of involvement in peasant life provide a more sensitive indication of differences in language choice than the dichotomous categories "worker" and "peasant." As a result, implicational scales provide the more useful model of language shift in Oberwart.

However, the choice of implicational scales for representing change in language choice leaves unsolved the problem of how alternation between old and new forms affects the communicative strategies of the speakers involved in change. In Oberwart, as the use of German expands in the community, speakers alternate between Hungarian and German in just those situations in which categorical use of Hungarian has been abandoned but has not yet been replaced by categorical use of German. The communicative function of this variable language choice contrasts with the uses of categorical language choice. In addition, since the varieties in Oberwart's linguistic repertoire include not only the two languages but also styles in each language, these changes in the functions of the two languages eventually involve the social uses of styles as well. In the course of language shift, as previously categorical language choices become variable, there is a reshuffling of the styles and languages used for particular communicative purposes.

The expressive uses to which linguistic varieties are put can be divided into two categories. The expression of a particular social status is separate from all other functions. The invariable choice of languages is utilized for this purpose. In Oberwart, when language choice is invariable, choice of style, both marked and unmarked, is used for all other purposes: conveying attitudes such as intimacy toward the other participants and communicative intentions such as to insult, to express anger or authority. This particular division of labor among linguistic forms has also been reported in the study of phonological change, where one set of variants, when they were categorically used, served to express the status of speakers as group members, while a different set of variants was used to convey other social, rhetorical meanings (Labov 1965).

In Oberwart the segregation in functions holds for those who still use the oldest pattern of language choice, those who invariably choose Hungarian and thereby identify themselves as peasants. It holds as well for many in the youngest generation, those for whom the language shift is almost complete. They have become industrial workers and signify their status by invariably choosing German in most situations. In both cases, whereas invariable choice of language asserts the speaker's identity in relation to the peasant–worker distinction, marked and unmarked choices of styles within each language are used to express rhetorical meanings and intentions. The two types of variation have complementary functions.

During the course of linguistic change—in language shift as in sound change—this separation in functions breaks down and linguistic variants, which formerly were used categorically, become variable and are used to convey both status distinctions and expressive functions. It is at this point that language choice serves the same functions as style-shifting. Invariable language choice becomes variable for a part of the middle generation of speakers in Oberwart. They are the people who are also socially in the middle, committed neither to the peasant nor to the worker way of life. They can, in many situations, choose between their two languages in a marked, unexpected way. In short, they engage in conversational language switching. By juxtaposing the two languages in a single exchange, they contrast the social categories and values—peasant and worker—that the languages represent and create a range of contextually interpretable rhetorical meanings based on the status distinction that is most salient in their lives. By thus alluding to the contrast in social statuses, this generation uses language choice as a symbol for many sorts of interactional contrasts. The unexpected switch from Hungarian to German in an exchange of advice, for instance, can be interpreted as the difference between friendly suggestion (Hungarian) and expert counsel (German).

Conversational language switching, to be intelligible, requires listeners to use their background knowledge about the connotations of linguistic varieties and the contrasts in values and statuses current in the community. It thereby ties the particular conversation to the larger historical context of social change in which the interaction is taking place. Significantly, such rapid switching between languages is not practiced by all speakers in Oberwart, nor does it occur in all bilingual communities. Rather, it is characteristic of communities undergoing language shift (Gumperz 1976b) and of that subset of speakers that, at any particular time, is in the midst of the social change that the contrast in languages symbolizes.

Although historically limited in occurrence, conversational language switching is of particular interest because it underlines the fact that in linguistic change the movement from invariable use of the old form to alternation between old and new forms occurs when variants take on social meanings that speakers can manipulate in interation. In this way the structure of linguistic variation is tied to the functions for which speakers use it and these uses in turn provide the fuel for linguistic change. In the case of Oberwart, while large-scale social changes lead to changes in the statuses and networks of speakers and in the association of languages with social identities, language shift occurs only when new generations of speakers use the new connotations of the linguistic variants available to them in order to convey their changing identities and intentions in everyday linguistic interaction.

2

From Felsőőr to Oberwart

Felsőőr means "upper sentry." It is the original Hungarian name of an ancient village settlement that has become a small commercial city within the last century. The name accurately describes the location of the village up near the source of the Pinka River and the military assignment of the early settlers, who were sent to guard Hungary's western frontier. Oberwart, the word for word German translation of this, is now the town's official name and many of the inhabitants now use German rather than Hungarian not only for naming their city but for many other linguistic functions as well. The change in language use is related to the newly urban character of the town. In fact, I will argue that social diversity and class stratification, which make Oberwart today seem like a city despite its small size, have created the conditions encouraging language shift within the bilingual neighborhood.

It is best to start by locating the Hungarian–German bilingual community both socially and geographically within present-day Oberwart and by tracing the historical processes that have created social diversity. Some of these developments have had a direct bearing on language use—for instance, Oberwart has been surrounded by German-speaking villages for at least 400 years. Other aspects of the history, though less directly related to language, prove equally important. Some changes have influenced the social position of Oberwarters with respect to their neighbors

23

and, hence, the relative prestige of the languages spoken by each. Other changes, such as the introduction of sources of livelihood other than local agriculture, have affected the economic usefulness of each language. In short, an account of Oberwart's social history will explain the motivating forces of change in language use.

OBERWART'S SOCIAL DIVERSITY

There are two kinds of Hungarian speakers in Austria. Those who emigrated from Hungary during or after each of the world wars of this century and after the 1956 Hungarian uprising were urban Hungarians who have settled in Vienna, Linz, and other Austrian cities. Oberwart's Hungarian speakers do not belong with these relatively recent arrivals. Rather, they are among the indigenous inhabitants of five agricultural villages in the middle of Austria's easternmost province, Burgenland (see Map 1). These five villages, first settled a thousand years ago, have remained stationary while the boundaries of empires and states have fluctuated around them. The changes of the past 70 years have been particularly dramatic. Starting the century as subjects of the King of Hungary they became citizens of Austria, then of the German Third Reich and now Austria again. The villages are arranged in two clusters, three to the south, two to the north. Oberwart is the largest of the southern communities.

In contrast to the other, smaller and more homogeneous Hungarian villages, people in Oberwart distinguish among themselves according to ethnic origin, language and religion. In addition to the Hungarian–German bilinguals, there has been a German mother-tongued ethnic group, as well as a Gypsy settlement for over a century. Partially crosscutting these distinctions are the Catholic, Lutheran, and Calvinist churches.

Only during this century have the Hungarian speakers of Oberwart become the minority. In 1920, Hungarian was spoken by three-fourths of the Oberwart population. By 1971, the town had grown substantially and only one-fourth, or less than 2000 of the inhabitants, could speak Hungarian (Table 2.1). All the Hungarian speakers are bilingual in German and all are peasant agriculturalists or the children of peasants. However, although most are Calvinists (the Reformed Church of Hungary), several hundred are Roman Catholics. The traditional antagonism between bilingual Catholics and Calvinists in Oberwart is most clearly represented by their separate neighborhoods. Because of the social and geographical distance, during the year I spent in Oberwart I could not be in both places at once. I chose to spend most of my time observing and participating in the Calvinist neighborhood for several reasons. The larger size of the

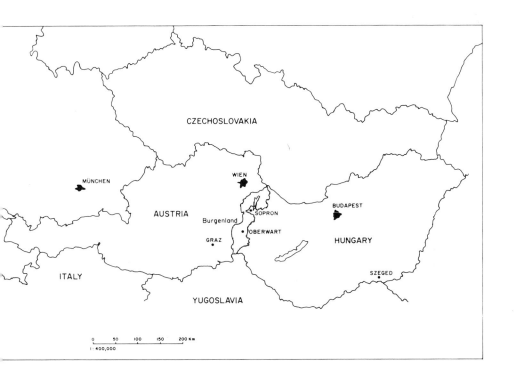

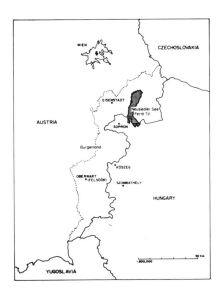

25

TABLE 2.1[a]

Mother Tongues in Oberwart

Year	Hungarian	German	Mixed	Croatian or other	Total[b]
1880[c]	2701	999			3700
1910[d]	3039	1148			4187
1920[d]	3138	965			4103
1934[e]	2176	2008			4833
1939[d]	1482				
1951[f]	1603	2854	577		4713
1961[f]	1206	3011	424	99	4740
1964[g]	1934	2726			
1971[b]	1486	4175			5661

[a] All of these figures have to be considered approximate at best, because the question of mother tongue in censuses has been taken to mean national loyalty and there were often political considerations involved in identifying oneself. Further, until 1951 "mixed" was not one of the census categories and even after 1951 the wording of the Austrian national census questionnaire was confusing as to whether the question concerned first language, language used in the home, or language used by the majority of the town's inhabitants.

[b] The total population figures come from different sources than the mother tongue figures and they do not always add up. The totals are from *Bundesamt für Stastistik, Statistisches Handbuch für die Republic Österreich*, Vienna, 1928, 1937 and from *Österreichisches Statistisches Zentralamt, Statistisches Zentralamt Volkszählungs Ergebnisse, 1951, 1961, 1971*. The totals are provided here simply to give a general idea of the proportions represented by the mother-tongue numbers.

[c] From Wallner 1926:26.

[d] From Nagy 1937:50–51.

[e] From Gyenge 1973:42.

[f] *Die Zusammensetzung des Wohnbevölkerung Österreichs nach allgemeinen demographischen und kulturellen Merkmalen, 1951, 1961*. Vienna: Österreichisches Statistisches Zentralamt, 1964.

[g] *Statistisches Jahrbuch österreichischer Städte 1971*. Vienna: Österreichisches Statistisches Zentralmt, 1972.

community and the completeness and accessibility of the church records contributed to my decision. But perhaps equally important was the fact that my first and most helpful acquaintances in Oberwart were Calvinist bilinguals who encouraged me to get to know them, their families, and their neighbors.

The number of Calvinists in Oberwart has stayed remarkably stable since the early nineteenth century. It has been mostly immigration of German mother-tongued Lutherans and Catholics from neighboring villages that has caused the steady increase in Oberwart's population in the past 100 years. The newer settlers have been attracted by work opportunities: Oberwart is the administrative center of the county, has a weekly regional market, and a large shopping district. In addition, the only hospital, the secondary school, and the trade schools of the county are located here. It is primarily this steady immigration that is responsible for Oberwart's transformation from a peasant agricultural village similar to its smaller neighbors to an economically stratified, and ethnically diverse, town.

The physical appearance of Oberwart's several neighborhoods is the most striking evidence of its social diversity. The town is about 100 km south of Vienna in the hilly transition zone between Alpine Europe and the Carpathian Basin. It was built along the Pinka river, on the main north–south route of Burgenland. A portion of this main road is the center of town, called *Fötér* in Hungarian and *Hauptplatz* in German (see Map 2). Here one finds the branch offices of three national banks, two department stores, and two supermarkets. There are also several fashionable clothing and shoe stores. Each of the numerous shops offers its own specialty, including electrical appliances, hardware, sporting goods, furniture, and decorative porcelain. The town's sports-car dealership is next to a store which sells nothing but wallpaper. Two stationery stores regularly carry the Austrian and German papers as well as French, Italian, and American news and fashion magazines. On the same street there are also hotels and restaurants, a travel agency, a movie house, and five Viennese-style cafes. Just a block away from this central area are the new, poured-concrete Catholic church, a municipal swimming pool and a sauna. The three large apartment buildings of the main street, built within the last 10 years, house doctors' and lawyers' offices, as well as apartments.

This list of stores and services is perhaps the most direct way of demonstrating the busy, urban and commercial atmosphere in the central section of town. At the same time it also suggests that there is a demand in Oberwart for a wide range of consumer goods and for such sophisticated diversions as foreign travel, sauna, and the international press. The modern apartment buildings house part of the local population that supports these services. For those with more money, a neighborhood of private houses has sprung up in the past 20 years on the eastern hills of the river valley, overlooking the main street. The doctors, the teachers, the lawyers, and some of the civil-service workers live here, and they are the people who use the pools, the sauna, and the travel agency, who frequent the cafes, and who buy the sporting equipment. They are overwhelmingly German monolinguals and newcomers to Oberwart. Their houses are all large, usually with two floors, two baths, basements, and central heating. At least one family has its own private swimming pool. The people living

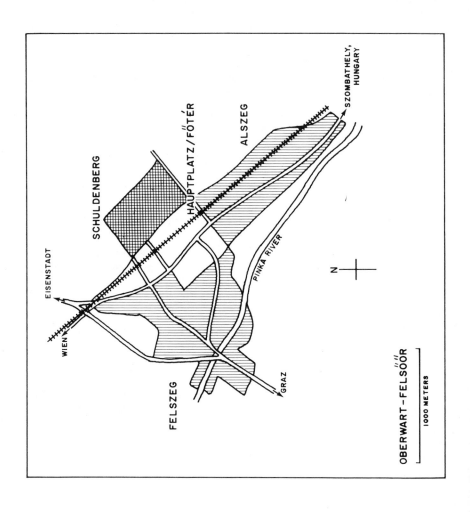

OBERWART–FELSŐÖR

1000 METERS

SCHULDENBERG

HAUPTPLATZ / FŐTÉR

ALSZEG

FELSZEG

EISENSTADT

WIEN

GRAZ

PINKA RIVER

SZOMBATHELY, HUNGARY

N

28

in the flatlands of Oberwart ironically call this section of town the *Schuldenberg* (*Schulden* 'debts'; *Berg* 'hill'). The joke is that ordinary people would have to go into debt to live on that hill. The *Schuldenberg* is the only section of town that has no Hungarian name corresponding to, and predating, its German name.

In contrast to the modern, centrally located *Hauptplatz* and *Schuldenberg* are the two old flat ends of town, the *Felszeg* to the north (in German *Obertrum* 'upper end') and the *Alszeg* (in German *Untertrum* 'lower end') to the south. Each is a peasant village in itself. The *Felszeg,* for instance, has two inns, a blacksmith, and several small grocery stores. The people of the *Alszeg* and the *Felszeg* use the main street only for buying clothes and some major household appliances. Some *Felszeg* people have never stepped inside a cafe; certainly not the municipal pool. And it is a rare *Felszegi* who is not a bit nervous in the main street's expensive clothing stores.

Both the *Felszeg* and the *Alszeg* are widely known as the Hungarian sections of town. The *Felszeg* is mainly Calvinist, the *Alszeg* mainly Catholic. Although the *Felszeg*, with about 1500 inhabitants is much larger, there is nevertheless a feeling that the two are matched opponents. This kind of division into neighborhoods is typical of Hungarian villages and even when there are no religious differences there is often antagonism and competition between opposing sections (cf. Fél and Hofer 1969:365). In Oberwart, there is widespread agreement on the geographical boundaries of each neighborhood. Being a native of one or the other is an important part of a person's identity and, until recently, it restricted choice of marriage partner because the neighborhoods were largely endogamous. In addition, each section imputes habits, beliefs, and personality characteristics (generally negative) to the other. Traditionally *Alszeg* people considered those of the *Felszeg* 'wild folks' (***vad nípek***).[1] They were said to be quick tempered, prone to fighting, tough, and stubborn: ***vastag nyaku kálvonisták*** 'thick necked Calvinists'. The *Felszeg* people on the other hand called those in the *Alszeg* 'papists' (***pápista níp***) and ridiculed their supposedly blind obedience to church rules and especially the dictates of the local priests. The social opposition was most clearly played out by the young men of the town. Until World War II, bachelor gangs and school boys from the two neighborhoods fought each other regularly, especially at the weekly dances, when a young man from one section asked a young woman from the other to dance.

In the *Felszeg*, where I spent most of my time, the streets are narrow

---

[1] German and Hungarian words in conventional orthography appear in italics; those written in phonetic or dialect atlas orthography, in order to indicate their local pronunciation, are in italic boldface.

A peasant yard in full operation.

compared to the *Hauptplatz* and *Schuldenberg*. Some are wide enough only for a wheelbarrow and several are unpaved. The typical house resembles the traditional houses of peasants all over western Hungary (Tóth 1971). It is a whitewashed stucco structure, one story high, built in a provincial neoclassical style. Although all of these houses now have electricity, very few have bathrooms or toilets. Each consists of a kitchen and one or two rooms. The narrow edge faces the street and on the longer side of the house a row of columns connected by arches encloses the doorway and porch. Between 1830 and 1930 so much of the *Felszeg* was built in this style that whole sections of streets appear identical to the outsider. But subtle distinctions were appreciated by the original owners: the more columns and arches on the house, the richer the peasant family that built it. The majority with three or four could hardly measure up to the ones with six columns, or to the house with eight built by the congregation as the Calvinist minister's home.

Today it is not the number of columns but the condition of the yard surrounding the house that reveals social distinctions. The crucial difference is no longer between wealthier and poorer peasants but between peasants and wage-workers. A peasant family's yard is littered with farm implements and the manure heap takes central place. Cows and pigs are housed in a building contiguous with the kitchen and rooms. In the yards of workers' families, vegetable and flower gardens replace the implements and the manure. If workers' families own chickens and pigs they are restricted to a narrow back section, well out of sight and smell. In addition, the prestigious newly built houses in the *Felszeg* all belong to worker families. Most have modern plumbing, but central heating is rare. Without exception the new houses in the *Felszeg* have been hand-built by the owners themselves, without official building permits, but with the aid of kin and neighbors who are building craftsmen.

The *Schuldenberg* and *Felszeg* differ not only in the appearance of the streets but also in the appearance and public interaction of the people. The streets of the *Schuldenberg* are invariably quiet, with little activity. Neighbors talk only if they happen to be leaving their houses at the same time. One woman who has lived on the *Schuldenberg* for 10 years said that she had never met her three closest neighbors. *Felszeg* people, on the other hand, often stand on the street and talk. On spring evenings when the weather and the work pace allow, one can often see groups of peasant women, heads covered with kerchiefs, and peasant men with dark blue aprons gathering around benches in front of the houses.

But the social homogeneity within the *Felszeg* and the central sections of town should not be overdrawn. First, it is not hard to find some German monolinguals, Catholics, and Lutherans living in the *Felszeg,* as well as a few bilingual families in the center of town. Second, even among the

Calvinists of the *Felszeg* only about one-fifth are engaged in full-time agriculture (*Österreichisches Statistisches Zentralamt* 1972b; Somogyi 1966:40). Because the rest, and especially the young, are workers of one kind or another, they rarely gather in the street, preferring instead to ride in their cars. The year I was there many were keeping pace with Viennese fashion, young men sporting sideburns and bell-bottom pants, young women in miniskirts and platform shoes.

However, despite such differences within the neighborhoods, the physical contrasts between them are far more striking and reflect a greater social distance. It is first of all a matter of social class. On the whole, the people of the *Hauptplatz* and the *Schuldenberg* are professionals, bureaucrats, and intellectuals. They are richer and more educated than the peasants and workers of the *Felszeg* and *Alszeg*. Second, there is a break in networks of social relations and communication. It is harder to find kin and friendship links between the *Felszeg* and *Schuldenberg* than within them. Though people in the *Felszeg* and *Alszeg* often know the names, occupations, and reputations of the professionals on the hill, some of the adolescents growing up on the *Schuldenberg* have never been in the *Felszeg,* know little about it, and have no acquaintances there. This last is not surprising in view of the educational segregation, common all over Europe, which is in force from the earliest grades. Most of the children from the *Schuldenberg* and *Hauptplatz* go to a demanding academically oriented school (*Gymnasium*) which prepares them for the university; the bilingual children in the *Felszeg* usually attend trade schools or the mandatory high school.

Because of Oberwart's particular history, the linguistic distinction between Hungarian and German speakers and the geographical distinction between the *Felszeg* and the center of town have been correlated with each other and with an economic and cultural distinction. The correlation is far from perfect, and yet, knowledge of local Hungarian dialect nevertheless suggests a peasant background, relative poverty, lack of sophistication, and an address in the *Felszeg* or *Alszeg*. It is the rest of Oberwart that is considered rich, educated and, in comparison, prestigious. Professionals, bureaucrats and intellectuals tend to be monolingual in German and to live in the middle of town. A trivial yet telling indication of these distinctions and the value placed on them by Oberwarters in all neighborhoods, is provided by official street names.

Until about 5 years ago, the streets of Oberwart had no official names; they had only folk designations. When names were finally given, three basic principles were followed: all names were to be in German; those streets that already had folk names based on obvious landmarks would retain the name, translated to German when necessary; and, following the countrywide custom, the main thoroughfares would be named after the

A house on the *Schuldenberg*, and one in the *Felszeg*.

largest city to which they lead. In accordance with this, *Pinkaszer* became *Pinkagasse* 'Pinka Street' because it runs parallel to the Pinka river, and the north–south main street leading to Vienna became *Wienerstrasse*. But this left a set of new streets in the *Felszeg* and most of the streets of the *Schuldenberg* with no names at all, and so the municipal authorities had to create some. The *Felszeg* streets became: *Sensengasse* 'Scythe Street', *Pfluggasse* 'Plow Street', *Strohgasse* 'Straw Street', *Getreidgasse* 'Corn Street' and *Eggengasse* 'Harrow Street'. The streets of the *Schuldenberg* became *Mozartgasse, Beethovengasse, Schubertgasse, Brahmsgasse* and *Prinz Eugenstrasse*—the last an Austrian national hero, and all five the stars of Austro-Germanic high culture.

EARLY HISTORY: THE GUARDING SETTLEMENTS

Before the nineteenth century, three developments had major effects on Oberwarters and indirectly on their language use. Each of these changed the terms in which they have since viewed themselves and outsiders. Oberwarters gained nobility status, the village became a speech island, and was divided internally by the Reformation.

Nobility was gained very early, in the eleventh century. The Hungarian-speaking villages of southern Burgenland were established by mandate of the first Hungarian kings to guard the one border of their recently conquered Carpathian Basin which did not have a natural boundary. Defense consisted of maintaining a broad uninhabited strip of land, called a *gyepű*, in which rivers were flooded creating an impassable marshy waste. The edges of this marsh were patrolled on horseback with bow and arrow (Tagányi 1913; Burghardt 1962: 108). It was in return for this service that the communities guarding the boundary were granted some noble privileges. They retained this distinction even though by the 1200s the military strategy itself had become ineffective and was replaced by a new defense system: a string of stone fortresses closing off each river valley.

There has been some controversy among Hungarian and Austrian scholars about this account of Oberwart's early history and about the linguistic evidence of place names and field names on which all accounts are based. Ethnic and linguistic origins, precedence of settlement, and historical information generally constitute the idiom through which political claims to territory are usually expressed in East-Central Europe. The scholarly controversies concerning the history of this region reflect, in part, the fact that in the twentieth century Burgenland has been a strongly contested territory (cf. Moór 1936 and Kniezsa 1938:398, for an early and linguistic phase of the debate, and Zimmerman, Zimányi, and Burghardt 1972 for a recent version of it, centering on historical issues).[2]

However, there can be little controversy about the written charter granted in 1327 by a Hungarian king to the guarding communities. It implied that the villages were well established and were already enjoying noble status because it stated that the inhabitants could *retain* their nobility as long as they remained within the community. The charter specified that noble privileges were granted to each village as a corporate group and not to individuals. It went on to list the clans or families who were granted nobility, a list that included most of the surnames of the present Hungarian-speaking families of Oberwart: Adorján, Fülöp, Benkő, Pál, Gál, Imre, Zámbó (Gyenge 1973:27; Kovács 1942:78–79).

The fortresses that formed the new line of defense were built by noblemen whose privileges accrued to them personally. They were given huge tracts of land around each fortress and charged by the Hungarian king with populating the previously uninhabited area. They turned the lands into manorial estates. Many of the peasants who came to work the estates were German speakers from the west. Their growing numbers and influence are indicated by the increase in German place names during this time (circa: 1100–1200) and the change from Hungarian to German names for some villages (Kranzmayer 1972).

The noble privileges of the guarding communities allowed them to retain, over the centuries, a certain degree of independence from the surrounding manorial estates. However, it did not protect them from poverty. Their way of life was never very different from that of the serf villages around them (cf. Gaál 1966:11–15; Gaál 1969:15–29; Kovács 1942:30–61; Wallner 1926). The special privileges were limited to somewhat lower taxes, no corporal punishment, and the freedom to move around to engage in trade. Yet retaining even this degree of independence was a continuous struggle, because the great estates repeatedly attempted to bring the former guarding communities under their control or at least (especially between 1600 and 1800) to take gradual possession of their fields.

[2] Related to these controversies is the fact that the use of either 'Felsőőr' or 'Oberwart' in reports about the city can be interpreted as an indication of pro-Hungarian or pro-Austrian sentiments. No such implication is intended here. Rather, in using primarily the German form I am following ethnographic tradition by adopting the more common pattern of present-day native usage. Similarly, although there are German as well as Hungarian names for the neighborhoods of the city discussed above, among native bilinguals the Hungarian forms are more common in most cases and there too I follow their usage. However, in designating the people themselves, I depart from native norms (discussed on pp. 105 and 162) and use instead non-native descriptive phrases which highlight analytical distinctions: for example, bilingual Calvinist Oberwarters, the Hungarian-speakers, the peasant community.

Perhaps it was their reluctance to give up their privileges that explains why the guarding communities, though suffering casualties during the Turkish invasions of the 1500s, did not abandon their villages, while many others did. During the Turkish siege of the Kőszeg fortress (about 30 km northeast of Oberwart) in 1532, most of the remaining Hungarians of the area migrated to the east to escape the invaders. But the guarding communities did not flee. After the invasions, the nobility tried to repopulate their lands with a serf work-force that was again recruited in the west, sometimes from the Austrian manorial estates of the same noble families. These new settlers were again ethnically and linguistically German. Another group of settlers came from the south: Croatians escaping the Turks. The resettling occurred in waves during the late 1500s and the 1600s (Breu 1970; Burghardt 1962:208, 276).

For the Hungarian-speaking guarding communities, the result of the formation of estates and then of the Turkish invasions was that, perhaps as early as the 1200s, but certainly by the end of the 1500s, they formed a speech island totally surrounded by German- and Croatian-speaking villages. They were separated by 40 or 50 km of densely inhabited countryside from the majority of Hungarian speakers. At least since that time there have probably been some bilinguals in Oberwart who facilitated whatever communication there was with other villages.

Despite the influx of German and Croatian speakers, Oberwart remained politically and culturally within the Kingdom of Hungary. For this reason the Protestant Reformation reached it quite late and not from the west, through Austria, but from the east, through Hungarian preachers and noblemen (Kovács 1942:53). By the 1570s, Oberwart, along with all the other villages in Western Hungary, became Protestant. However, as a result of the Counter-Reformation, and Oberwart's refusal to counter-reform, it became the only Calvinist congregation in the province and as such was given official permission in 1681 to build a church and school (Gyenge 1973:29).

The Reformation had created a split within the Hungarian-speaking speech island. The smallest village became Lutheran; Alsóőr (Unterwart), Catholic, and Oberwart, mostly Calvinist. Although the Protestant nobility of eastern Hungary was able to combat the Counter-Reformation in the east, the Protestants were less powerful and less successful in the Western half of the country, which had been directly under Catholic Habsburg rule during the Turkish wars. In this period the Kingdom of Hungary, while remaining a political unit, became part of the Habsburg Empire and, despite the permission to congregate, Oberwart's Protestants were persecuted. Even today, the Protestants of Burgenland consider themselves an oppressed minority. In largely Catholic Austria they are indeed a minority, but with privileges protected by law. Yet ministers still recall the injustices of the Counter-Reformation as if the events had occurred within their own lifetimes. The events of the Counter-Reformation set the Catholic and the Protestant families of Oberwart against each other, and the distinction remains important today.

With respect to changes in language use, Oberwart's early history suggests two questions: how did Oberwarters communicate with the people of other social classes (the great nobility, government bureaucrats, merchants, clergy) who were necessarily a part of their lives, and how much did they interact with Croatian and with German villagers?

Since Oberwart was administratively within Hungary, and the local nobility was largely Magyarized (Burghardt 1962:111), Hungarian was doubtless used with social superiors. Although Latin was the official written language of Hungary until the early 1800s, the teachers, preachers, and government officials who had to interact with peasants probably spoke Hungarian. For instance, the minutes of a court hearing held in the early 1600s in which Oberwarters brough suit against a great estate for infringement of property rights was written, and therefore certainly conducted, in Hungarian (Kovács 1942:51, Footnote 105).

As to contacts with neighboring peasant villages, what limited relations did exist were probably facilitated by a few bilinguals or the churches. More generally, the first few hundred years saw the formation of institutions and circumstances that served to reinforce Oberwart's isolation from other villages. Oberwart was a closed corporate community with noble privileges; it was surrounded by manorial estates whose villages were organized by different principles; and Oberwart's Calvinists in particular were surrounded by what they characteristically thought were hostile Catholics and Lutherans.

At the same time, such factors as trade and the army brought individuals from neighboring communities speaking different languages into contact with each other. Although it is not clear how important those factors were before the nineteenth century, there is little doubt that by then the Hungarian-speaking Calvinists' connections with those they considered outsiders were expanding and beginning to have profound effects on the community's values and way of life.

THE FORMATION OF A TOWN

During the nineteenth century, Oberwart became a socially diverse commercial center rather than a peasant village. The indicators of this change are numerous. First, the population increased rapidly. The rise is important because it reflects not primarily a natural increase in the large native, Calvinist population and the smaller Catholic one, but rather the establishment, in Oberwart, of a German–speaking Lutheran group, a small Jewish community, as well as the immigration of Catholics. By 1820 there were three churches, each with its own school.

The development of this religious diversity can be traced through census figures (Table 2.2). The Calvinists' numbers stayed relatively stable, thus, they did not contribute much to the rising population. The sudden appearance of Lutherans and Jews in Oberwart's records makes it clear that they migrated into Oberwart. Although there had been a small group of Hungarian–speaking Catholic peasants in Oberwart since the Counter-Reformation, in less than a century (between 1681 and 1777) the number of Catholics increased fourfold—certainly by immigration. In addition, the 100% increase in Catholics and Lutherans between 1851 and 1869 can also only be explained as immigration.

The immigrants were not only religiously but also linguistically distinct from the natives. There had been some German-surnamed individuals in Oberwart since the fifteenth century, but their numbers had always been small—about 10% of the population. Moreover, despite the common

TABLE 2.2[a]

Religion in Oberwart

Year	Calvinist	Lutheran	Catholic	Jew	Total
ca. 1681[b]	1013	/	103		1116
1777[b]	1189		546		1735
1830	1391	200	552		2143
1836	1266	368	576	9	2219
1846	1492	387	600	14	2493
1851	1400	300	613	10	2323
1869	1375	601	1105	43	3124
1880	1480	684	1158	75	3397
1910	1566	635	1601	108	3910
1920	1612	613	1845	89	4159
1939	1701	658	1796[c]	1	4479
1951[d]	1495				4713
1961[e]	1557	911	2382		4850
1971[d]	1577	855	3186		5661
1973[d]	1359	1080	3319		5788

[a] All figures are from Kovács 1942:63, unless otherwise indicated.
[b] Data are from Gyenge 1973:29–33.
[c] This excludes 323 Gypsies, and it is not known how many Gypsies were excluded or included in previous and subsequent years.
[d] From *Statistisches Zentralamt Volkszählungs Ergebnisse, 1951, 1961, 1971.*
[e] Here the census figures available at the Oberwart Town Hall differ from the nationally published figures and have been used instead. They were collected May 26, 1961.

assumption made by scholars that a German surname indicates an ethnically and linguistically German individual, surnames in Oberwart are a deceptive measure of the number of German speakers. For instance, a single German-surnamed male, marrying into the community can leave several sons who, although otherwise assimilated to the Hungarian community, continue to hand down their German surnames. Recognizing this, Kovács (1942:62) suggests that by 1800 all Calvinist Oberwarters, regardless of their names, were ethnically and linguistically Hungarian. It was not until the Lutherans settled in Oberwart that there was a sizable number of native Oberwarters who considered themselves ethnically German, who spoke German as their first language, who conducted their church services in German, and who taught only German at their school.

In addition to the increasing size and heterogeneity, there were other, more direct signs indicating that Oberwart was becoming a town and a commercial center. In 1841 it received the legal privilege of holding a weekly market, during the mid-1800s it became a county seat, and in 1881 a main stop on the newly built railroad. By 1900, Oberwart had two large factories, more than 100 artisan's shops, two savings banks, and many stores and inns (Éhen 1905:34). Among the villages of the region, Oberwart most directly felt the effects of the developing capitalism that reached this corner of the Austro-Hungarian Empire at the end of the nineteenth century (Jászi 1929, Chapter 7).

It has been suggested that people were attracted to Oberwart because of its centralized geographical location within the county and later by its railroad and market. In addition, as a village with noble privileges it originally enjoyed a certain freedom in trade and movement that others did not. These may be the reasons why Oberwart, rather than some other village, became a commercial center. But more generally, as a border community inside Hungary but only a few kilometers from two Austrian provinces, Oberwart profited from the increase in trade following the abolition of tariffs between Austria and Hungary after the 1848 Revolution. Trade also flourished because at this time Hungary was in many ways an agricultural colony of the more industrialized regions of Austria: Bohemia, Styria, and Vienna (Hoffman 1967; Jászi 1929:186–189). At least some of the grain which Hungary supplied to Styria and to the rest of Austria went through the hands of Oberwart merchants, as did return trade in Styrian lumber.

For the original Hungarian-speaking peasants of Oberwart, the growth of the village and the religious and ethnic diversity were important primarily because they corresponded to a new economic stratification. Ethnic and linguistic differences (German versus Hungarian), religion (Lutheran versus Calvinist), and differences in source of livelihood divided the population into the same groups, with little crosscutting. Only the

Catholic immigrants complicated this neat dichotomy. It was the historical sequence in which people migrated into Oberwart and the skills they brought with them that established the major divisions. As I will try to show later, networks of friendship and economic aid, and endogamous marriage patterns maintained and continue to maintain distinctions that are at once ethnic, religious and class based.

Immigrating Lutherans, Catholics, and Jews did not come to Oberwart to join the existing agricultural community as peasants nor to establish parallel peasant communities. Instead, most of them came as merchants, tradespeople, artisans, and bureaucrats.

It was the Lutherans who were usually, and in fact are today, the merchants and artisans. Most cabinetmakers, carpenters, mechanics, and millers are Lutherans. The Jews were tradespeople running small grocery and dry-goods stores, and later at least one large lumber mill. And some Jews were doctors or lawyers. Significantly, the Catholics were more divided, participating in craft and commerce but also in the professions and, perhaps most of all in the government bureaucracy. Catholics and Lutherans also opened inns and hotels, which profited from the market and the increased commercial traffic.

The newcomers settled in the relatively empty middle section of town, between the Catholic *Alszeg* and the Calvinist *Felszeg*. By 1910, the former small commercial centers of the *Felszeg* and the *Alszeg* had been superseded by the new center of shops, services, and railroad stop located between the two old ends of town (Wallner 1926:27). The Lutheran church and the Jewish synagogue were built in the center of this middle section, neatly representing in geography the social separation between the old population and the new.

Even before the nineteenth-century growth of the town there had been some social stratification in Oberwart. There were relatively rich peasants, very poor ones, peasants with noble privileges, and some who had lost their lands or had married in and so had no such privileges. However they had all been part of an agricultural community in which many of the necessary crafts, such as weaving and shoemaking, had been side occupations for people who were primarily peasants. Some, such as the blacksmith, may have been full-time artisans, but they did not form a separate stratum or class in the village (Gaál 1969:27). Particularly after noble privileges were abolished following the 1848 Revolution, the economic and legal distinctions among Oberwart peasants were minimal. Even though some peasant families were marginally richer or considered socially "better" than others, the differences among the peasants were very slight compared to the obvious differences they saw between themselves and the merchants, administrators, and professionals.

Some of the artisans, particularly cabinetmakers, mechanics, and millers, were rich enough to hire workers and to be able to buy their food. They and their families did not have to do agricultural work. Others, such as carpenters, coopers, innkeepers, and storekeepers, kept animals and owned fields but could hire others to do the work and even to take care of their children. This provided sources of money for poor peasants, but it also underscored the social distance between the native peasant population of Oberwart and the richer people living in the middle of town. There was vitually no relationship in which the peasant Calvinists and Catholics were on equal footing with the newly arrived Lutherans and Catholics. Even in the 1920s, when Calvinist young men became apprentices in the artisans' shops, they remained only assistants. Few could open their own shops and the social distance remained. Marriage between Oberwart Lutheran merchants or artisans and Calvinist peasants was very rare.

When I asked Calvinist women in their seventies and eighties to list, in order of preference, the kinds of men they would have liked to marry when they were young, they all replied a *gazda* 'peasant freeholder' with lots of land. When I inquired about artisans and tradesmen they answered that those would certainly be preferable, but that such *jobbfajta nípek* 'better kinds of people' would not even consider peasant girls as potential wives. One might still assume that it was strictly religious or ethnic differences that discouraged intermarriage. After all, most artisans and tradesmen were Lutherans and ethnically German. No one denied that such differences mattered, but they pointed out that although they themselves could not hope for it, a very rich peasant's daughter could indeed marry a carpenter, a mechanic or a storekeeper. The man generally recognized as the richest Calvinist peasant at the turn of the century had two daughters: one married a school teacher, the other the son of a Lutheran innkeeper. Clearly, added to and correlating with religious or ethnic differences was a strongly felt economic one.

From the point of view of ethnicity and language, we find that Oberwart consisted of ethnically Hungarian peasants on the bottom of the town's prestige hierarchy and a rich, artisan–merchant class of German Lutherans at the top. But this clear distinction is complicated by the Catholics who migrated into Oberwart during the 1800s. Most of these Catholics came from various parts of Hungary and considered themselves Hungarians. They were either professionals (lawyers) or local representatives of the Hungarian state, the Hungarian bureaucracy, and the Hungarian banks. Their numbers first increased after 1867 (Table 2.2), when the Compromise between Austria and Hungary led to the independent and equal status of Hungary within the Empire and therefore to the strengthening of its internal administration. The Catholic population increased again around the turn of the century, when more administration was apparently needed for the forced assimilation of the minorities within Hungary. This was when Magyarization became the official policy of the Budapest government. In Oberwart, Magyarization meant that, because Oberwart was the county seat, those who administered the county lived there in relatively large numbers and formed a stratum of Hungarian-speaking and strongly nationalistic elite.

Magyarization can be viewed as a belated and coercive effort to turn a state formed on the basis of a historical and geographical principle (loyalty to the Crown of St. Stephen and hegemony over the Carpathian Basin) into a "modern" nation–state on the Romantic model, held together by ethnic and linguistic homogeneity. Forcing Germans, Croats, Slovaks, Romanians, and others to speak Hungarian and to Magyarize their names was meant to achieve such unity. Large-scale assimilation was never accomplished, but Magyarization did have linguistic effects. Because of Hungary's new educational policy, knowledge of Hungarian was a prerequisite for high school and higher education, both of which were necessary to enter the professions, public administration, and commerce. In the German-speaking area around Oberwart, as in the rest of the country, the Magyar language became the major tool to achieve upward mobility. A woman in her seventies from Stadt Schlaining, a small city near Oberwart, provides an example. She explained that, although she was born Lutheran with German as her first language, she chose to go not to the German-language, Lutheran school but to the state-run, Hungarian one. This, despite the stigma attached to the school: that all the Jews in town went there. Her motive, she explained, was simply that she wanted to get places, to become someone. In cases like hers, and in cities generally, Magyarization contributed to a change in linguistic evaluations. By the start of the twentieth century," [T]he use of Magyar became a sign of intellect and cultured bearing, a status symbol, an entry into groups and circles that 'mattered' (Burghardt 1962:149)."

So, in Oberwart during the first decades of the twentieth century, the prestige language, the language of the administrative elites, the teachers, the lawyers, and the doctors was Hungarian. Yet an important, rich and prestigious group within the town, the Lutheran merchants and artisans, although bilingual in German and Hungarian, definitely maintained their use of German. They identified themselves as German and continued to teach German in their school to the extent that the Hungarian education laws allowed. In fact in 1879 they established a German-language newspaper (a descendant of it is still in operation) called the *Oberwarter Sonntagszeitung*. In addition, a Lutheran-run *Gymnasium*, which stressed the teaching of German and had ties with cities in northern

Germany, was in operation in a town near Oberwart during the entire Magyarization period. Many of the children of Oberwart's Lutheran merchants and artisans attended (Burghardt 1962:152; Oberwart school records). In short, German had a certain prestige. It was a language used for intellectual and political purposes within Oberwart, although it was not backed by the power and authority of the state.

The 1921 transfer, from Hungary to Austria, of all of the territory which is now Burgenland, drastically contributed to the ultimate change of this situation. The transfer was part of the post–World War I division of the Habsburg Empire by the Allies on the basis of ethnic self-determination. Ethnic group had been interpreted as linguistic group since the German Romantic movement had first equated the two ideas in the early eighteenth century. The region which is now Burgenland was 75% German-speaking and, according to Allied principles, certainly belonged with German-speaking Austria (Macartney 1937:40–48). However, some scholars have argued that the decision to take this strip of territory from one part of the losing Empire (Hungary) and to give it to another part (Austria) was determined as much by Allied enmity toward the temporary Communist government in Hungary as by a commitment to ethnic self-determination. With the exception of the city of Sopron which voted for Hungary, no general plebiscite was held in the region, and the territory was given to Austria (Burghardt 1962:207–223; Soós 1971:2–27; Wambaugh 1933).

In Oberwart, as in the rest of the newly transferred territory, the Hungarian administrators and intellectuals fled to Hungary. But none of the indigenous peasants left and so by the 1930s the Hungarian-speaking population of Oberwart consisted of the mostly Calvinist peasantry. As a result, since the local government continued to consist of the members of the most populous local group, the Calvinists, it continued to be conducted in Hungarian (Imre 1973a:124). In addition, the Hungarian press remained available and contacts with the nearby Hungarian market town of Szombathely were maintained, as were marriage contacts with Calvinist Hungarian villages on the other side of the new border. The Calvinist church remained totally Hungarian in its services and its school. However, the Hungarian county administration was replaced by an Austrian one. Consequently, not only the merchants and artisans, but the county government and the courts used German.

By the 1920s two social worlds had existed for decades side by side in Oberwart and, despite regular interaction and interdependence, they remained separated by class and ethnicity. A clear and symbolically important split had been forming, and was completed by the 1921 transfer: the rich merchants and the prestigious ruling elites of Oberwart spoke German. The peasants, although bilingual, were the only ones who spoke

Workers' houses; carefully kept yards.

Hungarian and who continued to look to Hungary for preachers, for higher education and for religious leadership.

THE CALVINIST PEASANTS

The gradual enlargement of Oberwart in the nineteenth and twentieth centuries resulted in a division into social strata of which the original peasant community became the bottom layer both in wealth and in prestige. By the 1960s, the growth of Oberwart resembled, in miniature, the pattern of great urban centers that include in their periphery villages that have been surrounded by the expanding urban complex but that still partly function as agrarian entities (Simić 1973:1–12). The existence of this urban center and the gradual industrialization of the entire country has had important effects not only on the vertical relations between the peasants and other social strata, but also on the horizontal relationships of peasant Oberwarters with other peasant villages.

I have used the word "peasant" to refer to those Oberwarters engaged primarily in agriculture. There has been some controversy concerning the definition of this term—as opposed to "farmers" who engage in agriculture for profit—and whether it can be applied at all to present-day European cultivators. Oberwart's agriculturalists, even of the twentieth century and certainly the centuries before, fall within the social, structural, and economic definitions of "peasantry." For instance, in their relations with the wider world they formed a part society, having to deliver a share of their production in the form of taxes and dues to a bureaucratic and aristocratic class that had the power to force such payments and that lived off them (Wolf 1966:Chapter 1). This is true despite the former noble status of Oberwarters because, by the early 1500s, the small nobility of which they were a part was taxed in much the same way as the serfs, and because they owed service, usually in the army, to a provincial nobility (Kovács 1942:39–41, Footnote 51). In addition, they participated in a market system—which became the legally recognized weekly market of Oberwart itself—that linked them to local and regional middlemen.

In the social organization of their production and consumption as well, Oberwarter cultivators can be distinguished from farmers. Producing primarily for subsistence, they did not specialize in any one crop but planted almost equally large quantities of wheat, winter barley, oats and buckwheat, as well as potatoes and cattle turnip. For those still involved in agriculture today the main crop is wheat, but with the exception of buckwheat, all the others listed above are also planted in similar quantities. No peasant family specializes in raising one kind of animal. Instead, they all have cows, pigs, chickens, and sometimes lambs and rabbits. Even today, families that farm are relatively self-sufficient in food. Only sugar, coffee, tea, beer, and some canned goods are bought.

In Oberwart, marriage, death, and number of children were, and for older cultivators still are, inextricably mixed with the economic considerations of land inheritance (cf. Shanin 1973:70). So, choosing a marriage partner to consolidate the property of the two families was not uncommon as recently as the 1930s. If the property in question was big enough, even first cousins married, despite the folk belief that the children of such a marriage would be sickly or deranged. The family farm continues to be run not as a business enterprise in which labor has to be made as efficient as possible for maximum profits, but as a household—at once a consuming, producing, and laboring unit (Chaianov 1931:144–145; Erdei 1938). For instance, Oberwart agriculturalists today do not invest in a potato-planting machine, which allows one worker to do the work of eight or ten in less time, as long as there are several generations of women household members and other kin available to do it for payment in crops and labor rather than cash. It is true that, in contrast to their ancestors, Oberwart agriculturalists must be seen as peasants living in a larger, industrialized economy in which the peasant mode of production is no longer predominant, or even very important (Franklin 1969:1). Nevertheless in economic decision-making, as in other aspects of life, Oberwart landowners still follow traditional peasant strategies.

Moreover, Oberwarters who still engage in agriculture (at least those over forty or so) identify themselves as peasants (*paraszt*). For many purposes they divide the world into "us" and "them." The "us" group includes anyone in their experience who works the land. Recently, industrial wage laborers who work with their hands also have been included in this category. The "them" group, *urak* 'gentlemen, gentry, nobility' includes everyone who does not work the land. The opposition between the two recalls a feudal society, but is used to characterize present social relations. It is seen in terms of politics ("they" have the power; "we" don't), economics ("they" are rich; "we" are not), and educated sophistication ("we" are ignorant of high culture and manners with which "they" are familiar). The common saying **Urnak ur e baráccsa** 'The gentry's friend is the gentry' is often used resignedly in political discussions. It assumes social inequality and expresses Oberwarters' belief that people of the same class always stick together. It expresses the conviction that the **urak** who are in power will arrange things to benefit others like them but never to benefit the peasant.

In contrast to **ur, paraszt** is a low-prestige category with pejorative connotations. This is not to imply that older Oberwarter agriculturalists do not feel a great deal of pride in being *gazdák*, 'heads of independent peasant households'. They are proud of attaining positions and symbols of high prestige and respect within the peasant value system, including land, animals, a reputation as a strong, hard worker, and being elected to serve as presbyter of the Calvinist church. But that set of values is in constant contrast to the evaluations of urbanized Oberwarters. Peasants know that those outside their own value system hold them in contempt. One expression of this contempt is well known to the peasants themselves: they are often said to smell of manure. This dichotomy between the peasant social order and the affluent urban world is of crucial importance in understanding Oberwarters' attitudes toward the languages that have come to symbolize the two.

VILLAGE LIFE IN A TOWN

Poverty was the most important feature of Oberwart peasant life from the nineteenth century through the early 1930s. Despite their nobility, by the start of this century, Oberwart peasants were poorer than peasants in other parts of Burgenland, and owned less land. The amount of land and forest originally given to the guarding community was limited and, being surrounded by large aristocratic estates, could not be increased. Also, the clay-like land was generally not good for grain production: they call it *sovány* ('infertile'). As the population of the guarding settlements increased, reaching 1000 by the year 1600, arable land could be expanded only by burning the community's woods. A large section of the fields is called *irtás* 'deforestation, clearing' and another is called *rácirtás* 'the Rácz family's clearing,' testifying to the fact that over the centuries forest was cleared repeatedly. Yet the holdings of any one family remained very small. By the turn of this century most Oberwarters had fewer than 5 holds of land (1 hold = .57 ha = 1.42 acres [Kovács 1942:76]). Informants now in their seventies and eighties remember only one family that had as many as 22 holds at that time. This is in contrast to a village in northern Burgenland described by Khera (1972b:351) in which more than one-third of the village had more than 9 holds and many had as much as 49.

When asked to list the rich peasant families in Oberwart at the beginning of this century, informants invariably answered that there were no rich families, they were all poor. The male informants' judgments were based on their experiences in the army and in seasonal work, which took them to northern Burgenland, the Austrian province of Styria, or to other parts of Hungary. Compared with the enormous single-family holdings they often saw in these places, no Oberwarter qualified as rich in land. But

When the field is too small to be worked with a tractor, cows are used.

judging by Khera's figures, these informants were also right in another sense. Not only was there less land, but Oberwart peasant holdings were also relatively equally distributed. There were fewer landless people, but also fewer very rich ones than elsewhere.

Nevertheless, some stratification according to wealth did exist in Oberwart, and, when pressed to list those families who were rich by Oberwart standards, the old informants independently came to the same limited list of six to eight families. Those with more land also owned two or more horses and up to six cows. The poor or medium holders, owned, in addition to pigs, only two cows which they used for milking as well as for plowing. But, because the differences between families were relatively small, there was not a sizable group of richer peasants who could afford, or needed, to employ the poorer ones on a permanent, contractual, or customary basis. At the same time, there were relatively few who were landless and who would, therefore, have wanted to attach themselves permanently to richer households. Instead, the poor retained their tiny holdings and did day labor for wages at harvest and during other labor-intensive periods.

Because Oberwarters practiced divided inheritance of land, the children of a richer family could easily become poor unless marriages among rich families were carefully arranged. In addition, property was usually divided only at the death of the parents. Only one child, usually a son and his wife, could stay in the parental household. The rest had to find separate residences and had to work on part of the land they would later inherit and on any other pieces of land they could manage to buy or rent. This meant that most Oberwart peasants, including many of the children of the richer families, were chronically short of land and money. They needed extra income, sometimes for necessities and often to enlarge their holdings to viable size.

Older informants relate stories of their own parents indicating that even in the nineteenth century Oberwart men traveled for jobs, especially during harvest season. They worked in the north of Burgenland on the huge Eszterházy manor lands and in southwest Hungary on similar estates. Some also worked as contract laborers for rich peasants in other villages. In addition, cattle and horse trading with neighboring villages was a specialty for some (Gaál 1969:26).

But once Oberwart became a commercial center, the major source of extra income for a large part of the peasant community was transporting freight between Hungary and Austria. It had the advantage of being mostly winter work, leaving part of the summer to work on one's own land. Well into the 1930s freight hauling was an important second livelihood for peasant men. By contracting with Oberwart merchants, peasants were kept busy transporting raw wood from Styria to Oberwart, where it was processed into boards. They then took the boards to southern Hungary, where the boards were sold for grain and wine, which was taken back to Oberwart and eventually to Styria. The peasants made none of the profits in this lucrative commerce; they simply worked for wages. There are few peasant men over 60 who have not spent a good part of their lives transporting wood or grain.

This source of supplemental income, perhaps even more than the others, brought Oberwart men into contact with German speakers in Styria and in neighboring villages. Although a few of the men in German villages spoke Hungarian, some knowledge of German was a useful resource for the Oberwart men engaged in trade and freight hauling. An indication of the felt importance of German was the *dzserëk csere* 'child trading' that was practiced before the turn of the century and until the 1920s. Richer peasants would send their sons to live in a German village for a year with a German-speaking family, which would "trade" a similarly aged boy to the Oberwart family for the same time. As long as the region was part of Hungary, the German-speaking villagers had reason to want their children to learn Hungarian, so the practice continued.

However, children were exchanged only by the richer peasant families in Oberwart. The poorer ones could not indulge in such special arrangements. Because their major concern was money, their young children, girls as well as boys, went wherever money could be earned. It is important to note that they did not usually have to leave Oberwart to find part-time work. In the nineteenth century, young peasant women worked as nursemaids, housemaids, and in inns for the merchants and artisans of Oberwart. Young men were employed in stores and shops and as temporary farmhands. However, the wage labor paid badly and remained essentially a necessary evil. It did not provide an economically viable substitute, much less a preferable alternative, to peasant agriculture. Yet, because by the nineteenth century Oberwart provided work opportunities in a way that other villages did not, a peasant family could use wage labor and farming to supplement each other, perhaps a century before large-scale industrialization made this a general practice in the rest of the region.

As a result, while at the turn of the century huge numbers of people from small peasant villages emigrated to cities or abroad because of unemployment, lack of land, or simply starvation, Oberwarters could find work and stayed. Most of the emigration from Hungary at the turn of the century was from agricultural regions like Burgenland and up to 5% of the country's population emigrated overseas (Benyon 1939:226). There is hardly a Burgenland family that does not have an American branch. (Most of the Hungarians are in Chicago). Yet the migration from Oberwart was significantly less than from smaller villages. A good comparison is the Hungarian-speaking village of Alsóőr (Unterwart), a few kilometers south of Oberwart. With a population of about 1400, by 1910 Alsóőr had sent 314 people overseas. In that same year, Oberwart's population was three times larger, its peasant population at least 1566, but the number abroad was only 185 (*Magyar Statisztikai Közlemények* 1910:124).

Despite the relative availability of jobs, Oberwart peasant men who did wage work used their money to buy land. Although by the 1930s there were jobs in road building, the railroad and the re-routing of the Pinka River, no one could live on wages alone. Land, owning as much of it as possible, remained not only an economic necessity, but also the basic goal of peasant life. The accumulation of land remained the only route to high status and prestige; the values of the peasant community stayed alive. Those few independent peasant *gazdák* who did not have to do wage work or who needed all their children to work the farm were the men with the highest prestige. Such men or their children were considered the most desirable marriage partners. Young women preferred to be married to a peasant with a lot of land rather than to a man who had to go to work. Old women informants recount that girls in the early decades of this century expressed their preference for peasant husbands in the saying: Why should I have to buy food in the store if I can arrange to have my own storage attic, where I can get it free?

Women's preference for peasant husbands before the mid-twentieth century is clearly reflected in the city's marriage records. Because some people from German villages came to Oberwart to work in inns and stores, and because some Oberwarters worked for peasants in German villages, there was a small but steadily rising number of marriages between Oberwart Calvinists and German monolinguals from neighboring villages (Table 2.3) during the nineteenth and early twentieth centuries. But before 1940, very few of these marriages with people outside the peasant community involved Oberwart men whose main or only occupation was agriculture (Table 2.4). On the one hand, a man who had land wanted to be sure to marry more of it. A woman outsider could never bring land as an inheritance or a dowry because she and her family would not own land within the Oberwart fields. On the other hand, the fact that *gazdák* rarely married exogamously also suggests that they were highly valued as marriage partners within the community and had their pick of marriageable local women. In either case, the marriage pattern reflects the importance of land as source of both livelihood and prestige before World War II.

TABLE 2.3

Percentage of Exogamous Marriages of Calvinist Oberwarters

Year	Percentage of Exogamous[a] Marriages	Total Number of Calvinist Marriages
1896–1900	20	66
1901–1905	15	65
1906–1910	22	63
1911–1915	31	45
1916–1920	25	80
1921–1925	23	57
1926–1930	31	59
1931–1935	37	51
1936–1940	29	59
1941–1945	34	47
1946–1950	27	111
1951–1955	38	66
1956–1960	48	64
1961–1965	50	58
1966–1970	82	66
1971	79	14
1972	65	17

SOURCE: *Register of Marriages*, Community (later City) of Oberwart.
[a] This means marriage to someone who is not Calvinist, including non-Oberwarters and Lutheran and Catholic Oberwarters. Because so few Oberwart Catholics and Lutherans are bilingual and because Calvinists marry Oberwart Catholics very rarely, exogamous marriages are, as a rule, marriages to German monolinguals.

TRANSITION: THE WAR

The 1930s and 1940s were transitional years for Oberwart's peasantry in several ways. First, the 1930s were the last decade in which land was of prime importance to peasant Oberwarters not only for subsistence, but as a measure of social standing. In the 1920s and 1930s some sons of Oberwart's poor peasants were able to get higher education and to enter government administration and teaching. In small villages, such native sons would have had to emigrate permanently to cities to find work, but in Oberwart they did not have to move away to be upwardly mobile. The point is not merely that higher education was now possible, since only a small number of people were actually able to get it. Rather it is important that, on returning from school, these educated children of poor peasants entered the bureaucracy and professions and largely replaced the richer peasants as leaders of the Calvinist community. In prewar Oberwart, the mayor was a rich peasant (by Oberwart standards) and the Calvinist

TABLE 2.4

Endogamous Marriages of All Male Calvinist Oberwarters and Male Peasant
Calvinist Oberwarters

Year	Percentage of Endogamous Marriages of All Calvinist Males	Percentage of Endogamous Marriages of Peasant Calvinist Males
1911–1940	71	87
1941–1960	65	54
1961–1972	32	0

SOURCE: *Register of Marriages*, Community (later City) of Oberwart.

church's leaders, the presbyters, were also among the richer peasants. Today, the son of a bricklayer–peasant is the business manager and a presbyter of the Calvinist church. He had become a teacher before the war. Another presbyter is the son of a carpenter–peasant. He had become a teacher before the war and then school superintendent for the entire county. A postwar Calvinist minister of Oberwart was himself a native Oberwarter, and the son of a landless washerwoman.

Another important change that began in the 1930s was the end of Oberwart's centuries-long dual orientation to east and west. Because of their trade and location, Oberwarters perceived themselves to be facing both Austria and Hungary, while being part of neither. 'Going to Hungary' has always been expressed as going *be* or *lë* 'in' or 'down' to Hungary. At least implicit in this is the conception that if Hungary is a separate place one goes into, then Oberwart is not itself in that place, not inside Hungary. Similarly they say that one goes *kü* 'out' to Austria, implying that Oberwart does not belong there either (Sozan 1974:161). In higher education for those few who could get it, Oberwart Calvinists showed a similar dual view. While some people were sent to Budapest and Pápa (in Hungary), others were sent to Vienna. The transfer of Burgenland to Austria in 1921 did not change this. It was the 1938 *Anschluss* of Austria with Nazi-led Germany that severed most of Oberwart's ties to the east and strengthened those toward the west. The subsequent Soviet occupation of Burgenland also contributed by creating ill feeling. The Soviet restrictions and Hungary's postwar Communist government not only minimized commercial and cultural activity between Oberwart and Hungary, but also drastically changed—for the worse—Oberwarters' perceptions of Hungary.

The strengthening of Oberwart's western orientation was accomplished in several ways, some directly involving language. When Burgenland became part of the Third *Reich*, the teaching of Hungarian was outlawed and the church schools that had taught it were replaced by state schools that mixed the religions and taught in German. In addition, a year of *Pflichtarbeit* 'mandatory labor' was demanded of all young people. This took them to various parts of the *Reich*, as far away as the Danish border, to work in groups with others their age from different regions of Germany. As a result, large numbers of young women and men traveled outside Oberwart to work. These changes, as well as the economic boom that preceded them and that, for the first time, provided industrial work in Austrian cities for many of Oberwart's men and women, made knowledge of German more than a convenient and helpful resource. German became and remained indispensable during and after the war. This was also true for the older men drafted into the German army. For most of them, the war and their participation in the German army was the most important and memorable event of their lives. After 35 years, war exploits are still the major topic of conversation at the local inn after the first round of wine. For the men, their war experiences often constitute ultimate proof of the need to know German in contacts with the outside world.

For the women, children, and old men who stayed behind, the war meant mostly fear. While they themselves participated in the deportation to concentration camps of the large Gypsy community on the outskirts of Oberwart, they were at the same time threatened by rumors that after the Gypsies and Jews the Magyars, as an inferior race, would also be deported and resettled in the "east." These rumors gained credence from the fact that the neighboring Lutheran villagers, and in fact many in Oberwart, were enthusiastic Nazis. (In 1974, a Lutheran-owned inn in Oberwart hosted a large celebration attended by, and in honor of, Burgenland's former SS officers.) With the Soviet liberation, the women's fear centered on the Soviet Army's looting and raping.

Oberwart's break with the east came after the war. While much of Western Europe was Marshall Planned back to economic well-being, Burgenland, occupied by Soviet forces, suffered economic stagnation until the neutrality treaty of 1955. Soviet policy not only failed to spur industry and commerce but rather shut down any development and siphoned off—as war reparations—whatever wealth there was in industry and minerals (Bader 1966, Chapter 6). Oberwarters' suspicion and fear of the Soviet Union and the socialist countries solidified during the 10 years of occupation.

Viewed historically, this animosity and fear are not surprising. Politically, Burgenland had been a right wing area during the polarized 1930s. It was one of the agricultural regions sympathetic to the Austrian rightist 'Christian Corporate State' (*Christlicher Ständestaat*) (Stadler 1971, Chapter 2). Recently, however, nearly half of Burgenland and half of

Oberwart have voted for the left-leaning Socialist Party in national elections (*Österreichisches Statistisches Zentralamt* 1972a:98). There are many reasons for this, a major one being a shift in the province's economic base. Before the war, 46% of Burgenland worked in agriculture; today it is only about 18%. Many workers have voted for the Socialist Party because it has supported wage and health-care legislation, enabling workers to enjoy the unprecedented well-being brought by the industrialization of the 1960s—a standard of living comparable to western Europe and unmatched further to the east. Yet, while most Oberwarters no longer support a right-wing government, their attitude toward the Soviet Union and, by extension, toward Hungary has remained the same: contemptuous, condescending, and somewhat fearful. It was most ironically expressed by Oberwart's young Catholic priest as we drove on the road that runs parallel to the many kilometers of border that Burgenland and Hungary share. The Austrian side of the border is unguarded; on the Hungarian side, a barbed wire fence, armed sentries in a string of look-out towers, and a mine field mark the boundary. It is the socialist workers paradise, the priest said, pointing east to Hungary, and they go to such lengths with the mines and the fence just to make sure our workers don't rush in.

In short, at the very time that Oberwarters' experience of the German-speaking west was increasing and knowledge of German was proving to be more economically advantageous than ever before, contacts with Hungarians to the east became harder to maintain and less economically desirable. Only the local Calvinist church sustained some links with seminaries in Hungary where its ministers were educated. The lack of contact was due not only to Oberwart's views about communism, but largely to Hungary's postwar isolation and relative poverty.

The war and its aftermath clearly marked a change in Oberwarters' perceptions of their position relative to outsiders and larger political units. But it was the turn away from the land as source of both subsistence and prestige, as well as the more recent economic boom, that have made many of these new perceptions relevant to language use within the bilingual community.

ECONOMIC BOOM

The post-1955 prosperity in Burgenland meant more jobs and more consumer products. Oberwarters who had formerly been peasants were recruited to work locally on electric, gas, and water works or in the many newly opened small businesses and light industry (*Bundesministerium*

1972:11). Alternatively, some commuted weekly to the cities of Wiener Neustadt or Vienna to work in heavier industry for higher wages. In fact, the expansion of Austria's industry and social-welfare legislation after the 1955 independence had so transformed the workers' economic situation that in Oberwart peasant agriculture, with small holdings and lack of machinery, could not compete with the benefits and high wages of industrial and business employment. By 1964, of Hungarian-speaking Oberwarters, almost all of whom had before the war engaged in agriculture to some extent, only 18.8% were full time agriculturalists and only 19% were peasant–workers. More than one-third were employed in business and industry (Somogyi 1966:56).

Hungarian-speaking Oberwarters became more and more a part of the German monolingual world of wage labor, business, and consumer economy. The young in particular saw their future in Austrian business and commerce and in the German-language trade schools, which would prepare them for such jobs. In addition, Oberwart itself was transformed, growing steadily in the 1960s as more German monolinguals from neighboring villages moved to Oberwart to take jobs in administration, commerce and the professions.

In short, 10 years later than the rest of Austria, Burgenland experienced the kind of "rural industrialization" that has been characteristic of postwar Europe (Dovring 1965; Franklin 1969). Movement of industry into the countryside is one part of it and mechanization of agriculture is the other. Socially, peasants and landless agriculture laborers all over Europe have been transformed into workers of various kinds, peasant–workers (who do industrial work all week and leave agriculture to their families and weekends), and farmers, that is, capitalist producers specializing in food, sugar beets, wine, or some other cash crop.

In Austria, in the entire Alpine region, and in much of Germany as well, *Arbeiter* 'worker' and *Bauer* 'peasant' are the conceptual distinctions used by villagers to classify their fellows. Usually the distinction implies differences in style of life and attitudes toward work. In most reports it is clear that the distinction does not involve political opposition or social tension. In fact, the regular social interaction between workers and peasants often includes cooperation and the exchange of economic favors (cf. Cole 1973; Friedl 1972; Honigmann 1963; Khera 1972a). Because of impartible inheritance of land, one member of a family may be a *Bauer* and another an *Arbeiter*. People can change from one to the other, though it is admittedly more difficult for a worker to get land than for a *Bauer* to find a job. Most important, in the ethnographic literature *Arbeiter* and *Bauer* seem generally not to be ranked categories—in the social organization of

many middle European villages one is as prestigious as the other (see especially Honigmann 1963).

Khera (1973) has shown that the villages of northern Burgenland constitute an exception to this central European pattern. The rule of partible inheritance of land has led richer peasants to marry each other in order to maintain the size of their holdings. They have thereby formed a class of rich *Bauern* within the village who have higher prestige than workers, and who cut themselves off from the workers. The rich peasants perpetuate the ranked social status system of the prewar period in which the landless poor of the village worked for the rich peasants and had hardly any hope of changing their low social position within the village. Workers are now economically as well off as the rich peasants, but still considered socially inferior. Not surprisingly, peasant and worker oppose each other politically. The rich peasants vote for the conservative party, the workers for the socialist party. It is the rich peasants who send some of their children to professional schools and universities. These children then move to large cities, leaving the village in its traditional form, run by the remaining landholders.

Oberwart fits neither of these patterns of postwar change. This is primarily because of Oberwart's urban character and the relative poverty of its peasantry. The part-time, small-holder peasant who needs the farm to supplement wages and the wages to supplement the farm is not a postwar phenomenon in Oberwart. Where such poor peasants in small villages before World War II either emigrated or became the permanent dependents of rich peasants, in Oberwart they stayed and depended on the town's growing commerce. By the postwar years, there was already, among bilingual Calvinist Oberwarters, a range of peasant to worker types.

On one extreme of this range are those children of poor peasants who were able to get an education before the war and who, upon their return to Oberwart became professionals and bureaucrats. Many of these people physically moved out of the *Felszeg* and into the center of town. Some of them severed relations with people they had known, even with kin who remained peasants. Others, who stayed in the *Felszeg* despite occupational mobility, became patrons or "connections" for the peasants in local government bureaucracies and took the leading offices of the Calvinist church. Still others, especially the postwar young and those with very little land, became full-time workers but stayed in the old neighborhood. Some, who had been trained as assistants in artisan's shops or who got industrial jobs, continued to work their small land holdings and not only stayed in the *Felszeg*, but continued to rely on their neighbors and kin for the traditional exchange of agricultural labor (called *összesegités*

(H), *össze* 'together', *segités* 'help') which allowed peasants to survive without investing in machinery. Finally, at the other extreme, are the full-time peasants who also participate in *összesegités* and who continue many of the other prewar traditions and modes of agricultural production.

In contrast to the situation in northern Burgenland's small villages, Oberwart's full-time peasants have, since the war, lost prestige and respect. They had never provided steady work for the landless. In fact, even some of the richest peasants had themselves been dependent on the commercial activity of Oberwart's merchants to earn supplemental income. Moreover, even in the 1930s and before, when land was highly valued, the full-time, relatively rich peasant was lower on the broader Oberwart social scale than the Lutheran artisans and merchants and the government bureaucrats and professionals. Far from being able to consolidate their lands, switch to capitalist production and maintain their position, full-time peasants in Oberwart since World War II have relinquished their high social standing among bilinguals to well-paid workers.

Workers have much readier access to money than peasants and are thus able to acquire the new symbols of high social status, adopted from urban Austria. For workers, land itself is no longer a potent symbol. Rather, such consumer products as cars, washing machines, deep freezes, new clothes, and, in particular, new houses are the signs of success. These can be acquired relatively easily by workers. But peasants face a dilemma. First of all, farms in Oberwart have always been too small for specialization and even for certain kinds of mechanization. Those who do full-time agricultural work today are the descendants of the richest peasants of the 1930s, yet they must still augment their personal holdings with equally large numbers of rented fields to make mechanized farming economically worthwhile. Second, even with larger farms, peasants can no longer gain respect from workers through the accumulation of land. Yet they also cannot spend what little cash they have on consumer goods. To maintain their farms when there is no cheap labor, and when fewer people are in need of exchanging agricultural labor, cash income must be invested in farm machinery and land rental.

Young Calvinist women of marriageable age specifically state that they do not want to marry peasants because peasant life provides few prestige-enhancing prospects. In addition, they feel the work is much harder, dirtier and uglier than holding a job (in terms of number of hours this is certainly true, cf. Franklin 1969:37–44). Men say that *Paraszt legin nem kap nüöt* 'Peasant lads can't get women' because, as one old man observed about a particular young couple: *Az a Trüumfba jár, oaz fog neki tehen szart lapáni?* 'She works at (the local bra factory), is she going to shovel cow shit for him?' While the trend in Oberwart since World War II has been toward exogamous marriages with non-Calvinist, nonbilinguals (Table 2.3), the marriage data for peasant men show a considerably greater percentage of exogamous marriages since 1960 than for men with other occupations. And for peasant men this represents a drastic shift since the 1930s, when they tended to marry inside the community far more frequently than workers. The marriage records reflect the attitude that peasant men are no longer good matches.

In Oberwart today there are few young people who have chosen agriculture as their sole source of livelihood. Peasants are often those over 50 or 60 who did not change their lives after the war, or younger people who inherited relatively large amounts of land and were unable to get training of any kind. Today's peasants, young and old, continue to value land and, in sharp contrast to workers who want leisure and evaluate jobs on the basis of how little work is demanded of them, the peasants continue to respect hard work and to admire those who do it. There is also a sense among the younger peasants in Oberwart, as in other parts of central Europe (cf. Golde 1975) that agricultural work should be considered a *Beruf* 'occupation' like any other. The establishment, in Burgenland, of agricultural high schools, where people are trained in the latest techniques of grain, dairy, and livestock production, contributes to this attitude. But despite the nascent professionalization of agricultural work, it remains unattractive for Oberwart's young people. Of men in their early twenties in the bilingual Calvinist community, almost all of whom own some land or will own some, only 1%, about five individuals, are making agriculture their main occupation.

Given this negative evaluation of agricultural work in contrast to desirable wage work, it is hardly surprising that Hungarian, the language used by and now associated solely with the peasant community and its Calvinist church has lost respect, while German has gained prestige among bilinguals. Although the ways of life and social groups that each language represents have changed somewhat since the symbolic dichotomy between them first took shape before the start of this century, the early prestige ranking between them has been underscored and, most important, has now been adopted by the peasants themselves. Although the prestige hierarchy has long existed, it is only since the war that the bilinguals have accepted these evaluations of the two languages as relevant to their own lives. As a result, for young people German is no longer just the potentially useful language of outsiders such as the Lutheran merchants and elites, standing in opposition to "in-group" Hungarian. Rather, German has gained prestige for bilinguals because it has become associated as well with the world of employment to which the former

The Wednesday market in the *Hauptplatz*.

peasants and their children aspire and which they are entering in increasing numbers.

CONCLUSION

The broad outlines of the relationship of social change to language use in Oberwart over the last seven centuries can be briefly characterized in the following way: The peasants of Oberwart (Felsőőr) have been speaking Hungarian since about 1000 when they settled in what is now the easternmost province of Austria. Between 1200 and 1500 the village became a speech island, completely surrounded by German- and Croatian-speaking communities. Probably there have been German–Hungarian bilinguals in Oberwart since that time. By the nineteenth century the majority of Oberwart peasants were bilinguals.

It was during that century that Oberwart grew from a peasant village to a religiously and ethnically diverse and socially stratified town. Its location on the trade route between Austria and Hungary encouraged commerce. The village grew not primarily because of an increase in the indigenous (and by this time largely Calvinist) population, but by the immigration of other groups. In particular, Lutheran Germans and Catholic Germans formed a wealthy, urban, and prestigious class of merchants, artisans, and bureaucrats. In the social hierarchy of the growing town, the Hungarian Calvinist peasants were the lowest, poorest, and least prestigious stratum. A symbolically important dichotomy was formed: the rich local elites spoke German, the peasants were bilingual and were the only ones who spoke Hungarian. After Burgenland was transferred from Hungary to Austria in 1921 this dichotomy was underscored. German was not only a local elite language, but became the national language as well.

But although this prestige ranking of the two languages clearly existed, peasants did not recognize its applicability to their own in-group, where different values, different prestige hierarchies and contacts with towns inside Hungary were maintained. As long as subsistence agriculture remained economically feasible and Hungary remained accessible, the Hungarian language retained, for peasants, its value as a symbol of group identity. German, on the other hand, was seen by them merely as a convenient resource. It proved very useful in earning supplemental income through wage labor for local German artisans and merchants. However, such labor was not lucrative or regular enough to replace peasant agriculture and the land-centered value system associated with it. Whatever its place in relation to German, for the peasant community, Hungarian remained a symbol of pride and the primary language.

Only since World War II have industrial, commercial, and bureaucratic jobs become widely available and economically preferable to peasant agriculture. Since the war, upward mobility through wage labor has been possible for large numbers of peasants and their children. Because German is a prerequisite for education and training, and therefore for employment of almost every kind, knowledge of German is no longer simply convenient but is considered an economic necessity. More importantly, as young people today consistently enter the Austrian labor force and not peasant agriculture, the peasant value system that Hungarian has represented for centuries is being abandoned in favor of one based on money, on the ownership of consumer goods, and on a more sophisticated urban view of clothing, housing and entertainment. The children of Oberwart's Hungarian-speaking peasants are no longer using German simply as a means of earning money. They now accept the higher prestige of German and scorn Hungarian because they are attempting to adopt the way of life and values of the *Hauptplatz*, the German-speaking Austrian urban center that for over a century has been developing around them.

3

Styles of Hungarian and German

The link between the broad social changes of the last century and the process of language shift is found in the pattern and function of Oberwart's synchronic linguistic heterogeneity.

Although it is well understood that among monolinguals there are no speakers limited to a single style, the investigation of stylistic variation has rarely been extended to bilingual communities. With few exceptions descriptions of bilingual communities have concentrated exclusively on the choice between the two languages, treating each language as internally homogeneous. However, the evidence from Oberwart demonstrates that bilingual speakers do, in fact, regularly use a range of styles within each language. In addition, contrary to one current hypothesis, style-shifting does not depend simply on the degree of attention paid to speech. Rather, it serves expressive functions for the bilingual speaker. The distinction between these two explanations of style-shifting is important because, if style-shifting is indeed used for expressive purposes, then questions are raised about the distribution of communicative functions during language shift. Many studies have suggested that in bilingual communities the choice between languages serves the expressive functions conveyed by style-shifting among monolinguals. Yet Oberwart's bilingual speakers, who have styles as well as languages to choose from, use style-shifting within one language in much the same way and for the same purposes as monolinguals.

SOURCES OF EVIDENCE

Tape recordings provided the major source of linguistic evidence. During the first few months of my stay in Oberwart, I taped a set of relatively structured interviews. In each of these, I was alone with one or two people in their homes. The interviews were usually my first or second contact with informants and lasted an hour or more. Although the Calvinist minister and his family and the Catholic priest gave me the names of some people who they thought might be interested in talking to me, the first people I actually interviewed were those I met while looking for a room to rent and those who worked in the neighborhood inn where I frequently ate dinner. In addition, people I had already interviewed often suggested that I talk with their kin and neighbors. All of these first interviews were conducted in Hungarian. This seemed the most advantageous choice for several reasons. I am a native speaker of Hungarian and politeness demanded that, at least at first, people speak Hungarian to someone identified as a native of Hungary. Also, Hungarian was then easier for me than German. Later, with the help of a local German monolingual student I was able to interview many of the same people in German, as the presence of a monolingual made use of German mandatory. I also taped interviews with a number of children, two friends at a time, aged 11 to 14. They were asked about their daily lives, sports, and records and then were asked to tell a story, first in one language and then in the other. These interviews were supplemented by several traditional, linguistic-elicitation sessions.

During the interviews with adults, I asked about each person's family history, language-learning history, early life and, if appropriate, war experiences. This last was a favorite topic for older men and women and was meant to evoke exciting personal narratives, following the technique described by Labov (1972:90–94). During most interview sessions I was asked to explain my background and answered questions about the research, my family, and life in America. With some informants, especially young women my age, it was quickly possible to commiserate about parental restrictions. Older people frequently expressed concern and sympathy about my being away from my home and family. We exchanged stories about separations and loneliness. Men whom I interviewed joked about my being alone and without male protection. All of these topics seemed to me to be outside the formal interview. They were not directly related to my prepared set of questions, often they involved some reversal of the roles of interviewer and interviewee, and appeared to be leading toward more familiarity. However, despite such attempts at sampling more "casual" speech through the standard sociolinguistic methods of encouraging involvement and informality, a frustratingly narrow range of styles was used by everyone in the early tapes. The event remained an interview and retained its formal character. My status as a stranger to the community with no kin or friendship ties, as a university student from the U.S. and as a speaker of standard Hungarian, made these initial interactions with Oberwarters anomalous and strained, despite most people's attempts at friendliness. As is often the case in sociolinguistic fieldwork, my daily experiences in the bilingual neighborhood indicated that people actually varied their speech considerably more in the course of everyday interaction than they did during the interviews.

Much more productive than these early interviews, at least from the point of view of recording a range of speaking styles, were the tapes I made during the second half-year of fieldwork. This was after several months of living in a family's spare room, attending church, regularly helping two households with their agricultural work, being the object of *Felszeg* gossip—in short, doing participant observation. This second set of tapes included recordings of naturally occurring conversation in a wide variety of settings. It was possible to make such recordings only when mutual interest, familiarity and sympathy developed between some members of a family and myself. In all, the members of eight households and visitors, having initially given permission to be recorded, were taped over the course of several months. These speakers ranged in age from 3 to 74. They were recorded during various daily activities, including card playing, dinner conversation, and housework. In these situations, my concern with ethnographic and linguistic information was not the focus of attention. By this time my presence was somewhat less strange and people often spoke more to each other than to me. In several cases I was not in the room during the bulk of a recording: the tape recorder was left running on the kitchen table while I went on an errand or worked in another room. No doubt these conversations were different in numerous ways than they would have been without the presence of the tape recorder. However, the recordings make a striking contrast to the original interviews and reveal a range of variation in style that would have been difficult to document in other ways.

Information from all of the tapes was used for the following description of Oberwart's linguistic repertoire. In addition, tapes of four speakers, two children and two adults, were selected to provide the evidence for a more detailed analysis of style-shifting. By first choosing several linguistic variables in each language, the speech of these four people in the early interviews was compared with their speech in everyday household interactions.

THE RANGE OF STYLES

It is useful to think of bilingual Oberwart's linguistic repertoire as a set of possible choices ranging from standard Austrian German to local German and from local Hungarian to standard Hungarian (Figure 3.1). The

Figure 3.1.   Schematic representation of Oberwart's linguistic repertoire.

varieties of German are not mutually intelligible with the varieties of Hungarian. Within each language the labels "local" and "standard" do not denote bounded linguistic entities or separate structural systems. Rather, in this instance as in the many well-documented cases of stylistic variation in stratified monolingual communities, most linguistic differences between variants within each language are matters of degree. Instead of forming two structural wholes, educated Austrian German and local Oberwart German can be described as a single system. The same is true of standard Hungarian and local Oberwart Hungarian. In each case, many phonological elements remain constant while a limited number have a range of possible realizations, being linguistic variables in Labov's sense (1964:166). Morphological variation also exists within each language, but most grammatical categories such as noun classes, cases and verb tenses remain the same. The morphological differences within each language are also best described as variables in one grammatical system.

To define strict boundaries between variants or to distinguish a set number of styles between the local and standard extremes in such a system would be difficult and arbitrary. Nevertheless, the notion of local dialect as opposed to a standard remains useful if it is understood to mean that, from the linguist's point of view, both German and Hungarian include linguistic variables that covary, tend to co-occur with particular lexical items, and, depending on the nonlinguistic context, can be used to convey social meanings. At the same time, certain of these lexical items and some realizations of linguistic variables are identified by native speakers as more educated and prestigious variants while others are taken to be less prestigious local forms. Speakers are therefore able to sound more "local" or less "local" in either language, depending partly on their choice of words, on the phonetic realizations of variables, and on the relative frequency with which particular values of linguistic variables occur in their speech.

All the informants in this study are bilingual—they are able to communicate in both languages. However, individuals vary in the range of styles they control in each language. The degree and types of experiences with each language are among the important determinants of how closely any individual is able to approximate the prestigious standard forms. The language in which a person was educated and the number of years of education make a difference, as does the amount of contact a person has in everyday activities with monolinguals. Generally, interaction with both Hungarian and German monolinguals has made Oberwart bilinguals aware of monolingual pronunciation, lexical choice, syntax, and style that do not correspond to their own bilingual usage. It has thereby provided linguistic models for those who want them.

As a broad overview of variation in stylistic range, it is fair to say that people who learned German relatively late in life (these are often men and women over 50) and who have little daily contact with monolingual German speakers, are least likely to be able to approach prestigious forms of Austrian German. Often these same people can be identified as bilinguals because of Hungarian interference in their German. On the other hand, those under 20 or so who have attended exclusively German-language schools and have rarely spoken to a monolingual Hungarian speaker are least likely to be able to approach standard Hungarian. However, there are also many speakers, often in their thirties and forties, who are not easily identified as bilinguals because they show little or no characteristic interference in either language and who are also capable of a wide range of stylistic variation in both languages.

GERMAN

Austria, especially non–Alpine Austria, differs from the rest of German-speaking Europe in that there is less of a linguistic difference between the speech of educated urban speakers and the many local village dialects. Keller (1961:200) notes that in Austria no great "linguistic gulf" separates the regional dialect-speaking peasants from each other or from the upper, or educated, classes. This is partly because the educated classes of Vienna, and even the more geographically dispersed educated classes of what was once the Habsburg Empire, never accepted the North German *Hochdeutsch* 'standard'. They insisted that their own versions of the supraregional Austrian *Herrensprache* 'upper class, aristocratic language' had as much right to be considered prestigious, proper German as that of the northerners. The historical and political reasons for the relative lack of difference (Kranzmayer 1955:262–269, 1956:2) are less important here than the consequent linguistic circumstances of Austrian market towns such as Oberwart. If the dialect of peasant villagers differs relatively little from the careful, prestigious speech of educated urbanites, then the everyday speech of market towns differs even less. According to Austrian dialectology, market towns are the source of urban features that are later adopted by villages. In fact, the special terms *Verkehrssprache* and *Umgangssprache* have long been used to characterize regional forms that are neither educated urban speech nor village dialects (Waterman 1976:185). For instance, Keller (1961), writing as a dialectologist with notions of dialect purity, notes: "The inhabitants of [Austrian] country towns also speak dialect, but in a diminishing degree of genuineness [p. 201]." In the case of Oberwart one may expect even fewer linguistic peculiarities than in other market towns because this is typically the case in areas where a shift from one language to another has taken place (Gumperz and Bennett 1976:22–23).

Nevertheless, there are differences between the speech of educated urban Austrians and the everyday local speech of Oberwart, both in the view of linguists and in the view of natives. Oberwarters feel that, although as a city Oberwart has no provincial peculiarities of speech in the way small villages do, one nonetheless has a choice between speaking normally, or speaking better, that is, in the way first taught and practiced in school. This latter is sometimes called talking *nach Schrift* 'according to writing.' On the basis of certain criterial words and phonetic differences, dialectologists identify the local German spoken in the villages of Burgenland as a combination of Middle and Southern Bavarian characteristics (Hornung and Roitinger 1950:47–55; Pfalz 1951:380; Wiesinger 1967:129–130). It contains some features found primarily in the Middle Bavarian area of Lower and Upper Austria, as well as features found farther south in Styria. While the dialects of small villages in middle Burgenland are called, in German, *Heanzischen* or *Hienzischen* dialects (in Hungarian: *Hienc*) by both natives and linguists, no one has a special word for local Oberwart German.

The dialectological classification of Burgenland German rests on data gathered through linguistic questionnaires which specifically ask how something is said in local speech. As Blom and Gumperz have pointed out (1972:413–414), this data-gathering procedure itself assures that only the local forms most different from standard educated speech will be provided by informants. Data collected in this way always support the conclusion that the dialect is a distinct and separate system. These procedures are not designed to tap the community's range of linguistic resources, nor to provide information about patterns of style-shifting. Nevertheless such a traditional dialectological description is the starting point for studying speech use in everyday interaction. It is a way of locating possible linguistic variables as well as constants and it helps to identify what is considered typically "local" by native speakers.

Unfortunately the dialectological categorization and description of Burgenland is based almost exclusively on phonetic studies conducted in the north (Bedi 1912; Gräftner 1966; Puhr 1925; Rauchbauer 1932; Seidelmann 1957). Of the more southern region, in which Oberwart is located, there are only two studies (Karner 1930; Laky 1937). Both were done several decades ago and would therefore be more useful in a historical study of sound change than for investigating present-day use. Since the local German of Oberwart itself has never been described, a dialectological sketch of it is in order here. For this description I will use "dialect" to mean locally occurring forms deemed most different from urban, educated, *nach Schrift* speech. For brevity I will call this ideal of educated and prestigious speech "standard." My summary of the ways in which local Oberwart German is most different from standard is based on elicitation and observation; contrasts and comparisons were also made with data provided by Karner (1930), Keller (1960:200–247), Laky (1937), and Wiesinger (1967:81–184).

The consonant system of educated speech is based on a distinction between voiced and voiceless stops, fricatives and affricates in labial, alveolar, and velar positions. However, voicing is nondistinctive in final position. The dialect, on the other hand, has stops, fricatives, and affricates at the same articulation points, but does not use the voicing distinction at all. Rather, fortis obstruents *p t k f s x pf ts t* are opposed to lenis ones *b d g v z ž bv dz d* and all are voiceless.[1] While this contrast is maintained for final position, in initial position the dialect does not distinguish lenis from fortis; all stops and fricatives are closest to fortis. For example in the dialect the pairs *backen* 'to bake' and *packen* 'to pack' are homonyms **pokn**. *Ich fahre* 'I ride' and *ich war* 'I was' become *i foa*. Intervocalic *b* is often a fricative, *aber* 'but' **ovʌ**, *Arbeit* 'work' **oavat**.

While the standard has liquids *r* and *l* both before and after vowels (except that morphfinal *er* is vocalized), in the dialect they do not occur after vowels. After vowels, *r* is omitted and if *r* occurs after a back vowel,

---

[1] The IPA orthography is used for describing the German used in Oberwart except that the symbols usually used to distinguish voiced from voiceless (e.g., *b, p*) will be used here to represent the lenis–fortis distinction. German words in conventional orthography appear in italics; those written in phonetic orthography are in italic boldface.

the vowel is diphthongized; *l* is also usually deleted after vowels. If the vowel is unrounded it becomes a diphthong, but if it is a rounded front vowel it is unrounded. For instance *Dorf* 'village' *duof*, *Garten* 'garden' *koadn*, *wollte* '(he) wanted' *vujd* and *Gelt* 'money' *kɸd*. Final -*ç*, -*x* do not occur in the dialect, so *ich* 'I' is *i*, *auch* 'also' *a*, and *noch* 'still, yet' *no*.

In the dialect as in the standard there are labial, alveolar and velar nasals, but in the dialect one-syllable words ending with a nasal often lose it: *ein* 'one' *a*, and sometimes the previous vowel is nasalized, e.g., *Mann* 'man' *mão*, *Kann* '(I) can' *kão*. In compounds, the nasal remains: *einheizen* 'to heat the room' *anhatsn*. Final *en* in forming the infinitive verb or in words such as *Ofen* 'oven' and *oben* 'upstairs' is a syllabic nasal, which, in the dialect, is assimilated in its place of articulation to the preceding consonant, e.g., *ofm*. This assimilation occurs even when the consonant is itself deleted as is often the case with intervocalic lenis stops *b, d, g: oben om, geben* 'to give' *kem, sagen* 'to say' *soŋ, Augen* 'eye(s)' *aəŋ*.

As in all middle Bavarian dialects, the length of vowels in Oberwart is dependent on the quality of the following consonants (Keller 1960:206–207). Long vowels are always followed by one or more lenis consonants, short vowels by one or more fortis consonants. The following applies only to vowels in stressed positions in a word. Generally, the back vowels of the standard are raised in the dialect. The standard's low back vowel as in *Vater* 'father' is *fodʌ*, *acht* 'eight' is *oxd*, *ab-* 'off, away' *op*. The dialect does have a low back vowel, which corresponds to the standard's diphthong *aj* as in *Heim* 'home' *ham*. Before nasals the dialect's low back vowel is diphthongized *oā*. The standard's mid-back vowel, as in *wohl* 'well,' is raised to *u* when followed by nasals or liquids as in *wohl fu, sonst* 'otherwise' *sunst, kommt* '(he) comes' *kumt*. The highest back vowel of the standard, as in *gut* 'good' is a diphthong in the dialect *kuʌd~kuid*, *Mutter* 'mother' *muajdʌ*, *Schuster* 'shoemaker' *ʃuazdʌ*.

The rounded front vowels of the standard are systematically unrounded in the dialect so that *für* 'for' *fi*, *früh* 'early' *friʌ*, *Glück* 'luck' *klik*, *fünf* 'five' *fimf*, *möchte* '(I) would like' *mixd*, *Vögel* 'birds' *fegl*, *blöd* 'stupid' *pled*, *schön* 'beautiful' *fē*. But, although the standard's rounded vowels are unrounded in the dialect, the dialect has its own full series of rounded front vowels in words where the standard has a front unrounded vowel followed by a liquid. For instance: *viel* 'many' *fy*, *spielen* 'to play' *ʃpyjn*, *Gelt* 'money' *kɸd*, *Zelt* 'tent' *tsɸd*, *mehr* 'more' *mɸ*, *eingesperrt* 'locked in' *aŋkʃpyt*.

The high front unrounded vowels of the standard tend to be lowered in the dialect. For instance, the standard's short high front vowel *i* is often close *e* in the dialect: *nicht* 'not' *net*, *sitz* 'sit (imperative)' *sets*. When it is in final position, however, it remains high: *dich* 'you (acc.)' *di*, *mich* 'me (acc.)' *mi*. What is a long high front vowel in the standard, as in *lieb* 'cute' is, in the dialect, a lower front diphthong *leap*, *ihm* 'him (dat.)' *eam*. The standard mid-front vowel *e* is lower in dialect: *gelegt* 'put' *klɛkt*, *nächsten* 'next' *nɛkstn*. But the lower mid-front unrounded vowel of the standard *ɛ* is higher in the dialect: *essen* 'to eat' *ejsn*, *jetzt* 'now' *jetst*. The lowest front vowel of the dialect, a very fronted *a*, occurs in words which, in the standard, have the diphthong *au*, such as *auch* 'also' *a*, *Baum* 'tree' *pam*, *kaum* 'hardly' *kam* and *kaufen* 'to buy' *kafm*.

Most of the diphthongs in the dialect have already been mentioned: they occur where standard liquids are omitted and in place of standard long *i* and *u*. In addition, the standard's diphthong *oj* in words like *neu* 'new,' *heute* 'today,' *Deutsch* 'German,' and *Freund* 'friend' is also a diphthong in the dialect, but usually a lower front one: *naj*, *hajt*, *tajtf*, or occasionally a slightly higher *tɛjtf*, and *frajnd* or *frɛjnd*. The other diphthongs found in the standard are monothongs in the dialect. As mentioned above standard *au* is dialect *a* and standard *aj*, as in *kein* 'none', *weiβ* '(I) know,' and *einmal* 'once' is, in the dialect, the lowest back open vowel *ka(n)*, *fas*, *amo*, or rarely, a close mid-front diphthong: *Fleisch* 'meat' *fleaf*, *klein* 'small' *klean*.

Unstressed vowels, especially in articles and prefixes are usually lost, as in the standard's prefixes *ge-*, *be-* and *de-*. And in Oberwart, as in most Bavarian dialects, the final *ə* of the standard in nouns, the first person singular of most verbs and in most adjectives is lost: *Sprache* 'language' *fprox*, *Schule* 'school' *ful*, *ich habe* 'I have' *i hop*, *ich sage* 'I say' *i sog*, and *gerade* 'straight, direct' *krod*. However, the final *ə* remains when it marks the plural, *Stein* 'stone,' *Steine* 'stones' *ftanə*.

In sum, the number and type of simple vowels is the same as in the standard although their distribution is different. There are some diphthongs that do not occur in the standard:

Rounded Front		Unrounded				Diphthong	
y		*i*		*u*		*uʌ~ui*	
φ		*e*		*o*	*ej*		
		ɛ	*ə*		*ea*		*uo*
			ʌ	*a*	*aj*		*oɑ*
		a					

Other salient characteristics of the local German include: the past participle of verbs beginning with a vowel a liquid or a fricative have the prefix *k* instead of the standard *gə*; those beginning with stops have no prefix at all, and verbs with separable prefixes also have no past participle prefix. So for instance: *hat gesehen* '(he) saw' *hot ksenk*, *ist gegangen* '(he) went' *is koŋ*, *ist gekommen* '(he) came' *is kumn*, *hat eingekauft* '(he) shopped' *hot nkaf*, *hat hingezeigt* '(he) presented, displayed' *hot hintsak*. The present indicative conjugation of several frequently occurring strong verbs differs from the standard. This is the case with the verb *sein* 'to be', both as substantive and as auxiliary:

Local forms

I am	*bin*	*pi*
you are (fam.)	*bist*	*pis*
he is	*ist*	*is*
we, they are	*sind*	*saŋs~sɛns*
you are (fam. pl.)	*seid*	*sats*

Some particles of motion are included in the local dialect, as in the standard, but their forms differ:

Movement away from speaker		*Toward speaker*	
	Local forms		Local forms
out of	*hinaus-*	*nasi*	*heraus-*	*asi*
into	*hinein-*	*naŋni*	*herein-*	*anə*

Dialect nouns and articles differ from standard in several ways. For instance, the noun class without distinction for number is much larger in the local than in the standard. 'Church' *Kirche*, and its plural *Kirchen* are both *kirxn*. Other such nouns include: *Gasse* 'street' *kosn*, *Sache* 'thing' *soxn*. The declensions of both definite and indefinite articles differ between standard and dialect. For instance, for the indefinite articles local dialect does not distinguish gender in the nominative case at all, nor does it distinguish between masculine and neuter in any of the commonly used cases. It also does not distinguish between the feminine dative and accusative (see below). However, masculine and neuter are distinguished by the dialect in both the definite article and the demonstrative pronoun systems.

Indefinite articles

Masculine		Feminine		Neuter	
Local forms		Local forms		Local forms	
Nom. *ein*	*a*	*eine*	*a*	*ein*	*a*
Dat. *einem*	*am*	*einer*	*anə*	*einem*	*am*
Acc. *einen*	*ən*	*eine*	*anə*	*ein*	*ən*

As in many nonstandard forms of German, the standard's genitive declension of nouns and articles is not used but is replaced by prepositions and, in the case of the possessive function, by a dative paraphrase: *den Seper sein Sohn* for 'Seper's son', *den Kirch sein Tochtl* 'Kirch's daughter'. And finally, the personal pronouns in post-verbal position, as in questions and imperatives, are sharply abbreviated retaining only the consonant in *du, dich* 'you', *sie* 'they, she, you' and *es* 'it', *wir* 'we' is *miʌ* in pre-verbal position and *ma* in post-verbal position. This produces: *haben Sie* 'do you have' *homs*, *sagen Sie* 'say, tell (imperative)' *soŋs*, *hast du* 'do you have' *hosd* and the very frequently heard *gehen wir* 'let's go' *kema*.

This brief summary of salient contrasts indicates that the differences between "standard" and "local" speech can be described as morphophonemically different realizations of the same grammatical categories.

GERMAN VARIABLES

Having given some indication of local speech in terms of the traditional dichotomy of dialect and standard, it is now possible to examine the range of variation in speakers' performances by using the concept of linguistic variable. This will provide a much more faithful description of the linguistic situation in everyday interaction. To do this two sets of tapes were compared.

The first set consisted of two tapes, made at different times, each a structured interview with a 14-year-old girl. Each girl was asked to tell a fairy tale she knew well. It happened that both told *Hansel and Gretel*. Each interview took place in my room with only the informant, one friend of hers and myself present. Although the girls and I were friendly, the task of telling a story first in one language and then in another was probably perceived as a school-like test situation. To contrast with the story-telling, a tape was chosen of each girl as she interacted with her own family on a weekday afternoon. Each girl's speech on one tape was contrasted with her own performance on the other tape. Admittedly the two situations differ on many dimensions. While not specifying the exact social differences between the two events, this comparison nevertheless demonstrates the existence and gradualness of intraindividual linguistic variation. Each story was timed and a similar short stretch of the girls' speech at home was used for comparison. Since the results for the two girls were very similar they were pooled.

Some of the differences identified above between dialect and *nach Schrift* speech turned out not to vary between these two situations. For instance, even in telling the story the girls did not distinguish lenis from fortis initial stops and fricatives. Nevertheless many of the elicited phonological differences between dialect and *nach Schrift* speech appeared on the tapes as variables.

Three related phonological differences mentioned above were examined in detail: (*1*) the raising of the back vowel *a* in all positions except before *r* and nasals, (*2*) the diphthongization and nasalization of the low back vowel *a* before nasals, and (*3*) the omission of *r* when it follows a low back vowel and the diphthongization of the vowel.

In the case of the back vowel *a*, speakers do not alternate between two totally different and distinct points of articulation. Rather, in these tapes there are at least three positions of articulation: the low back open vowel *a*; a higher and more closed vowel *ɔ*; and an even higher vowel with lip rounding *o*. The same holds for the back vowel followed by a nasal. Three versions may be distinguished: *an* again, the lowest, furthest back of the three; *ʌn*, which is a low central vowel with no lip rounding, and the diphthong *ʌon*, which is higher and has some lip rounding. In these environments *o* and *ʌon* are the forms most different from standard.

In the case of omitting *r*, although it may be said that there are two versions, one with *r* and one an *r*-less diphthong, it is not the difference itself but the frequency of occurrence of each version that distinguishes the speech in the two situations. This is true of the other two variables as well. So, for all three linguistic environments of *a*, both girls used more dialect forms in family interactions and fewer dialect forms in the interview, but both standard and dialect forms appeared in all tapes. Table 3.1 contains a summary of this variation. Notice also that the variables covary, so that when the frequency of the more standard value of one variable is highest, then in that tape the same is true of the other variables as well.

Although morphological differences did not occur frequently enough in the course of the storytelling to allow for a quantitative analysis, it is noteworthy that the standard forms of the indefinite article that occurred at all, occurred during the storytelling, although not all indefinite articles in the story were full standard forms. The same is true of particles of motion.

In sum, Table 3.1 shows not only that in the German speech of individuals there can be several realizations of one linguistic variable, but also that the frequency of occurrence of these can vary with the situation. As one might expect, in the situations considered here, the values in the direction of the dialect were more frequent in the home conversation while the others were more frequent in the interview story.

TABLE 3.1

Frequency of Occurrence of Values of German Phonological Variables in the Speech of Two Girls in Two Situations

Linguistic variables	Values	Interview story	Home conversation
No. 1	*a*	.47	.07
a	ɔ	.51	.80
	o	.02	.13
		n = 39	*n* = 53
No. 2	*an*	.65	.05
a + nasal	ʌ*n*	.31	.43
	ʌ*on*	.04	.52
		n = 19	*n* = 13
No. 3	*ar*	1.0	.15
a + *r*	*oa*	0	.85
		n = 2	*n* = 8

HUNGARIAN

Bilingual Oberwarters consider their local Hungarian to be peculiar to Oberwart, differing in identifiable ways from the prestigious Hungarian standard on the one hand and from the speech of neighboring Hungarian villages on the other. They name two ways of speaking Hungarian. To say something *üöriesen* 'in the Felsőőr way' refers to local forms. Such speech lacks prestige because use of it identifies the speaker as a native of Oberwart and, by implication, a peasant. However, among Oberwarters, use of local forms is usually the only appropriate choice. The association of local variants with community and peasant identity and the social pressure to use local forms are best illustrated by the case of a woman who, some 5 years ago, was overheard giving her own name at the town hall with a standard rather than local pronunciation. Even though the setting was the town hall, the person she was speaking to was another native Oberwarter and her speech was judged to be inappropriate. It was sanctioned at the time by ridicule. This single instance of inappropriate speech is still remembered and was recounted more than once, each time with the same moral: the woman was showing off, but no matter how she says her name she is just a peasant like the rest of us. Local speech has its acknowledged specialties that contrast with the similarly well-known linguistic specialties of other Hungarian villages in Burgenland. In contrast to this, the speech of educated Hungarians is called *röndes madzsar* 'proper Hungarian', and they are said to speak *irásilag* 'according to writing'. Such standard forms are felt to be esthetically superior to local ones. In the presence of those who usually speak standard Hungarian, Oberwarters invariably deprecate their own speech, saying that they admire and prefer the clarity and beauty of the standard. Note that these attitudes about Hungarian differ considerably from Oberwarters' conception of the German they speak. The German of Oberwart can be spoken well or badly, but its forms are neither deprecated nor held to have local peculiarities such as those typical of the German spoken in nearby peasant villages. Judging by language attitudes and conceptions, it appears that in its German speech Obertwart is considered a city, but in Hungarian it is a peasant village.

The linguistic difference noted by Oberwarters between standard Hungarian, spoken by educated urbanites, and the local forms is also of importance to linguists. Hungarian dialects generally differ very little from each other or from the standard, but communities such as Oberwart, which are speech islands outside of present-day Hungary, are notable exceptions to this. It has been suggested that the longer the community has been a speech island the more divergent its dialect is likely to be. Dialectologists attribute the greater divergence of speech-island dialects to the lack of constant influence from the standard and from neighboring dialects. This, they argue, has permitted unusual innovations as well as retention of features that are archaic in the standard. Similarly, archaic features that have been retained in the standard may have been discarded by the dialect. Also recognized as a cause of divergence is the influence of the foreign language with which the speech island is necessarily in close contact (Imre 1971a:30–36).

It is not surprising, then, that, although the Hungarian dialect of Oberwart shares many features with Transdanubian dialects, it is different enough from them and from the standard to cause occasional problems of intelligibility for outsiders trying to understand the dialect (Imre 1977). On first trips to Hungary young Oberwarters often notice this, but can overcome it. This degree of divergence has made Oberwart's dialect particularly important for Hungarian linguists interested in historical reconstruction and in the language's structural possibilities. Partly because of its theoretical importance, the speech of Oberwart has been very thoroughly described in traditional dialectological terms. Perhaps also contributing to the abundance of information on Oberwart Hungarian is the fact that Samu Imre, one of Hungary's leading linguists, is a native of Oberwart and has been analyzing his dialect for almost 40 years. Imre's monographs and dictionaries carefully describe the phonology, morphology, and vocabulary, and, in keeping with dialectological tradition, explain the ways in which the dialect is most different from other dialects and from the standard (Imre 1940, 1941, 1942, 1943, 1971a,b, 1973a,b, 1977). There are also other sources of information relevant to a study of Oberwart speech. These works, which are generally less sensitive than Imre's to the effects of social factors, include a short early report by Varga (1903) and the dialect atlas of Őrség and Hetés counties, located within Hungary, southeast of Oberwart (Végh 1959).

One characteristic of Oberwart Hungarian that is mentioned at least briefly in many of these reports is particularly salient and deserves special attention here: the large scale borrowing of German elements into Hungarian sentences. Word borrowing is common in bilingual communities. It is to be distinguished from language switching, although both involve a combination of items considered to belong to separate languages. Borrowing consists of the introduction of single words or short idiomatic phrases from one language into the other, occasionally without, but most often with, phonological and even semantic changes in the borrowed item. In Oberwart, speakers' knowledge of monolingual norms, which deprecate borrowing, makes them reluctant to use words they know or suspect to be borrowings when speaking to strangers. Although in my first interviews with Oberwarters I rarely encountered such words, I heard them quite frequently later on, especially in people's everyday conversations with family and neighbors.

Hungarian elements are rarely used in structurally German sentences. The few exceptions include an exclamation (*nohát* 'well'), diminutives of some proper names (*Sanyi, Laci*) and the polite, personal address forms *néni* 'aunt' and *báccsi* 'uncle' which are used, along with the Christian name or surname, for any much older person.[2]

---

[2] The orthography to be used in the following description of Hungarian is that of the Hungarian dialect atlas. While it reflects dialect pronunciation, it uses mostly the letters of conventional Hungarian orthography with only a few additions. Hungarian words in conventional orthography appear in italics; those written in the dialect atlas' orthography are in italic boldface. Hungarian and German words are marked as such unless this is already clearly indicated in the text.

Following is a summary of the Hungarian dialect's phonetic inventory in the orthography of the dialect atlas, with approximate articulation points indicated and with the IPA equivalents in brackets.

But the case is very different in the opposite direction. First, local borrowings must be distinguished from more widespread ones because, as a glance at the *Hungarian Etymological Dictionary* (Benkő 1967a,b) will demonstrate, standard Hungarian has borrowed huge numbers of words from Austrian German, especially in the last few hundred years (Bárczi *et al.* 1967). These words are no longer heard as German by native speakers. They are pronounced with standard Hungarian phonology, they have been assimilated to Hungarian word classes and are incorporated into the Hungarian grammatical system. Examples are words such as *pucol* (H) and *putzen* (G) 'to clean,' and *suszter* (H) and *Schuster* (G) 'shoemaker'. However, in the local Hungarian of Oberwart there are many words of German origin that do not occur in standard Hungarian. They have entered directly from German into local speech and not by way of standard Hungarian. These have been assimilated to local Hungarian, not to standard. Perhaps they should be considered Hungarian dialect words

Footnote 2 continued

Vowels

Short

		Rounded		
front	*i* [*i*]	*ü* [*y*]	*u* [*u*] back
	ē [*ə*]	*ö* [*ɸ*]	*o* [*o*]
	e [*ɛ*]	a [*ʌ*]	

Long

		Rounded		
front	*í* [*i:*]	*ű* [*y*]	*ú* [*u:*] back
	ië [*iə*]	*üö* [*yɸ*]	*uo* [*uo*]
			á [*a*]

Consonants

	Bilabial	Labiodental	Dental	Palatoalveolar	Palatal	Velar
			Voiced			
Stop	*b* [*b*]		*d* [*d*]		*gy* [*ɟ*]	*g* [*g*]
Fricative		*v* [*v*]	*z* [*z*]	*zs* [*ž*]	*j* [*j*]	
Affricate			*dz* [*dz*]	*dzs* [*dž*]		
Liquid			*l* [*l*]			
Roll			*r* [*r*]			
Nasal	*m* [*m*]		*n* [*n*]		*ny* [*ɲ*]	
			Voiceless			
Stop	*p* [*p*]		*t* [*t*]		*ty* [*c*]	*k* [*k*]
Fricative		*f* [*f*]	*sz* [*s*]	*s* [*ʃ*]		*h* [*h*]
Affricate			*c* [*ts*]	*cs* [*tʃ*]		

with German etymology. Examples include: *intereszál* (H) from *interesieren* (G) 'to interest' and *mujder* (H) from *Mutter* (G) 'mother'. Since the process of borrowing is continuous, it is difficult to distinguish between (*a*) full-fledged loan words that were borrowed generations ago and are used by everyone, (*b*) words that are now used by most, though not all, speakers and so are presumably in the process of becoming loan words, and (*c*) words that are used sporadically or idiosyncratically. It is also hard to establish which words have already been accepted as new Hungarian words and which are still heard by many native speakers as German borrowings. The situation today is further complicated by the fact that virtually any German word equipped with Hungarian suffixes and grammatical markers can appear in a Hungarian sentence. Regardless of the number of such words in a sentence, it continues to function as a Hungarian sentence if the affixed grammatical elements (the number and case markers, person and tense markers, articles) remain Hungarian. The German word is used as any item of Hungarian lexicon would be. Imre (1971b) has recently compiled a list of German loan words regularly used in Oberwart Hungarian. He suggests that only the young engage in the kind of 'indiscriminate' borrowing that allows almost any German word into a Hungarian sentence. Yet my own data show that even speakers over 70 generously sprinkle their talk with German words, which must be considered new or idiosyncratic borrowings since they are not in general or regular use. The borrowings of older people do not differ from the similarly idiosyncratic use of German words in the speech of the younger generations.

Not surprisingly, nouns and verbs are the most commonly borrowed lexical items (Gal 1977). In these examples (1–4), only the German and its translation are in boldface:[3]

(1)   **Plicc**üt ez **aparát**.
        The **camera flash**ed.

(2)   Tegnap este **unfol**je vot e **moped**vje.
        Last night he had an **accident** with his **motorbike**.

(3)   Dzsere vacsorára, ne **blájdiguj** ingem.
        Come for supper, don't **offend** me.

(4)   Takaritnunk, dzsün e **svigerlájt**.
        We're cleaning, the **in-laws** are coming.

---

[3] These and all subsequent numbered examples are written in phonetic (German) and dialect atlas (Hungarian) orthography.

Local Hungarian has productive processes for assimilating German nouns and verbs. Nearly all borrowed verbs are assimilated to the class of Hungarian verbs ending in *l:* e.g., *lastn* (G) 'accomplish, perform' becomes the root *lájsztul* (H) with the same meaning and *psuxn* (G) 'to visit' becomes the root *peszukel* (H), also with the same meaning. Nouns are either used in their original German form e.g., *tinst* (G), 'service, duty' *tinszt* (H), or local German nouns ending in syllabic *n* are often incorporated with the suffix *ni* e.g., *hiftn* (G) 'hip' becomes *hiftni* (H), *tozn* (G) 'can(s), tin' becomes *tozni* (H), *plotn* (G) 'record(s)' *plotni* (H). German nouns ending in syllabic *l* including diminutives are assimilated with the suffix *li*, or *i*, for instance *medl* (G) 'girl' *médi* (H), and *fnitsl* (G) 'cutlet' is *snicli* (H). Also, as both Hungarian and German have separable verbal prefixes, many of which indicate direction of motion and often correspond in the two languages, some prefixes on borrowed German verbs are translated into the Hungarian equivalents *ein* (G) = *be* (H), *aus* (G) = *ki* (H), *auf* (G) = *fel* (H) 'in', 'out', 'up'. So for instance, *belodul* (H) from German *anlodn* (G) 'invite' and *küzeccül* (H) from German *aussetsn* (G) 'stop or discontinue'.

Borrowings are not limited to new technology or new semantic domains. On the one hand, recently introduced machines, Austrian political–bureaucratic titles and institutions, as well as obligations and privileges which Oberwarters have as Austrian citizens are named with German nouns and their Hungarian equivalents are known by few if any Oberwarters e.g., *medrɛʃʌ* (G) 'combine, harvester' is *médreser* (H), *feən-sen* (G) 'TV' is *fernszé* (H), *aliment* (G) 'alimony' is *aliment* (H). But there are also many German nouns and verbs now in use for which Hungarian dialect equivalents do exist and that are often used side by side with the Hungarian forms: *ádresz* from German as well as *cím* from Hungarian 'address'; *firtsoftul* from German as well as *gazdákod* from Hungarian '(he) farms'; *spitol* from German as well as *kurház* from Hungarian 'hospital,' *ja, jo* 'yes' from German, as well as *igën* from Hungarian.

Although rarer than nouns and verbs, modifiers, exclamations, greetings, and other frozen phrases from German are also often used in Hungarian sentences, e.g., *niksz cu mokn* from German 'nothing can be done', or *a so* from German, roughly 'oh, I see'.

Large-scale word borrowing is only one of the features of Oberwart Hungarian that distinguishes it from other dialects and the standard. However, since excellent dialectological descriptions of Oberwart Hungarian are available elsewhere, there is no need to provide a traditional summary here of the local forms most different from the standard. Rather it will be possible to move beyond a catalogue of dichotomous differences to offer an analysis of variation in the use of Hungarian.

HUNGARIAN VARIABLES

This discussion of variation in the Hungarian repertoire of Oberwart is based on three recordings. As with the German tapes, they were chosen for contrast, to show a range of variation in the use of Hungarian. One of the speakers was a man in his seventies, Miska báccsi, who had been a peasant all his life. He was now living as a pensioner. Although he was no longer working his land, he had quite a bit of land by Oberwart standards, had served as a presbyter of the Calvinist church, and as a representative on the town council. The other speaker was his wife, Anna néni, who was in her sixties and had also always been a peasant.

One tape is an interview with Miska báccsi and Anna néni at their house. It was the first time I had spoken to them at length. The interview started with questions about the land inheritance system in Oberwart, how it worked in general and how it had worked specifically in their case, and then proceeded to questions about their family history. The tape of part of this interview, in which Miska báccsi and Anna néni each spoke for about half the time, was compared to two other tapes. One of these was a conversation between Miska báccsi and a former neighbor, a man who had, as usual, come over to play cards in the afternoon. The second tape was a conversation on a different day between Anna néni and another man, a neighbor who had also come over to play cards. On this occasion Miska báccsi was temporarily out, but Anna néni and the neighbor proceeded anyway to exchange the latest news so that when Miska báccsi finally arrived they could get down to serious card playing. By the time these tapes were made I knew the couple and even many of their neighbors fairly well; I had talked to them daily for about a month and lived nearby. For most of each tape I was not in the kitchen with them—the tape recorder was, as usual, sitting on the kitchen table—and even when I was there my presence was acknowledged but I was only briefly drawn into the conversation. Miska báccsi's speech in the interview was compared to his speech when conversing with his neighbor; Anna néni's speech in the interview, to her conversation with the other neighbor. The data from the two conversations were similar enough to be considered together.

To accurately describe the range and use of the Hungarian repertoire it is first necessary to locate linguistic variables and then to determine the frequency with which each value of each variable occurs in the interview as opposed to the conversations. Often, one value of a variable is the form included in Imre's list (1971b) of the phonological, morphological and lexical items that distinguish the dialect from the standard. Here, as with the German material, the problem with a traditional list of dialect forms is that, by dichotomizing speech into dialect and standard it implies that the dialect is a separate structure, that local speakers must use either the dialect or the standard and that all dialect forms are used in the same way. However, in Hungarian speech, as in German, the dialect form is not invariably chosen by Oberwarters, even when speaking informally among themselves. Furthermore, when dialect–standard differences are viewed as linguistic variables, an analysis of their use shows that, far from being alike, they must be grouped into three categories according to the kind of variation they show.

For some variables the frequency of occurrence of each value did not change from the interview to the conversation—these variables showed no situational variation. The dialect form was always most frequent, although it did not occur invariably. Another set of variables did show situational variation, in the same way as the previously discussed German variables. In these, some values were much more frequent in the conversation than in the interview, while other values occurred most frequently in the interview. A third set of variables also showed this same pattern. The values most frequent in the conversation occurred least in the interview. But for this last group of variables the reversal was extreme: whatever values occurred in the interview never occurred in the conversation and those that occurred in the conversation never occurred in the interview. The dialect values of this third set are considered by Oberwarters to be peculiarities of local speech. As acknowledged and widely discussed local forms, they are subject to particularly strong stigmatization and suppression, if the situation demands. It is noteworthy that synchronic variation corresponding to these three types has been reported for monolingual communities, where the variables showing these characteristics are called "indicators," "markers" and "stereotypes" (Labov 1965:109–114).

Group I. No Situational Variation: Indicator

The presence or absence of *l* is the first variable in Table 3.2. The orthographic *l* usually pronounced by standard speakers can be omitted in most Hungarian dialects, but the rules for doing this differ from place to place (Imre 1971b:19–23). Of particular interest here is one of the environments in which *l* is often not pronounced in dialect forms. Hungarian has a class of verb stems ending in *l* such as ***csinál*** 'do,' ***meghal*** 'die,' ***felel*** 'answer.' Also, verbs can be derived from many nouns by adding a vowel and the *l* suffix. For instance, ***parancs*** 'command' becomes ***parancsol*** 'to

TABLE 3.2

Frequency of Occurrence of Values of Seven Hungarian Linguistic Variables in the Speech of
Two Informants in Two Situations

Linguistic variables	Values	Interview	Emotional Part of Interview	Conversation
No. 1	*l*	.05	.08	.03
	—	.95	.92	.97
		n = 132	*n* = 37	*n* = 31
No. 2	**gy/ty**	.61	.82	.10
	j	.09	.07	.20
	dzs/cs	.30	.11	.70
		n = 162	*n* = 28	*n* = 112
No. 3	***a***	.75	.78	.30
	oa	.25	.22	.70
		n = 138	*n* = 32	*n* = 43
No. 4	***el***	.27		0
	e	.64		.39
	je	.09		.61
		n = 11		*n* = 18
No. 5	***ez***	.98	1.0	.30
	jez	.02	0	.70
		n = 41	*n* = 2	*n* = 27
No. 6	***v***	1.0		0
	—	0		1.0
		n = 7		*n* = 6
No. 7	standard	.70	1.0	0
	local	.30	0	1.0
		n = 20	*n* = 6	*n* = 18

command'; *ének* 'song' becomes *énekel* 'to sing.' The vowels that may
occur before this verb-forming suffix are limited to *ö* and *u* in dialect
forms. So, for instance, 'command' would be *parancsul*. No such restriction holds for verb stems that are not derived from nouns. Tense and
person markers as well as other changes in the verb are indicated by
suffixes added to the stem. When a suffix ends in a consonant (and many

do) the *l* of the stem may be absent. If the preceding vowel is *a* or *e* then it is raised when the *l* is absent. For instance, *csal* 'cheat' with its suffixes becomes *csalt* '(he) cheated,' *csalnak* '(they) cheat,' *csalhat* '(he) may cheat.' But when the *l* is absent, these same forms are *csoat*, *csoanak*, *csoahat*. However if the preceding vowel is neither *a* nor *e* then it does not change at all. For instance, when suffixes are added to *röpül* 'fly' it becomes either *röpült* '(he) flew,' *röpülnek* '(they) fly,' *röpülhet* '(he) may fly', or, in the alternate realization *röpüt*, *röpünek*, *röpühet*. Table 3.2 shows that although *l* is frequently absent, this does not happen invariably. Further, there is no appreciable difference between the frequency of *l* pronunciation in the interview and its frequency in the conversations. There are other examples of this kind of variable, for instance the palatalization of *n* intervocalically in many nouns and in the infinitive verbal suffix *ni*. It is safe to say that if *l* appeared so rarely even in the interview situation then it is unlikely to appear any more frequently elsewhere. Oberwarters themselves do not discuss the frequent absence of *l* in any way and appear to be unaware of it, yet it is a characteristic of their speech in all situations.

Group II. Situational Variation: Markers

In Table 3.2 variables 2, 3, 4, and 5 belong in this group. The first of these involves differences in the realization of the first consonant in *gyerek* 'child'. There are three distinguishable points and modes of articulation for this voiced consonant. The standard form is a palatal stop: *gy*. Another realization is articulated further front and is a fricative rather than a stop: *j*. The third value is even more fronted; it is an alveolar affricate: *dzs*. Corresponding to the range of articulations of *gy/j/dzs* is a voiceless counterpart. A palatal stop *ty* is the standard form, the fronted palatal fricative *j* is another realization and the third is a voiceless alveolar affricate: *cs*. In the Transdanubian region, Oberwarters are unique in their use of *dzs* and *cs* for the standard's *gy* and *ty*. For example, the three pronunciations of 'clever, skillful' are *ügyes*, *üjes*, *üdzses*, and three possible pronunciations of 'dog' are *kutya*, *kuja* and *kucsa*. In final position, the voicing of this consonant assimilates to the voicing of the next word's initial sound, so that *dzs* may alternate with *cs*, or *gy* with *ty*, depending on the linguistic environment. However, linguistic environment does not influence the choice between local and standard values.

None of these realizations occurs invariably. Rather, the standard form is much more frequent in the interview, while the alveolar affricates are more frequent in the conversations. For instance, Table 3.2 shows that in the interview the palatal stops occur 61% of the time, while in the conversations the alveolar affricates occur 70% of the time.

Variable 3 involves the raising and diphthongization of *a* in a limited number of words. In the case of borrowed words that show this raising it is probably due to the influence of the local German in which, as we have seen, diphthongization of this vowel occurs regularly. However, it is unclear why some originally Hungarian lexical items of various classes are affected by this process and others, in which the vowel has the same linguistic environment, are not. To control for this irregularity the tapes were compared on the basis of only those words that, according to my own list and Imre's (1971b), had been heard pronounced with the diphthong. There are not many of these, but they occur frequently because they include the demonstrative pronoun *az* 'that' in its various forms. For the purposes of this analysis only two values of this variable were distinguished. The standard form is the vowel *a* and the dialect form is the diphthong *oa*. For example, 'that (acc.)' can be realized as *aszt* or *oaszt*, 'from that' can be *attol* or *oattu*, 'on that' *azon* or *oazon*. The values of this variable show the same reversal in frequency of occurrence between the interview and the conversation as the values of variable 2 did (Table 3.2).

Variables 4 and 5 show the same pattern. The first indicates the realization of the separable verbal prefix *el*. This prefix has a wide range of meanings including 'away' as in *eldob* '(he) throws away', *elmegy* '(he) goes away', and is a marker of completed or one-time action. Three realizations of this prefix occur in the tapes. One is the standard form *el*, another is *e* which occurs when *l* is not pronounced. The third value is *je*, reflecting the fact that in a limited number of environments, including this separable prefix, *j* is added to initial *e*. This last is the most divergent from standard. Only those prefixes attached to verbs with initial consonants were counted as examples of *e* and *el* in order to exclude the possibility, suggested by Imre (1971b:12), that when *el* occurs in Oberwart speech it is not the standard form but merely the allomorph of *e* which occurs before vowels. The three renderings of the prefix are: *elmënt* '(he) went away', *emënt* and *jemënt*, or when separated as in *vüdd el* 'take (it) away', *vüdd e*, *vüdd je*. Again, the dialect forms occur more frequently in conversations and less frequently in the interview.

The fifth and final variable of Group II concerns the realization of the demonstrative pronoun 'this' and its various forms. There are two values of the variable, *ez* the standard, *jez* the local form. This demonstrative pronoun and the separable prefix discussed above are the only two cases in which *j* is added to an initial *e*. Table 3.2 shows the difference in frequency of occurrence of *ez* as opposed to *jez* in the interview and in the conversations.

Group III. Stereotypes

Variables 6 and 7 are those which not only show more extreme situational variation than those in Group II, but are also the subject of discussion by native speakers. They are consciously perceived features of what Oberwarters conceive of as their way of talking. Variable 6 registers the presence or absence of intervocalic *v*. The presence of *v* is the standard value of the variable and its absence is the dialect form. Intervocalic *v* occurs in many verbs, nouns and adjectives, but most particularly in those called *v*-root words. The stem form of these words ends in a vowel to which a *v* is added before the addition of certain suffixes that begin with vowels (e.g., possessive, accusative, person markers and plural). The *v* thereby becomes intervocalic and is sometimes dropped. For example *ló* 'horse' can become *lovam* or *loam* 'my horse'. Other examples include: 'blacksmith' *kovács* or *koacs*, 'bread starter' *kovász* or *koasz*, the name of a neighboring village *lövő* or *lüö* and 'chilly' *hüvös* or *hüös*. When asked what characterizes their way of speaking, Oberwarters usually give some of these words as examples of local peculiarities. As Table 3.2 shows, in the interview not one *v* was absent, while in the conversations not one *v* appeared.

The use of one or the other of certain word pairs also shows the same all-or-none pattern. The existence of such pairs was noted by many informants during discussions of local speech. They identify one word of the pair as local, or *üöries* 'Felsőőr way', and the other as *röndes* 'proper', or the way it is said in Hungary. Examples include: 'duck' *kacsa* (standard) *riëce* (dialect), 'manure' *trágya* (standard) *ganaj* (dialect), 'peas' *bab* (standard) *borsuo* (dialect). Variable 7 concerns the choice between dialect and standard lexical items. The fact that some dialect words were used in the interview (30%) does not argue against the extreme situational variation of the variable because in each case the speaker corrected himself or herself immediately afterwards by giving the standard version.

It should be noted that, with the exception of variable 1, when more standard values of one variable were used, more standard values of the other variables were also used, in a pattern not of strict co-occurrence but of covariation. This covariation was not limited to phonology but included choice of morphological variants and lexical items. In all, speech in the interviews sounded quite different from the conversations although most of the differences were matters of degree.

FUNCTIONS OF STYLE: EMOTIONALITY AND INTENTIONALITY

My aim until now has been to show that linguistic differences within the two languages exist and that individuals are able to vary their speech within each language. I have not specified what it was about the interviews, as opposed to the conversations, which could account for the demonstrated differences in the way people spoke. In the first place, the differences were in a common-sense expected direction. People spoke in a more standard way in interviews and in a more dialect way in conversations with each other. Second, the social situations differed on so many possibly relevant dimensions (e.g., the identity of the participants, the formality of the situation, the purpose and topic of talk) that if one wanted to separate the effects of these factors a simple comparison between these particular situations would be inadequate. However, correlating styles of speaking with such independently measured aspects of the social situation is only one, and perhaps the least useful, approach to explaining the factors which produce and account for the use of different styles.

Two other approaches to the problem of style-shifting appear to be more applicable here. Both consider style-shifting from the point of view of the speaker, but each presents a different analysis of the reasons for shifting and the interactional functions served by shifting. One approach emphasizes the audio self-monitoring which the speaker engages in when using a careful style. The other emphasizes the rhetorical, expressive function of style-shifting; the way in which it serves to convey the speaker's intent. The two approaches differ in the extent to which they impute to speakers communicative purposiveness, that is, the intention to make a socially significant impression. The data gathered during the interviews described above provide a basis on which to compare and evaluate these two approaches.

The first view is one of the explanations of style-shifting originally proposed by Labov and later adopted generally in urban dialect surveys. It is based on data from Labov's ingenious linguistic interview techniques, which were designed to obtain as much variation as possible in the speech of each informant by manipulating the context of speech within the interview. The following outline is based on Labov's most recent discussion of techniques first developed in the study of linguistic stratification in the Lower East Side of New York City. An interview itself defines a rather formal situation in which people use "careful speech" (1972:79). Of central interest for the present discussion is the effort made to obtain speech variation in the direction of more casual speech. One was to tape interaction between interviewer and informant after the official interview was over, or at any point in the interview where interruption by others, or an offer of coffee or beer to the interviewer, broke up the interview situation. The second method was to get the speaker to produce "spontaneous speech" by creating a context in which "the emotional state or attitude of the speaker overrides any formal restrictions and spontaneous speech emerges (1972:91)." Spontaneous speech is defined as speech which is structurally the same as casual speech but occurs nonetheless in formal contexts, or rather, in spite of formal contexts. Speech is spontaneous, in this view, when the speaker is paying a minimum of attention to it. Therefore, Labov's strategy was to "break through the constraints of the interview situation by various devices which divert attention away from speech and allow the vernacular to emerge (1972:209)." Elsewhere Labov described the technique of obtaining such speech this way: "We can involve . . . the subject in questions and topics which recreate strong emotions he has felt in the past or involve him in other contexts (1970:47)." In the Lower East Side study this was done by asking the informant if he or she had ever been in danger of being killed. Channel cues such as changes in tempo, pitch, volume and breathing, or changes in laughter, were then used along with context as the formal definition of least careful vernacular speech. Primarily on the basis of the results obtained in these interviews and in anonymous recording of natural speech, Labov (1970) has suggested:

> [S]tyles can be ranged along a single dimension, measured by the amount of attention paid to speech. The most important way in which this attention is exerted is in audio-monitoring of one's own speech, though other forms of monitoring also take place. This axiom (really an hypothesis) receives strong support from the fact that speakers show the same level for many important linguistic variables in casual speech, when they are least involved and excited speech, when they are deeply involved emotionally. The common denominator for both styles is that minimum attention is available for monitoring one's own speech [p. 46].

The hypothesis suggests that during interruptions of the interview, or when the interview is felt to be suspended, the vernacular occurs because the speaker forgets to pay attention to speech. Within the formal, high-monitoring situation of the interview, it is presumably the speaker's involvement with the emotion-laden narrative that distracts the speaker from paying attention to speech and results in the speaker losing control.

Unable to maintain a careful style, the speaker falls back into casual speech. In a mechanical application of this view, changes in style would be attributed to changes in attention and audio-monitoring. Intentionality would not be imputed to the speaker and the possible interactional functions of style-shifting, in either the casual or the careful direction, would be ignored.

An alternative view recognizes the existence of a continuum along which informants' speech may vary, but stresses the selection of a particular style, including the most casual, for achieving particular social purposes. Gumperz's work on code switching exemplifies this approach. "Codes" are the linguistic varieties in a speaker's repertoire including, in the case of bilinguals, different languages as well as different styles. Choice of styles or languages is seen as a strategy on the part of speakers trying, for instance, to present themselves as individuals with particular socially defined qualities, or, as another example, trying to convey a particular attitude or impression concerning a topic of conversation. In addition, the ability of the listener to interpret code switching is made the object of investigation (Gumperz 1974:16). The view is that "code switching is a communicative skill which speakers use as a verbal strategy in much the same way that skillful writers switch styles in a short story (Gumperz and Hernandez 1971:328)." The method used to investigate the use of code switching consists of taping code switches that occur in speech among acquaintances at meetings or in other naturally occurring conversations. Later, with the speakers' help, the meaning of the switches within the conversation is examined in the light of culturally defined assumptions about the values associated with each of the codes.

An example of code switching used by speakers to present themselves in a particular way is contained in Blom and Gumperz's (1972) study of style shifting in discussion groups in Hemnes, Norway. They note: "Our analysis of these sessions . . . revealed that when an argument required that the speaker validate his status as an intellectual he would . . . tend to use standard forms . . . [p. 430]." Labov takes this same view of the function of style-shifting when he comments, in his Lower East Side study, that after the interview, the interviewer could encourage casual speech by changing roles and presenting himself differently. He could end his role as interviewer and act instead like the tired employee who, having finished the job, is free to "be himself" (1972:88, Footnote 5).

That code switching can be used to express an attitude or to create an impression concerning a topic of conversation is made clear in Gumperz and Hernandez's (1971) study of Spanish–English code switching in California. Here the codes are languages, not styles, but the analysis is the same. They give an extended example of a woman alternating between

English and Spanish while discussing her problem of giving up smoking and then they comment that the juxtaposition of Spanish and English is used to depict the speaker's attitude toward smoking. The content and intonation of the Spanish phrases, along with the association of the language itself with an in-group, serve to convey intimacy and personal feelings. The English phrases, both in content and associations, contrast with this. As a result, the entire passage expresses vacillation between personal involvement and clinical detachment, a vacillation that accurately and artfully reflects the speaker's ambivalence about her smoking. Labov also implies that stylistic variation functions as "expressive behavior" (1972:109) when he describes the interactional constraints put on informants by the danger-of-death question, the interview question which was most successful in producing "casual speech" in the Lower East Side interviews. The question was put in such a way that the informant had first to answer yes or no: "Have you ever been in serious danger of being killed—where you thought to yourself, this is it?" If the informant answered yes, the interviewer was free to ask, "What happened?" As Labov notes, in such an exchange the informant "stands in a very poor light if it appears that there was no actual danger." In fact, he is under "some compulsion to show that there was a very real danger of being killed [p. 93]." In short, the speaker is constrained to try to convince the listener that he was frightened, that the situation was indeed emotionally charged and dangerous. It is true that the situation being described may evoke emotion in the speaker. But, by pointing out the interactional constraints on the speaker and alluding to the interactional risk he runs, Labov underscores the importance, to the speaker, of skillfully conveying emotionality. In fact this implies that the speaker is under pressure not to lose control, but rather to choose the kind of speech which will make the desired impression on the listener. In sum, this second approach to style shifting emphasizes the speaker's selection of a particular style for the achievement of particular social–interactional purposes.

Some evidence from one Oberwart interview allows an evaluation of the relative merits of these two approaches. Although informants were clearly attending to their speech during various phases of the interview, the self-monitoring hypothesis alone cannot account for the pattern of variation.

The Hungarian interview with the elderly peasant couple took an unexpected turn when, in collecting the family history, I routinely asked Anna néni how she felt about having had to live with her mother-in-law for the entire forty years of her own marriage. I asked because this is a quickly disappearing living arrangement and people disagree on its merits. Many women complain bitterly and openly about their mothers-in-law and about the horrors of sharing the same kitchen. In this case, however, the mother-in-law had recently died and apparently both Miska báccsi and Anna néni had had a great deal of respect and love for her. In strongly defending the character of her mother-in-law and in describing the (unusual) loving, motherly treatment she had always received from her husband's mother, Anna néni's voice broke and she began to cry. The tape of her from this point on includes small whimpers and sobs. Both Miska báccsi and Anna néni then proceeded to describe in detail and with paralinguistic signs of emotion the day the old woman died and the particulars of her admirable stoicism in the face of death.

During the short time that this emotion-laden personal narrative, accompanied by changes in channel cues (crying, slower speech, sobbing, broken voice) was taking place, Miska báccsi and Anna néni did not vary their speech in any significant way from what it had been during the rest of the interview. As Table 3.2 indicates, the frequency of occurrence of the variables changed very little between the main body of the interview and the emotional narrative. In Oberwart such lack of change during an interview was not at all a unique phenomenon peculiar to this couple. On the contrary, for instance, a woman recounting an incident during World War II, when a soldier had attempted to rape her, did the same thing, as did another *Felszeg* woman describing her near death in childbirth and a man describing his escape from a prisoner-of-war camp.

The first approach's predicted correlation between emotionality of the narrative, channel cues indicating involvement, lack of monitoring and increase in the frequency of vernacular (dialect) features does not hold in these and many other cases. Despite the nature of the story and the crying, Miska báccsi and Anna néni continued to pay attention to their speech. One indication of this is self correction of dialect forms. Another is the pauses made before the use of words that have both a dialect and a standard version (e.g., *anyósom* (standard), *napam* or *svigermujderom* (dialect) 'my mother-in-law'). In their speech they both continued to approximate the standard. This is an apparent anomaly for which the second of the two approaches provides an interpretation and a path for investigation.

If we take this second approach and accept the view of style shifting as expressive behavior motivated by the speaker's intention to get his or her message across, then we can explain, by the same mechanism, both New York style-shifting, in which the vernacular emerges during emotional narratives, and the Oberwart case, in which it does not. We need to remember that in Oberwart use of dialect features, in contrast to standard, implies that the speaker is not only a native of Oberwart but also a peasant. Oberwarters, in front of standard speakers (such as the interviewer), invariably express embarrassment because of what they say they consider their unclear local speech. Recall also that nowadays, in front of educated strangers, Oberwarters are ashamed of the peasant identity—implying lack of sophistication and poverty—that is associated with local Hungarian.

Let us accept, as the evidence indicates, that both in the New York case and in Oberwart the personal narratives were emotion-laden and emotionally involving for the speakers. We can then hypothesize that in the New York case the interviewer was perceived as a person for whom the vernacular would be meaningful and to whom use of the vernacular would effectively convey the speaker's feelings of fright within the danger–of–death situation and thus would convey the truly dangerous nature of the situation. Hence, in New York, both the emotional involvement of the speaker and the expressive constraints on the speaker would encourage a move in the direction of the vernacular. In this view the story functioned not only as a distraction, but also as an occasion for putting into action a verbal strategy different from the one used in the rest of the interview.

In Oberwart, while the narrative was equally emotion–laden and, presumably, emotionally involving for the speaker, the expressive constraints of the situation were very different and so the relative importance of distraction and expressive aim may be compared. We can hypothesize that from an Oberwarter's point of view, dialect features, when used to a standard speaker, primarily convey the speaker's peasant status and not his or her involvement in the narrative. It might even be supposed that, to impress a standard-speaking stranger with the importance of an emotion-laden incident, the Oberwarter would strain toward the standard to maximize intelligibility and convey seriousness in the listener's own terms; that is, in the linguistic variety most likely to be meaningful for the stranger.

Thus, on the one hand it may be that in a community such as Oberwart, where the local dialect is associated with a stigmatized social status, the speaker's concern with making as good an impression as possible—presenting oneself as less of an unsophisticated peasant—overrides all other concerns in a formal interview with a standard-speaking outsider. On the other hand, it may be that to communicate the gravity and importance of the emotional incident to an outsider unfamiliar with the dialect and, presumably, with the feelings it can convey to insiders, the Oberwarter's strategy is to approximate the standard and thus convey those important feelings in what is defined as the stranger's own terms. The data do not allow us to choose between these two suggestions. However, either one supports the view that expressive considerations override the effects of distracting emotional involvement in the narrative and are therefore more important in determining speakers' style-shifting strategies.

In sum, for Oberwarters, style-shifting within each of their languages resembles style-shifting in monolingual communities. It is quantitative rather than categorical, it is characterized by three types of linguistic variables (indicators, markers and stereotypes), and it serves expressive functions. However, because Oberwart is a bilingual community, style shifting utilizes only one part of its linguistic heterogeneity and serves only some aspects of its speakers' communicative purposes.

4

Synchronic Variation in
Language Choice

In any conversation, bilingual Oberwarters have to choose among the languages available to them. The choice *between* languages is more salient linguistically and more important socially than style differences within each language. Yet in Oberwart there is a great deal of variation in the outcome of language choices. What appears to be the usual pattern for one speaker in a range of situations is rarely the same as anyone else's pattern. In fact, the nature of this variability renders static models of bilingual language use inadequate to the task of describing it. It is more useful to extend to language choice a model of variation derived from recent theories that link synchronic linguistic heterogeneity to diachronic change. In this way it is possible to describe Oberwart's present patterns of language choice so that they can be understood as both the products of social–historical forces and the sources of future changes in language choice.

Inseparable from the problem of describing language choice is the set of evaluations and social presumptions with which Oberwarters approach each of their languages. These attitudes provide part of the justification for considering choice between languages as a process separate from, and more socially significant than, style-shifting. In addition, the pattern of language choice itself suggests that its determinants differ from those of style-shifting as do the communicative purposes to which language choices are most often put.

SOURCES OF EVIDENCE

The argument of this chapter rests primarily on analysis of systematic observations made during the year I spent in Oberwart. After 6 months, I also constructed an interview schedule about language choice and related matters (Appendix I). The purpose of the interview schedule was to provide a picture of language choice patterns that could in some ways supplement direct observation. All my notes were necessarily based on a limited access to people's lives; I could not hope to observe each informant in every situation of interest. The interview, by using folk categories, was able to tap people's observations of their own behavior. In that sense it reflects a much larger and broader sample of choices than I had access to. In addition, the interview responses and my own notes could be used to check each other as they were limited in complementary ways. First, it is true that my presence influenced people's language choices to some extent. Yet, because my observations continued for a year and included a wide range of situations, they could not be affected by people's impression management in the same way as a one-shot set of questions. Second, the interview schedule facilitated comparisons and generalizations by providing the same amounts and kinds of information about everybody. In contrast, my own observations and tapes did not cover all speakers equally, but often did include information that would not have been revealed in direct questioning.

In addition, tapes provided fine-grained data about linguistic events that are difficult for speakers to recall and verbalize as, for instance, the details of an instance of conversational language switching. The examples quoted in this chapter were drawn from the everyday conversations I recorded in eight households. The people from these eight households were included among the men (31) and the women (37) whose language choices I systematically recorded. With the exception of four people, the 21 men and 28 women who answered the interview questions were also among those systematically observed.

Members of the eight households formed the core of people I worked with most closely and knew best. They consisted of five families, three of which had split into two separate nuclear-family households some time after the marriage of the oldest child. Because conversations often involved visiting relatives, the tapes include exchanges within and between three generations. It is important that the individuals who were taped included speakers of varying ages, because in choosing the rest of the informants I also aimed to represent a range of ages. The youngest of the 68 speakers was 3 years old and the oldest was 80, with at least one person representing every 5 years in between. Another aim was to select people who occupied different points on a dimension I later specified with measures of education, appearance, and social networks, but which I first thought of impressionistically as "peasantness—urbanness." I chose these two dimensions because they seemed particularly important both in predicting how a speaker would use German and Hungarian and in the way others interpreted that speaker's choices.

A MODEL OF LANGUAGE CHOICE

A few weeks of observation in Oberwart made it clear that no single rule would account for all choices between languages. Statements to the effect that one language is used at home and another in school–work–street, would be too simplistic. However, after accumulating many examples it was possible to predict the choices of particular people in a variety of situations. In formalizing my own intuitive predictions about the contexts of use for each language, I attempted to specify the situational factors (e.g., participants, occasion, location) associated with each language. In addition, I expected to be able to rank the factors according to their generality and applicability, so as to construct a model of the community-wide constraints on choices.

In this way I was following a common sociolinguistic strategy: taking the alternation among variants as the starting point and trying to predict the choice of variant from a knowledge of the factors present in the social situation. Numerous studies have done this, either to predict language choice in multilingual communities (e.g., Sankoff 1972), or to predict the use of some other sociolinguistic alternate such as address form or personal pronoun. However, there are two problems with the models of language choice based on this strategy. In many cases, including some in Oberwart, it is not possible to predict language choice through knowledge of its situational correlates. In addition, the models, usually formalized as decision trees or flow charts, assume that patterns of language choice are static. As a result, the kinds of variability that reflect change over time cannot be accurately represented in them.

Language choice cannot be completely predicted in conversational language switching, where the social situation and its components remain the same, but speakers nonetheless move from one language to another. Although one language may be unmarked or more expected in the situation than the other, speakers can also choose the unexpected language. This constitutes the violation of a sociolinguistic norm and such violations are commonly interpreted by listeners as a reflection of the speaker's momentary communicative intent. Alternatively, they can be viewed as the speaker's strategy for expressing such intent. Either way, interpretation of the intent or meaning behind a switch requires knowledge not only about the social context of the utterance, but also about the values associated with alternate forms. Precisely because conversational language switches depend on the momentary intent of the speaker, it is not possible to predict them. Instead, conversational language switching can be explained by providing an interpretation; a hypothesis about its effect or function in the interaction—a hypothesis that ideally either corresponds to that given by speaker and listener, or is considered plausible by participants.

Even those models of language choice that accurately represent the difference between marked and unmarked choices are not able to incorporate the kind of interinformant variation that reflects changes over time. The fact that change occurs in sociolinguistic systems has been recognized by Ervin–Tripp (1972) and others. But, perhaps because the process of change itself has not been studied, the inadequacy of the models has gone unnoticed. Rather than describing variation within a group, decision trees or flow charts have either modeled the choices of only one individual (Ervin–Tripp 1972:218–220; Geoghegan 1969), or have explicitly included "only those dimensions which seem to set the pattern for the group (Rubin 1968:516)." In fact, however, the decision–tree formalism itself does not require the investigator to choose between individual data and homogeneous group data. It is capable of representing some kinds of interinformant variation. For instance, if women systematically choose languages differently from men in a multilingual community, then one node in a decision tree can be "sex of speaker." If a particular speaker is a woman, then one set of choices applies; if a man, then another set applies. In this way, the model can capture the pattern of the entire group without ignoring certain kinds of variation among individuals.

At first glance it would seem that if informants' usage differs by age, as it does in Oberwart, this too can be included in a decision–tree model in much the same way that sex differences can be included. However inclusion of age differences presents special problems. For instance, in Oberwart the choices of a 60-year old were very different from the choices of a 15-year old. If the same decision tree, with a choice point for age, is used to describe the choices of both the 60-year old and the 15-year old, then the model is assuming age-grading of language choice. Such a decision tree applies to the entire group and implicitly states that an individual of 60 did, at the age of 15, make the choices predicted by the model for present-day 15-year olds. Correspondingly, the model assumes that the

15-year old, upon reaching 60, will behave as the 60-year old does today. In short, the decision tree assumes that synchronic variation that is correlated with age is necessarily a reflection of life-cycle changes and not change over time in the community. When, as in the case of Oberwart, independent historical evidence shows that the age differences in usage are *not* correlated with individual life cycles but reflect change over time, then the decision-tree model is an inaccurate representation.

Because both conversational language switching and variation between speakers of different ages occur in Oberwart, some alternative formalism, which could accurately incorporate both, was required. I found that two components of the situation—characteristics of the speaker and of the listener—allow for the prediction of language choice in a majority of cases. Thus, it was possible to conceptualize and display the observed language choices of the 68 Oberwart speakers as part of a matrix, as in Tables 4.1 and 4.2. In these matrices, speakers are ranked on the vertical axis (women in Table 4.1, men in Table 4.2). On the horizontal axis is a list of interlocutor types, people with whom the speaker interacts. In both tables each row of letters represents the language choices of one informant and each letter represents the language(s) chosen.

Both speakers and interlocutors are ranked in such a way that the language choices fall into an implicational or Guttman scale. Scales such as these are well known in some of the social sciences (Guttman 1944), but have only recently been used in linguistics as a way of organizing data and thinking about variation and change (e.g., DeCamp 1971; Elliott *et al.* 1969). In Tables 4.1 and 4.2 the habitual usage of individual informants can be read across each row. For example, informant 11 in Table 4.1 uses Hungarian (H) with her grandparents (2), Hungarian and German (GH) with her brothers and sisters (7), and only German (G) with her spouse (9). At the same time, by reading down each column it is possible to see the kinds of differences that exist across informants regarding language choices with a particular interlocutor. For instance, although informants listed toward the top of the list use only German with their age-mate pals (6), those in the middle use both languages in such interaction and those at the bottom use only Hungarian. The problem of representing age differences that are not life cycle differences, is solved because, although speakers of different ages appear as individuals in the matrix, the relationship between the choices of individuals and the pattern of the group is explicit and apparent when one scans the matrix vertically.

Although the interlocutor categories and language categories of these scales are culturally defined, the matrices themselves make no interpretations of communicative strategies or intentions, but simply summarize

TABLE 4.1

Choice of Language by Women
(Observations)

Number of speaker	Age of speaker	Interlocutors												
		1	2	3	4	5	6	7	8	9	10	11	12	13
1	14	H	G		G	G	G	G	G				—	
2	14	H	GH		G	G	G	G	G				—	
3	25	H	GH	GH	G		G	G	G	G	G	G	—	
4	15	H	GH		GH	GH	G	G	G				—	
5	13	H	GH		GH	—	G	GH	G				—	
6	13	H	H		GH	—	G	G	G				—	
7	27	—	H		GH	—	G	G	—			G	—	
8	3	—	H		GH	—	GH						—	
9	4	—	H		GH	—	GH	GH	—				—	
10	17	H	H		GH	—	—	GH	—				—	
11	39		H		GH	—	—	GH	G	G	G	—	—	
12	52	H	H	—	GH	—	GH	—	—	GH	G	G	—	G
13	23	—	H	GH	GH	—	—	GH	G		GH	G	—	
14	22	H	H		H	GH	GH	GH	—			G	—	
15	33	H	H	H	H	—	GH	—	—	H	GH	G	G	
16	35	H			H	—	GH	GH	—	GH	GH	G	—	
17	40	H			H	—	GH		—	GH	GH	G	—	
18	42	H			H	—	GH	GH	—	GH	GH	G	—	
19	43	H			H	—	—	—	—	GH	GH	G	—	
20	35	H	H		H	—	H	GH	H	H	GH	—	—	
21	40	H		H	GH	—	H	GH	H	H	G	—	—	
22	40	H		—	H	—	H	—	H	H	GH	—	G	
23	50	H			H	—	H	H	GH		G	—	—	G
24	61	—	H			—	H	GH	—	GH	GH	—	—	G
25	54	H	H	H	H	H	H	—		H	GH	GH	—	—
26	55	H			H	—	H	H	—	H	GH	—	—	GH
27	61	H				—	H	H	—	H	GH	—	—	
28	59	H		H	H	H	H	H	H	H	GH	H	—	GH
29	50	H			H	H	H	H	—	—	H	GH	—	
30	50	H		H	H	—	H	H	—	H	H	GH	—	—
31	60	H		H	H	H	H	H	—	H	—	GH	GH	—
32	60	H			—	H	H	—	H	H	GH	—	GH	
33	63	H			—	H	H	H	H	H	H	—	GH	
34	64	H			—	H	—	—	H	H	H	—	GH	
35	66	H			—	H	H	—		H	—	—	GH	
36	68	H			H	H	—	H	H	H	H	—	H	
37	71	H			—	H		H		H	H	—	H	

Interlocutors: (1) God; (2) grandparents and that generation; (3) black market clients; (4) parents and that generation; (5) Calvinist minister; (6) age-mate pals, neighbors; (7) brothers and sisters; (8) salespeople; (9) spouse; (10) children and that generation; (11) nonrelatives under twenty; (12) government officials; (13) grandchildren and that generation.

usual unmarked usage. Interpretations of intention (or function) will be necessary to account for choices between German and Hungarian in those interactions indicated with (GH), where both are appropriate. In short, the problem of incorporating conversational language switching is also solved. The matrices do not predict when each language will be chosen in conversational language switching, but rather indicate when conversational language switching is likely to occur at all. Oberwarters' evaluations and conceptions concerning their two languages lend support to this model of language choice and to the division of the repertoire into three linguistic categories.

LANGUAGE ATTITUDES

In contrast to actual language choice, which is varied, values and aesthetic judgements about speech are widely shared. Bilingual Oberwarters realize that, because of their use of two languages and the way they speak each language, most people conform neither to the linguistic norms of German monolinguals, nor those of Hungarian monolinguals. They feel that their everyday speech and usage are stigmatized by both German and Hungarian monolinguals.

The effect of the difference between monolingual and bilingual language norms and the judgements accompanying it is a near universal lack of linguistic pride and confidence on the part of Oberwarters (Gal 1974). Even those who can approximate both standards feel unsure and insecure about their speech when talking to monolinguals or outsiders. In the language usage interview, I asked informants to rank their own knowledge of each of their languages on a scale of one to five. This was meant to be a rough measure of linguistic insecurity. Perfect Oberwart Hungarian and monolingual everyday Oberwart German were indicated by one. The other categories were given labels: very well but not perfect = two; moderately well = three; not so good = four; and hardly at all = five. The standard of excellence for both languages was the local form, and all of the 38 people

---

NOTE: In this table and in Table 4.2, 4.3, 4.4, and 5.1, informants were ranked along the vertical axis and interlocutors along the horizontal axis to achieve maximum scalability. When the choices of several informants were identical on all cells for which data were available, e.g., numbers 16, 17, 18, 19 in Table 4.1, then the ordering among them was arbitrary. When, despite the effort to gain maximum scalability, an informant's choice with an interlocutor did not correspond to the scale model, the ordering was also arbitrary, with regard to that cell. For instance, number 15 in Table 4.1 could also have been placed after number 19. This, however, would not change the overall scalability.

Scalability = 93%.

TABLE 4.2

**Choice of Language by Men
(Observations)**

Number of speaker	Age of speaker	Interlocutors											
		1	2	3	4	5	6	7	8	9	10	11	12
1	6	H	G		G	—		G				—	
2	7	H	G		G	—	G	G				—	
3	14	—	GH		G	—	G	G				—	
4	17	—	GH		G	—	G	G				—	
5	8	H	GH		GH	—	GH	G				—	
6	12	H	GH		GH	—	GH	G				—	
7	12	H	GH		GH	—		G				—	
8	13	H	H		GH	—	GH	G				—	
9	25	H	H	H	GH	—	GH	G			—	—	
10	25	H			GH	—	G	G			—	—	
11	42				GH	—		G	GH	G	G	G	
12	25	H	H		G	—		G		G	—	—	—
13	20	H	H	H	H	GH	G	GH				—	
14	22	H	H		—	GH	G	GH				—	
15	22	H	H		H	GH	GH	GH			G	—	
16	31	H			H	—	GH	GH	G	G		—	
17	62	H		H		—		H	GH	G	G	—	G
18	44	—			H		—	—	GH	GH	—	—	
19	41	H		H	H	—	H	H	H	GH	—	—	
20	43	H			H	—		H	H	G	—	—	
21	46	H		H	H	—		H	H	GH	G	—	
22	58				H	H	H	H	H	GH	—	GH	G
23	61	H		H		—		H	H	GH	—	—	GH
24	63	H		H		H	H	H	H		GH	H	
25	64	H		—		—	—	H	H	GH	—	—	
26	40	GH		H	H	—	—	H	G	—	H	H	
27	53	H		H	H	H	H	H	H	H	—	—	
28	68	H			—		H	H	H	H	—	—	GH
29	70	H		H		—		H	GH	H	—	—	GH
30	74	H			H	H	H	H	H	H	—	H	GH
31	80	H			—		H	H	H	H	—	—	—

Interlocutors: (1) God; (2) grandparents and that generation; (3) black market clients; (4) parents and that generation; (5) minister; (6) brothers and sisters; (7) age-mate pals, neighbors; (8) spouse; (9) children and that generation; (10) nonrelatives under twenty; (11) government officials; (12) grandchildren and that generation.

Scalability = 95%.

who answered the interview questions had spoken Hungarian every day since childhood and German for most of their lives. Nevertheless, only half scored themselves the highest category for Hungarian and only 21% scored themselves the highest on German. As many as 20% said they spoke Hungarian only moderately well and 37% said the same about German. Several people refused to rank themselves altogether, apparently out of embarrassment, saying only, "not too well." Because in other domains such as drinking, cooking, or baking Oberwarters are not generally reticent about their achievements, these self-rankings reflect insecurity rather than modesty. One young man echoed, verbatim, the statements of many others: *egisz ju se nímetet se madzsart nem tunnunk* 'We don't speak either Hungarian or German totally right.'

According to Oberwarters, standard Hungarian is spoken by *madzsarok* 'Hungarians', and although some Oberwarters over 60 consider themselves Magyar by nationality or ethnicity (though always and vehemently Austrian by citizenship), the word itself is invariably reserved for those who were born in present-day Hungary and who visit or have come to live in Oberwart. For instance, if a family has a branch living in present-day Hungary, often because of a marriage contracted before 1921, the relatives are referred to as *e madzsarok*. Local natives are not called Hungarians or Austrians, but *üöri* 'native of Felsőőr', in contrast to all others who are called *dzsütmënt* 'come and gone'. From the point of view of native Oberwarters, these last are migrants who may come to live in Oberwart, but who were not born there and so, regardless how long they have stayed, they can never really be accepted as natives. This division of the world is reflected in evaluations of linguistic forms.

Although standard Hungarian is lauded as clear and beautiful while local forms are deprecated, it is important that such judgements are offered most frequently in the presence of standard speakers. This is not to say that Oberwarters are less than genuine in their admiration of the standard. The symbolic contrast between stigmatized local forms and prestigious standard forms is powerful. Yet it coexists with other contrasts. The connotation of standard corresponds to the stereotype Oberwarters hold about Hungarians. Although seen as prestigious, friendly, and hospitable, Hungarians are also thought to be arrogant boasters. In fact, even friendliness is a two-edged characterization, as they are felt to overdo it and therefore to be insincere. One old man confided to me that there was so much *nadzszás* 'swagger' in Hungary before the war that they deserved the communism they got. Considering his negative feelings about the Hungarian government, this was quite a condemnation.

On the other hand, local Hungarian, as identified by its stereotyped features, is spoken only by the native bilingual community and is therefore identified with them. Among Oberwarters, if Hungarian is to be spoken at all, then the appropriate forms are local. Within Oberwart it is irrelevant whether the speaker is a peasant; the local Hungarian forms assert solidarity regardless of occupation. The standard, given its association with Hungarians, is likely to sound boastful and insincere among Oberwarters. Its use is often taken as showing off, rejection of the group, putting oneself above others. In fact, there is a great deal of informal social pressure to use only local forms. One woman, during an interview, expressed regret that she could not speak more beautiful Hungarian, but then added that if she ever did people would laugh at her. Another woman used the standard Hungarian word *gerebje* instead of the local *gerábla* while she was talking to me in a small group. Her choice of words was immediately noticed by the other women who commented sarcastically that she certainly had *uri* 'gentlemanly' manners. In short, it is the local Hungarian forms that are considered ideal for sincere, unassuming talk between native Oberwarters—if they are to speak Hungarian at all.

But the contrast between evaluations of standard and local Hungarian is much less important in Oberwart today than the contrast between Hungarian and German of any kind at all. When compared to German, even standard Hungarian carries some connotations of community solidarity. For instance, Calvinist natives all prefer to attend the Hungarian-language church services (conducted in standard) rather than the newly instituted German one. They prefer to pray and sing hymns in Hungarian and even prefer to hear the sermon in Hungarian although this is always delivered in standard by the Hungarian-born minister. They explain that this is the way they are used to it and that it is the Lutherans and Catholics who do it in German; "we" do it in Hungarian.

It would not be too extreme to say that Hungarian spoken mostly by peasants and former peasants symbolizes the old way of life, the old forms of prestige of the peasant community. These values are now being rejected by all but the oldest bilingual Oberwarters. In contrast, the educated upperclass of Oberwart consists of German monolinguals. The world of schooling, of employment, and of material success is a totally German-speaking world. The language itself has come to symbolize the higher status of the worker and the prestige and money that can be acquired by wage work. While Hungarian is the language of the past and of the old, German is seen as the language of the future, of the young people who are most able to take advantage of the opportunities that Oberwarters feel exist in the German-speaking world.

Hungarian is considered a useless language because only peasant work is possible without a thorough knowledge of German. People often say that you can't go far with Hungarian. This is meant both geographically, as most neighboring towns and cities speak only German, and socioeconomically, since upward mobility, they feel, requires perfect knowledge of German. The expertise and knowledge required for employment, and the sophistication that Oberwarters associate with Austrian urban life and that they seek, are both represented by the German language. Peasant parents often say of their grown children who are employed in bureaucratic or commercial work and who go to cafes and shop downtown: *Ü má egisz nímet* 'He–she is already totally German.' This does not refer to their nationality, which is always given as Austrian, or to their language abilities, as they are recognized to be bilingual and often speak Hungarian at home. Rather, it indicates the close symbolic relationship between the children's occupation, status, and the German language.

The relative prestige of the German and Hungarian languages for bilinguals in Oberwart today derives directly from local historical–economic circumstances and reflects the relative prestige and income of those who can speak Hungarian as opposed to those who speak only German. It also reflects the fact that those on the bottom can and do aspire toward the top of the prestige hierarchy. Bilinguals, especially the young, accept the values of monolinguals.

The higher prestige of German over Hungarian is demonstrated by the fact that today the children of a monolingual German speaker and a bilingual German–Hungarian speaker virtually never learn Hungarian regardless of which parent is bilingual. Even forms of German spoken in nearby villages, which are recognized to be provincial and are stigmatized in relation to urban educated German, are nevertheless valued as real German in contrast to mere Hungarian. Lately the prestige difference has been sharpened and refined. Bilingual parents no longer consider it enough that their children be able to speak German well enough to communicate with monolinguals in a variety of situations (including marriage). Now they are concerned that the German betray no trace of Hungarian influences. They proudly say that in their own speech or that of their children *Nëm vág bele e madzsar* 'The Hungarian doesn't cut into it.' In short, it has become a goal to be able to pass as a monolingual and thereby to be able, among strangers, to dissociate oneself completely from local Hungarian and, thus, from any connotations of a stigmatized peasant identity.

It is first of all the social primacy of the distinction between German and Hungarian that motivates the analytic division of Oberwart's repertoire into the categories that appear in the implicational scales. But linguistic considerations are also involved. Although there is variation within each language, for both linguist and native speaker, the linguistic distinction between German and Hungarian is more salient and far-reaching. Native speakers could remember whether a conversation was in German, Hungarian or both, but they would have trouble recalling and recounting whether local or standard forms were used most often. The difference between German and Hungarian is the one which dominates discussions about language. In addition, from the linguist's point of view, German and Hungarian differ from each other structurally much more widely than any forms within each language. Not even the local versions of German and Hungarian are mutually intelligible. Further, the restrictions keeping the two languages apart in their grammatical markers and syntax are co-occurrence and not co-variation rules. Even when lexical items can travel rather freely from German to Hungarian, grammatical constraints remain rigid. A phrase started with Hungarian grammatical markers does not ever end with German grammatical markers and the reverse is equally true.

As a result of the social connotations of each language, as well as the linguistic boundaries between them, my data on language use between particular speakers and interlocutors consistently and regularly fell into the categories German and Hungarian. People who habitually use Hungarian to each other almost never use German. People who habitually use German with each other very rarely use Hungarian. For instance, about twice a week and on Sundays the usual afternoon pastime for many retired men and women is playing cards. Card-playing groups are stable and made up of age-mate friends, usually neighbors. In one group that I visited on almost every card-playing day for several months, the three men and three women (all in their sixties and seventies) used various styles of Hungarian; they quoted in German, but never used an entire German sentence to each other. Similarly, during the many hours I spent with several children playing in my yard, they always spoke German to each other. Not once did they use Hungarian. The same was true of a brother and sister whose house I visited daily for about four months.

It is similarly easy to distinguish those few participants for whom both languages are the norm. The teenage members of the church's Hungarian dance group, even during the three or four evenings I spent with them, often used both languages. The same brother and sister, who never spoke Hungarian to each other, sometimes spoke Hungarian and sometimes German when addressing their parents. A husband and wife in their late twenties, with whom I often ate dinners and spent evenings, used both languages to each other repeatedly during each of our meetings. In short, it was rarely difficult to decide whether German, Hungarian, or German–Hungarian was the proper way to characterize interactions between any two people.

The social connotations of the two languages also influence momentary choice between languages in those interactions where both are equally appropriate, but in these cases the connotations have a more indirect effect.

GERMAN–HUNGARIAN: CONVERSATIONAL LANGUAGE-SWITCHING

There are two sorts of language uses in Oberwart that involve the juxtaposition of German and Hungarian (GH) utterances in one exchange. Both of these need to be distinguished from borrowing and quoting. In both borrowing and quoting, German elements are incorporated into Hungarian sentences, but structurally German and structurally Hungarian sentences are not juxtaposed. As a result, neither quoting nor borrowing qualify as GH usage. Also, in contrast to most GH use, quoting is relatively predictable. All one needs to know to predict the language in which most quotes will be spoken is the language in which the original utterance was spoken. So, for instance, a man recounting the death of his father in a hospital told this story about calling the hospital to get news. (Only German and its translation are in boldface):

(5)   Este hít orakkor fëhittam üket, aszonták
        In the evening at seven I called them, they said

        hodzs imm**ʌ** **ʃlextʌ**. No osztán akkor mielütt
        that he's **worse and worse.** So then before

        min munkába mënëk fëhijom üket, na akkor
        I go to work I call them up, then

        osztá monták hodzs **də fotʌ is um hojp tsvɸf ntslofn.**
        they said **Your father died at half past eleven.**

And a man describing life in the army in World War II said:

(6)   Mást nem lehetett mondani mint j**ɑvol** j**ɑvol**
        You couldn't say anything else but **yes sir**

        hɛr gɛnɛrɑl.
        yes sir, general.

Of the two kinds of GH use, one occurs most often between parents and children or grandparents and children and can be called "unreciprocal" because the older person consistently uses Hungarian while the younger person consistently answers in German. Lengthy conversations can be conducted in this unreciprocal way. For example the following is an excerpt from a longer exchange. Three people participated: two women friends in their late sixties–early seventies, Kata néni and Juli néni, and Juli néni's daughter Juli, who was about 30-years old. Since Kata néni had been gone for a long time, living with her own daughter in another village, they started by catching up on news about the family:

(7)   Juli: **fɑn sɑns kumn?**
                 when did you come?

      Kata
      néni: Csötörtökön. Regge fékelek, Mariska dzsün
                 Thursday. In the morning I wake up, Mary comes

                 na, e mënnünk haza! Na mandam, hála isten
                 well we're going home! Well, I say, thank God

                 hocs haza lehet mënnyi.
                 that we can go home again.

      Juli: **Ah so, jo jo si's kumn.**
                 Oh, yes yes, so she came (too).

      Kata
      néni: Ja ja (Pause) Van most ëdzs szíp szobájuk,
                 'Yes   Now they have a nice room,

                 ahun in feküttem, uj butor van.
                 where I slept, with new furniture.'

      Juli: **Ah so, und fo homs əs kaft?**
                 Oh, and where did she buy it?

      Kata
      néni: Eccer itt, Eccer ott, e jizibe (she names a store).
                 Sometimes here, sometimes there in the (store).

                 Van nadzs szekrinye ucs fë e poadlásig,
                 She has a big cabinet, up to the ceiling,

                 filig klump van, madarak meg minden. Meg
                 full of junk and birds and things. And

                 izivje van kü hodzs hijják, e - ?
                 it's also . . . how do they call it?

Juli: **Tɑpetn?**
          Wallpaper?

Kata
néni: Ja ja, a falan.
          Yes, on the wall.

Juli: **Deis hom mɑ nuʌ im tsimmʌ.**
          We only have that in the living room.

Kata
néni: Ja ja, ott izs van.
          Yes, we have it there too.

(a little later, after the two older women have talked to each other awhile).

Juli: **Un vi get's də Ilse?**
          And how is Ilse?

Kata
néni: Annak is ju mëdzs. Mindedzsiknek ju mëdzs,
          She's doing fine, they're all doing fine,

          pínz elig, minden.
          there's money enough and everything.

Juli: **Und vos moxt dʌ, dʌ Sanyi?**
          And what is Sanyi doing?

Kata
néni: Ja, annak is van, már van, már
          'He's got too, he's got a house

          háza neki, ipüt.
          already, he built.'

Juli: (Pause) **N'joa, i ge ɑ pissl fek, neni**
          Well, I'm going away a little, auntie

          i ge pissl fuot, nuʌ in di kirxn.
          I'm going out, just to church. (she leaves).

The younger woman, who had no trouble understanding the older woman's answers, could have asked her rudimentary questions in Hungarian, but she did not.

The other, more important, type of GH use occurs when there is no way of predicting which language two people will speak to each other at any one time, or in any particular exchange. Many of the switches between languages that occur here are examples of conversational language switching. In such cases all the predictive model can do is to specify under what circumstances, and between which speakers, such apparent unpredictability is likely to occur.

In many, though not all, cases the switch between languages can be understood—its meaning for the interactants and its function within the interaction can be interpreted—if (a) it is compared with a number of other switches that appear similar, (b) if the reactions of the listeners and the context of talk are taken into account, and (c) if the switch is interpreted in the light of the symbolic meanings and evaluations associated with the languages. Often the switch is a conversational tactic and at the same time a rhetorical device to express an emotion. This is the case in the following four examples, each from a different speaker and from different interactions, but all with features in common.

A small girl of about three, while playing in the shed, scattered a carefully assembled pile of fire wood with the help of her small cousin. Her grandmother, who was nearby, was too busy to notice, but when her grandfather walked into the shed he immediately commented on the mess and soon afterwards started yelling:

(8)   Grandfather: Szo! ide dzsüni! (pause) jeszt jerámunyi
                     Well, come here!   put all this away,

                     mind e kettüötök, no hát akkor! (pause)
                     both of you, well now!

                     Kum her! (pause) Něm koapsz vacsorát!
                     Come here!   You don't get supper!

In the course of the incident he first noted the mess, then in the piece quoted here he started with a command (come here) and as the children did not respond he went on to another command. Both of these Hungarian commands were ignored by the girls. Finally he repeated the original command, but in German. Apparently the response was not quick enough. After the third pause he stopped commanding and started to threaten (you don't get supper). It should be noted that he used a German command even though the family agreed that the small child and her cousin understood no German at all. The little girl did not go to school yet and, since her mother worked all day, she was in the care of her grandmother who spoke only Hungarian to her.

The next example also concerns the same small child who had apparently misbehaved all day and for various reasons was tired and whiny when the exchange below took place in the evening. This time her mother was home, as well as both her grandparents. The grandfather and the mother disagreed, as usual, about the proper way to discipline the cranky child. As the little girl whined and cried, the grandfather expressed his sympathy for her:

(9)

Grandfather:	Szëginke.
	Poor little one.
Grandmother:	Udzs ne jáccá ha má ámus vadzs!
	Don't fool around like that if you're sleepy!
Mother:	Ács csek ej ju pofont!
	Just give her a good slap.
Grandmother:	Hodzsne.
	Oh sure.
Grandfather:	(to child) Ju hocs e te mamád nincs itthun
	It's a good thing your mother is not home (all day)
	mer igën sok pofont kapná tülö.
	because you'd get an awful lot of slaps from her.
Mother:	**Jo, o**a**dnu**ŋ **mus s**a**jn!**
	You bet, there has to be order!
Grandmother:	Rossz is! e mëdzs cüpüt vennyi osztán e nenit
	She sure is bad! We go to buy shoes and she
	ju mëgrugdzsa aki mëgprobágassa melik
	gives the lady a good kick, the lady trying to
	pásszul neki. Szíp ë leán.
	fit her with shoes. Some nice little girl.

Much of the talk appeared to be addressed to the child but was actually a disagreement between the mother and grandfather. When the grandmother ordered the child to stop playing around, and the mother recommended a good slap, the grandfather indirectly commented on that suggestion. We see that the mother took this as disapproval of her methods of discipline because she proceeded to support her view by providing a màxim, a principled reason, in German for her methods. We can also see that the exchange was indeed a disagreement since the grandmother deemed it necessary to take a side, to support the mother by listing the child's misbehavior during the day (she sure *is* bad). The German comment was the end of the exchange between mother and grandfather. Its result was that the grandfather dropped the subject, or rather, he said nothing for several rounds of talk and nothing at all on the subject of slapping.

The third incident occurred between a husband and wife in their early forties. During one of my visits to their house, the wife offered me some pastry. The husband noticed it was not from the baker at the weekly market where she usually shopped but was from a different baker's stand. He wanted to know why, since changing shops is a violation of the implicit agreement between merchant and customer. She answered in the following way:

(10)

Wife: Vettem mer ippig ott vot annyira kéát, köszönt, no mondom, azir oda mëntëm hozzá, akkor itt vot tejnap szembe, neki mondom, veszek külön voamit moa. Mindig neked fizet hát, ne hodzs, ne hodzs aszondzsa hát—

I bought it cause he was there and he was yelling so much and he said hello to me so I went over, then yesterday he was here across the street, so I told him I'd buy something today. He always pays you, I didn't want him to be able to say, well to say—

Husband: Pindler, Pinlerho! Hát ne mond, mer oa
At Pindler, you went to [shopped at] Pindler,

adzsonvág akkor.
Well don't tell because he'll kill you (i.e., the original merchant).

Wife: Hát oaho is mëntëm, hát ûnálla's vettem,
Well I went to him too, I bought from him

látta.
too, he saw (i.e., the original merchant).

Husband: E mëglassa hoj e Pindlerná veszed akkor
If this one sees you buy at Pindler he'll

hoarakszik.
be mad.

Wife: I koɑn neks ojləs bɑj im kafm!
               I can't buy everything just from him!

Husband: (eating) nem ju ez.
              This stuff's no good.

Once again there was a disagreement in which at first the woman explained her reasons for having done what she did. The man emphasized the gravity of her act. She defended herself again, this time giving an excuse. He repeated again his original assessment of the dangers involved. On the third time around she responded angrily, in a loud voice and in German, again giving an excuse, in fact a paraphrase of the previous Hungarian one (i.e., she goes to both merchants). With this the incident ended. The husband responded to the German utterance by eating, but not liking, the pastry.

It is noteworthy that in the last two examples, as in many other cases of language switching in Oberwart, not only is the switch part of a disagreement, but the argument itself revolves around conflicts of values symbolized by the two languages. The traditional, and lax, method of child rearing is contrasted with the modern and strict; the traditional peasant allegiance to a single merchant is opposed to the notion that the customer can choose.

The final example of language switching concerns an older married couple, in their sixties. After dinner it was usual for the wife to go down to the cellar to get the husband a bottle of beer. This particular night he asked her to go but she was having coffee with her daughter (a woman in her forties) and me and she simply refused to go. After repeatedly asking he finally went for the beer himself and as he came back and started to drink his wife asked him for a sip:

(11)

Wife: Ide, itt tessik (she offers her glass to be filled with beer).
            Here, here please.

Husband: Hojne.
            Oh sure.

Wife: Ja, hát add oda
            Come on, give it here.

Husband: Hojne, ott csek idd e kávét (laughs) Niksz.
            Oh sure. Just drink your coffee there. No.

Daughter: Ne addzs, ne addzs!
             Don't give her any, don't give her.

Husband: Fë nëm hoznyi, de mëginnya. O ho, oaszt nëm.
             You won't bring it up but you want to drink it, oh no,
             no you don't.

Wife: Nëm is kë. Mer ha kë le mënëk osztá hozok.
             I don't even want it. Because if I wanted some, I'd just
             go down and get some.

Husband: Niksz, oh ho, nëm szabad neked.
             No, oh no, you're not allowed.

Wife: Nëm, nëm szorutam rá hoj te adzs nekem.
             I don't, I don't have to depend on you to give me.

Husband: Nekem nëm hozu fë, magadnag akko nem szabad
             If you don't bring it up for me, then you

             inna.
             can't drink it yourself.

Wife: In akkor iszok mikor in akarok. **Deis vird niks**
             I drink when I want to. **I don't even want**

             kbra k. Das vird niks kbra kt.
             it. I don't even want it.

Again the pattern of argument and escalation of anger is clear. This time the woman's daughter quickly came into the talk right after the German switch and suddenly made some very silly sounds. The wife broke up laughing after a moment. In fact everyone started laughing. There was no reason, it seems, for those sudden silly sounds except to defuse by laughter a situation that had apparently, even in the daughter's estimation, gone too far. Notice that once again the older woman's German comment was a verbatim repeat of a previous Hungarian one (Nem is kë = **Das vird niksz kbrakt**, literally 'it is not needed, wanted'), but with much more serious implications—she sounded angrier—and judging by the reaction of others, more serious possible effects.

These four examples of switching allow certain inferences to be made about the function of the switch and, indirectly, about the aims of the speakers. Each switch occurred in an argument as a culmination of escalating disagreement and hostility. When the German utterance was a repeat of a Hungarian phrase used originally at the beginning of the disagreement, (numbers 8 and 11, perhaps 10) the German phrase apparently had more force, sounded more distant and harsher; it ended the argument and served as a "topper"—a last word that was not outdone. Even though it added nothing more to the content of the argument, the German showed more anger, as if something had been yelled louder the second time. In each case, the German utterance was followed by a change in topic (in the first example a change from commands to a threat), or at least by a stop in the escalation of hostility in that particular exchange. The point is not that a switch to German is *always* used to express anger, to indicate the last and most effective increase in show of anger in an escalating disagreement, or to win an agrument. It is not. The point is, rather, that if a speaker wants to, switching to German at a particular point in an argument can accomplish these communicative purposes.

Conversational language-switching was used in other ways too. For instance, the expression or assertion of expertise and knowledgeability, either about an issue or in an area of activity, a skill or craft, was often accomplished by the speaker through a switch to German when giving a judgment or opinion. This often happened when opinions were solicited by others and such opinions were taken as definitive. Yet another use of language switching was what might be called emphasis or "validation." In a narrative of personal experience, the phrase that summed up the moral, or the reason for the telling of the narrative, was said twice, once in each language (cf. Labov and Waletzky 1967). In all, I have analyzed 40 taped instances of the use of both German and Hungarian within the same exchange. Four were extended unreciprocal exchanges, seven occurred as "toppers" in arguments. Seven more were instances in which expertise was asserted and two were markers of emphasis or validation. In sum, half of the instances were readily interpretable within this framework. What ties all these cases together is that the meanings conveyed through conversational language switching are related, though indirectly, to the conceptions Oberwarters have about the Hungarian and German languages. The most prestigious language, connoting urban sophistication, is the one that gives a statement added authority. At the same time, the fact that German is not the language identified with Oberwarters explains the feeling of social distance conveyed by its use among natives.

Just as the examples given here of conversational language-switching demonstrate its use in accomplishing interactional tasks (winning an argument, expressing emotion), so the examples of style-shifting in the previous chapter include instances of its use for similar interactional purposes (emotion expressed, persuasion accomplished). Whereas the language-switching examples were drawn from interactions in which both languages were used between speakers, the style-shifting examples came from situations in which only one was habitually used. The two girls (speakers 1 and 2 in Table 4.1) both used only German to their parents and siblings; Anna néni and Miska báccsi (33 in Table 4.1 and 30 in Table 4.2) used only Hungarian with their neighbors and with me. The major difference between the two kinds of variation is that, instead of categorical choices between separate languages, style-shifting depends on quantitative changes in linguistic variables. Nevertheless, both conversational language-switching and style-shifting serve the same kinds of functions: the expression of momentary communicative intents.

With this in mind, what is most striking about conversational language-switching is its infrequency. It is not an option for everyone in every situation. The implicational scales of language use indicate that conversational language-switching is relatively rare: for any speaker it occurs only with a limited set of interlocutors. In other interactions this kind of linguistic variability is not available for encoding meanings. Instead, when choice of language for two interacting speakers is always Hungarian or always German, then it is style-shifting within each language that can be used to express the conversational functions sometimes served by switching between languages. So, although in Oberwart both style-shifting and conversational language-switching are possible means of conveying intent, the two are largely in complementary distribution. Style-shifting occurs only where conversational language-switching does not.

PATTERNS OF CHOICE

The meaning conveyed by the invariable choice of one language between speakers can best be explicated by first returning to the question of how people choose between G, H, and GH. For any informant, the choice of language can be predicted if one knows the identity of the informant and of the interlocutor. Speakers and their interlocutors can both be ranked in such a way that the choices, when displayed in a matrix, form an implicational scale. This array illustrates the differences between individual choices as well as their relationship to the pattern of the group as a whole.

The language choices summarized in Tables 4.1 and 4.2 include only interactions between bilinguals. Each letter in each cell of these matrices is based on direct observation of the particular informant involved, but the numbers of instances represented by each cell vary. For more than half the men (15) and women (17), the observations are for practical purposes uncountable, as they are the result of a year of living in the same house or next door to them or of nearly daily interaction. For the rest, who were more distant acquaintances or neighbors, each cell represents at least five discrete instances, but often more. Exceptions to this are rarely occurring interactions such as with government officials or the minister. Empty cells mean that the cell does not apply in some sense. A 4-year old cannot have a grandchild, for example. A dash in a cell indicates lack of adequate data. An informant was rated as categorically using only H or only G with a particular interlocutor or set of interlocutors if the other language was never used during any of the interactions that I observed, or if I heard it used only a very small proportion of the time—for well-known informants three times or less during the year.

By reading across each row in Tables 4.1 and 4.2, we see that if a speaker uses H with an interlocutor then only H can appear to the left of that and H, G, or GH to the right. If the speaker uses GH with an interlocutor then H and GH can appear to the left of that and GH and G to the right. If the speaker uses G with an interlocutor then H, G and GH can appear to the left, but only G to the right. Thus, the occurrence of any of the categories in a cell implies the occurrence of particular categories in the cells to the left and right. The scales show that for any speaker there are no bilingual interlocutors in his or her life with whom GH is spoken unless there are some, listed to the left, with whom H is spoken. In addition there are no interlocutors with whom G is spoken unless there are some, listed to the left, with whom the speaker uses GH. For instance, if a boy uses G to his grandparents, as informant 2 in Table 4.2 does, then he probably will use G with his parents and his sibling as well. Knowing what language a person uses with a particular interlocutor allows us to predict that person's choices with particular others.

Note that the same ordering of interlocutors produces this pattern for all speakers, with one difference between men and women. Women do much more of the shopping than men, so the category of "salesperson" was inappropriate for the men. Otherwise the lists and the rankings are identical.

The ranking of interlocutors clarifies the relationship between one speaker's choices with different interlocutors. The ranking of speakers produces a pattern in the variation between them. Reading down any column in Tables 4.1 and 4.2 we can see how speakers differ in their choice of language with the same category of interlocutor. When speakers listed toward the top of the list use G, then speakers in the middle use GH and those toward the bottom use H. When those at the top use GH those in the middle and bottom use H. When those at the top use H, then all speakers use H with that interlocutor. Because speakers' ages are listed next to their identifying numbers, we see that younger people tend to be at the top of the lists and the very old at the bottom. Therefore, when one speaker's habitual language use with a particular interlocutor is known, it also gives information about the possibilities open to those higher up on the list—those likely to be younger—and those lower down on the list, who are likely to be older.

If the generalizations outlined above were completely accurate predictors of choice in each case, the tables would be implicational scales with scalability of 100%.[1] Although inspection of Tables 4.1 and 4.2 shows there are exceptions to the generalizations, their scalability of 95% and 93%, respectively, indicate that they come close to being perfect implicational scales.

The results of the language-use interview appearing in Tables 4.3 and 4.4 provide a different measure of language choice. Probably because the interviews were individually tailored to each informant by using the names of particular people and places, and because people knew that I was already aware of their language use in many situations, there was a high degree of agreement between observation and interview responses. Average agreement was 90% for men and 86% for women for all those people who appear on both the observation and the interview scales. Blank spaces on the interview scales also indicate inapplicable cells. The interlocutor types are the same in Tables 4.3 and 4.4 as in Tables 4.1 and 4.2 with the following exceptions: 'doctor' was left out of the observation list because such interactions were impossible to observe; 'nonrelatives under twenty' and 'minister' were not in the interview schedule because they emerged as categories from later analysis of observed incidents. For the observation and interview scales, the order of the categories is nearly identical and the same kind of implicational relationships hold for both with comparable numbers of exceptions: Tables 4.3 and 4.4 have scalability of 96% and 94%, respectively. The two sources of information, direct observation and self-report, corroborate each other.

ETHNOGRAPHY OF LANGUAGE USE

This description formally characterizes the present-day patterning of language choice in the community, as represented by these 68 informants. However, it requires a set of ethnographic examples to suggest the meaning conveyed by invariable choice, and to support the assertion underlying this formal model that, whatever the social situation, only the identity of the participants determines language choice. Further, because other situational factors such as audience, setting, occasion, and purpose have

---

[1] "Scalability" is the proportion of cells that fit the scale model. Inapplicable cells and those lacking data are omitted from the denominator.

TABLE 4.3

Choice of Language by Women
(Interview)

Number of speaker	Age of speaker	Interlocutors											
		1	2	3	4	5	6	7	8	9	10	11	12
1	14	H	GH		G	G	G	G			G		G
2	15	H	GH		G	G	G	G			G		G
3	25	H	GH	GH	GH	G	G	G	G	G	G		G
4	27	H	H		GH	G	G	G			G		G
5	17	H	H		H	GH	G	G			G		G
6	13	H	H		GH	GH	GH	GH			G		G
7	43	H	H		GH	GH		G	GH	GH	G		G
8	39	H	H		H	GH	GH	G	G	G	G		G
9	23	H	H		H	GH	H	G		GH	G		G
10	40	H	H		H	GH		GH	G	G	G		G
11	50	H	H		H	H	GH	GH	GH	G	G	G	G
12	52	H	H	H	GH	H		H	GH	G	G	G	G
13	60	H	H	H	H	H	H	H	GH	GH	G	G	H
14	40	H	H	H	H	H	H	H	GH	GH	GH		G
15	35	H	H		H	H	H	H	H	GH	H		G
16	61	H	H		H	H	H	H	H	GH	H		G
17	50	H	H	H	H	H	H	H	H	H	H		G
18	66	H	H		H	H	H	H	H	H	H	GH	G
19	60	H	H		H	H	H	H	H	H	H	GH	G
20	53	H	H		H	H	H	H	H	GH	H	GH	G
21	71	H	H		H	H	H	H	H	H	H	GH	G
22	54	H	H	H	H	H	H	H	H	H	H		G
23	69	H	H		H	H	H	H	H	H	H	GH	G
24	63	H	H		H	H	H	H	H	H	H	GH	H
25	59	H	H	H	H	H	H	H	H	H	H		H
26	60	H	H	H	H	H	H	H	H	H	H		H
27	64	H	H		H	H	H	H	H	H	H	H	H
28	71	H	H		H	H	H	H	H	H	H	H	H

Interlocutors: (1) God; (2) grandparents and their generation; (3) black market clients; (4) parents and their generation; (5) age-mate pals, neighbors; (6) brothers and sisters; (7) salespeople; (8) spouse; (9) children and that generation; (10) government officials; (11) grandchildren and their generation; (12) doctor.
Scalability = 96%.

each been shown to influence the form of speech in other communities, it is necessary to demonstrate rather than to assume the irrelevance of those factors to the Oberwart case.

The primary importance of participants in determining language choice is most easily demonstrated. When several people are present, though perhaps not all are participating in the conversation—as is usual in kitch-

TABLE 4.4

Choice of Language by Men
(Interview)

Number of speaker	Age of speaker	Interlocutors										
		1	2	3	4	5	6	7	8	9	10	11
1	17	H	GH		G	G	G			G		G
2	25	H	H		G	G			G	G		G
3	25	H	H		GH	G	G			G		G
4	42		H		GH	G	G	G	G	G		G
5	13		H		GH	G	G			G		G
6	12	H	GH		GH	GH						G
7	20	H	H	H	H	GH	G			G		G
8	22	H	H		H	GH	GH			G		G
9	22	H	H		H	GH	GH			G		G
10	31	H	H		H	GH	H	G	G	G		G
11	62	H	H	H	H	H	H	GH	G	GH	G	G
12	44	H	H		H	GH		GH	GH	G		G
13	63	H	H	H	H	H	H	H		GH		G
14	64	H	H	H	H	H	H	H	GH	GH		G
15	43	H	H		H	H	H	H	G	H		G
16	41	H	H	H	H	H	H	H	GH	H		H
17	54	H	H	H	H	H	H	H	H	H		G
18	61	H	H	H	H	H	H	H	H	G	GH	GH
19	74	H	H	H	H	H	H	H	H	H	GH	H
20	70	H	H		H	H	H	GH	H	H	G	H
21	58	G	H		H	H	H	H	H	H		H

Interlocutors: (1) God; (2) grandparents and their generation; (3) black-market clients; (4) parents and their generation; (5) age-mate pals, neighbors; (6) brothers and sisters; (7) spouse; (8) children and their generation; (9) government officials; (10) grandchildren and their generation; (11) doctor.

Scalability = 94%.

ens during the winter—choice of language by a speaker can signal in advance which of the people in the room is being addressed. For instance, in one household a young man of about 25 and his 13-year-old niece were joking together in the kitchen speaking German to each other. The man's mother was also there cooking. When the young man, in the midst of his conversation with the niece, asked his mother something, he said it in Hungarian, the language in which he always addressed his mother. The addressee was the only factor that had changed in this situation.

A similar incident occurred when I was taping an interview one evening with a worker in his early forties, at his home. His 14-year old son was also sitting at the table with us, listening. I knew from previous experience that the father and son spoke German to each other (speakers

3 and 11 in Table 4.1). The father and I were speaking Hungarian at the time and I was asking about the location of another family's house:

(12)

Ethnographer:	Hol laknak? Where do they live?
Father:	Itt, itt mindzsá. Here, just right here.
Son:	(whispering) **In di kirxngos** **In the church street.**
Father:	Udzsis e református—(Pause) **e di refuomirtn** **kirxnogs, net?**
	Just in the Reformed—**It's the Reformed-Church** **Street, isn't it?**
Son:	**Jo, drausn ∫on.** **Yes, out there.**

Note that the son understood my question, since he answered it, though in a whisper, before his father did. Further, to have understood the question and what it referred to, he needed to understand most of the preceding conversation. The father started to answer my question, but paused. Presumably he was unsure of the answer, because he then asked his son about the street. But when he turned to his son (and I assume he wasn't asking me what street, since I had just indicated that I did not know) he asked in German, despite the fact that the talk with me was in Hungarian. Yet the form of the question assumes that the son had understood the preceding Hungarian conversation, because it doesn't explain what house he is talking about, or even what he wants to know about the street. I stress this in order to emphasize that, for these speakers, the choice of language did not hinge on the speaker's or the listener's ability to understand either of the two languages, but on the felt appropriateness of using either one. This particular son for instance would never speak Hungarian to his father, nor would the father speak Hungarian to his son. Both told me emphatically that only the old people speak Hungarian, only the old peasants. This is not to say that this father and his son never speak Hungarian. On the contrary, they both know that they speak it with certain people. Rather, their statements about the speakers of Hungarian must be taken as stereotypes, as a reflection of their understanding of what it means to choose Hungarian. The fact that neither would choose to speak Hungarian to the other suggests that neither would ever make the symbolic statement to the other that he was old-fashioned or valued peasant life.

In addition to the identity of participants one other aspect of the situation has an effect on language choice: the audience to the interaction. This is true only in the case of monolinguals, particularly German monolinguals. If monolingual German speakers are part of the interaction bilinguals always switch to German. Although the use of only German in front of German monolinguals is now explained by Oberwarters as a gesture of politeness, so that the monolinguals will not feel that they are being left out or being discussed, it is in fact a rather new idea which developed only after World War II. It has far-reaching effects on language use within households where a monolingual has married in, and it is related to the lack of prestige of Hungarian as opposed to German. Since this is now close to being an invariant rule, situations in which a monolingual was part of the interaction were not included among the observations recorded in the implicational scales.

The lack of influence of other factors can be demonstrated by incidents or strings of incidents in which the participants are the same but other factors vary. It is possible to show for instance that the setting of the interaction does not affect language choice. Home, yard, the fields, church, the market, the inn (*kocsma*), the street, downtown, school and the town hall are the usual locations named by Oberwarters. Yet, in asking the interview questions, I mentioned all of these places separately and was often stopped by informants who said that it doesn't matter where we are, if it is my mother I talk to her in Hungarian. And in fact, children who speak to their friends only in German continue to do so even in church, during Hungarian prayers, songs and sermons. Women walking to market often called on each other at home, walked through the streets and into the market place speaking whichever language they started with. They did not switch languages when entering different locations. Acquaintances, both men and women, meeting in the market or downtown, spoke Hungarian if that was usual for them, just as they did at home, in the field, and in the yards. Even in the town hall, two people meeting by accident always spoke whichever language was usual between them. The bilingual head notary of Oberwart, who works in the town hall, gives instructions to the bilingual summons-server in Hungarian, despite what one might expect about the "Austrianness" of the location and the official purpose of their interaction. Only school demands the use of German by law, and this only in classes. Some youngsters who normally use both German and Hungarian to their siblings report using some Hungarian in the schoolyard, along with the usual German. However, I never witnessed this and school may well be the only example of location influencing language choice.

In a similar way, occasion and purpose of interaction seem to make little difference in language choice. The volunteer fire department is an official organization, sponsored by the municipal government, and therefore defined today as an Austrian institution. Monolingual Oberwarters participate in it along with bilinguals. If the nature of the occasion influenced language choice, one would expect that a meeting of this fire department would require use of German by bilinguals. At one meeting I attended, the bilinguals sat together in the back of the room, but not totally separated from the others. The meeting was conducted in German and the bilinguals participated and made suggestions in German. But when, for instance, one middle-aged bilingual man asked his friend to stand guard duty with him, he asked in Hungarian, the language which they usually used to each other. In another incident, the children who were preparing for their confirmation were asked to come on a Saturday afternoon to help one of the bilingual school teachers move the Calvinist church's library of Hungarian books from one building to another. Church is a location strongly associated with Hungarian, and all bilinguals attend Hungarian services. The purpose of the interaction was also associated with the Hungarian language, and it was a community project. In addition, they constituted a group of all bilingual children led by a bilingual teacher and minister. Yet those children who habitually spoke German to each other did so under these circumstances as well, even when giving instructions about the placement of books.

In sum, knowing who the participants are, is, by itself, adequate to predict language choice. But the interlocutors listed in the implicational scales appear to be arbitrarily selected from all the possible status categories in the community. They are not limited to a single domain such as kinship, they appear to have little in common, and seem to be noncomparable. Further, the reason for ordering them in this particular way is not self-evident, although it is important, because the horizontal scaling in the matrices is produced by this ranking of interlocutors. Again, ethnographic examples should clarify both the reasons for choosing these particular categories and the principle behind their ordering.

First, it will be helpful here to explain what is meant by each interlocutor type in the tables and to list those who belong in that category but are not specified. 'To God' refers to church services, the language of hymns and prayers (but not to the church as a physical location, nor services as an occasion). 'Grandparents and their generation' includes primarily grandparents, but also all bilinguals with whom the speaker is acquainted and who are approximately as old or older than one's grandparents. 'Black-market clients' are people of any age or sex who come to the home of the speaker for a black-market exchange. This is an unlicensed, and therefore illegal, service such as carpentry, electrical or heating repair, building or fixing houses, hair-cutting, shoe-fixing, and several others. 'Parents and their generation' includes uncles, aunts, and nonrelatives of that age group. 'Minister' and 'brothers and sisters' refer to no one else. In the category 'age-mate pals, neighbors' often called *kolega,* are included same-generation cousins as well as any acquaintance of one's own general age, related or not, who does not live in one's own house. 'Bilingual spouse' is again a very specific category, while 'children' and 'grandchildren' refer to one's own children as well as the friends of one's children and grandchildren. The exception to this is that nonrelatives under 20 are treated differently in language choice than one's own children and grandchildren. For those who are themselves under 20, this last category does not apply. 'Government officials' specifically refers to a group of people, ranging in age from 20 to 65, who hold offices or work at the town hall and whose jobs vary in importance from head notary of Oberwart (highest administrative nonelected official), to the assistant notary, to secretaries and messengers.

This collection of interlocutors, while heterogeneous, is nevertheless united by their order along a single dimension. They are ranked according to their degree of 'urbanization' or 'Austrianness', that is, the relative association of each category, in the conception of Oberwarters, with urban, educated, Austrian culture. Considering current attitudes toward peasant life and the Hungarian and German languages, it is not surprising that this dimension is roughly correlated with age. Older people, grandparents and parents are on the Hungarian extreme of the list, while younger people, including grandchildren, are on the other, Austrian end. However the other interlocutor categories indicate that, although the dimension is correlated with age, it is not age itself. Government officials are on the Austrian end of the list regardless of age, in contrast to God at church services. The local Calvinist church is the institution most strongly identified with the *Felszeg* bilinguals and most strongly supporting the use of Hungarian. Church services constitute the only public and ritual use of the language. In addition, the minister and his wife organize a set of youth-oriented projects, including a yearly dramatic production played in Hungarian, a Hungarian dance group, and confirmation classes where children formally learn Hungarian prayers and hymns. If speakers use Hungarian at all, then they will use it in thus addressing God. If speakers use German at all, then they will use it with interlocutors on the Austrian–urban end of this scale.

With these categories of interlocutors and this principle of ordering, an empirical question remains: How does one determine, without reference to language use and therefore circularity, which interlocutor category a particular person is enacting during a specific incident? This question hinges on the fact that usually one individual can legitimately play many roles, even vis à vis one other individual. A standard example is that doctor and nurse may also be sisters or friends. But note that, in the case of the categories listed for Oberwart, such overlapping is not generally a problem since most of the categories are mutually exclusive. For instance, it would be impossible to be both someone's child and parent at the same time. This is equally true of spouse and age-mate pal in a society that does not define husbands and wives as pals in any sense. It even holds in the case of the minister, who, as religious leader not only of Oberwart but also of all Protestant churches in Austria, holds such a high position that he is always addressed as 'Reverend' (*Tisztelendő Úr* in Hungarian and *Pfarrer* in German) by almost everyone outside of his immediate family. His status as minister overrides all other possibilities.

However, in choosing a language when speaking to government officials, salespeople and black-market clients, these statuses need not always be relevant. It is possible for Oberwarters to define such interlocutors in several ways, each used consistently by different sets of speakers. These cases are particularly interesting because answers in the interview showed that for these interlocutors, more than for the others, Oberwarters were able to directly discuss their own reasons for choosing one or the other language. Their explanations shed further light on the communicative effect of invariable language choice in all situations.

It might be argued, simply on the basis of attitudes toward the two languages that the invariable choice of Hungarian between two people is interpreted by each as an assertion of peasant identity, of solidarity with the peasant community's values. This is the hypothesis supported not only by normative statements and stereotypes about what kind of people speak each language (recall the opinion voiced by the father and son discussed above), but also by people's explicit remarks about why they choose the language they use with officials, clients, and salespeople.

In going through the language use interview, many older people, particularly those at the bottom of the implicational scales, would generalize that there was no need for me to ask about each particular person since Hungarian was used with all the people one knew well. When I got around to asking about their choice of language with the head notary in the town hall, these informants answered that they would, of course, use Hungarian because they knew him well. Then they usually offered one of several further justifications of their choice. Tacitly setting aside the fact that he is the head notary, some would explain that he, or more often his father, had been in their class at school and the notary was therefore a *kolega*, or almost one; others noted that he had been, or still was, their neighbor. Still others traced the kin network connecting them to him and explained that they had to use Hungarian since he was (or practically was) a relative. This range of explanations actually collapses into one because virtually every bilingual Oberwarter today can, if necessary, be linked to every other either by kin and neighbor ties, or on the basis of long acquaintance. Therefore, the statements can fairly be interpreted to mean that both the notary's status as part of the community and the speaker's status as part of the community override all other considerations. The notary is one of "us," and so only Hungarian is felt to be appropriate.

In contrast, younger people (particularly those at the top of the implicational scales) said they always used German with officials. They did not claim kin or friendship ties with either the notary, the assistant notary or any of the others. This was the case even though these younger people were the children or grandchildren of the older informants and therefore actually had comparable kin ties with the officials. Many also lived in or near his neighborhood and might well have been pals with him, his children or with younger government officials. Nevertheless, the younger people did not mention these links. Instead they said that if they didn't use German it would reflect badly on them. They said that the head notary and other officials I asked about are all representatives of the national government and one is expected to know that German is the national language.

This difference between choice of a language (H) to emphasize two speakers' statuses as kin and neighbors, as opposed to stressing the official or service aspects of their identities, applies to women's interactions with salespersons as well. The additional fact that each language is associated, in the conceptions of Oberwarters, with opposing social statuses (peasant versus worker) suggests that the contrast in language choice between the older and younger informants is related to the way in which they define themselves; whether or not they present themselves first and foremost as members of the local, peasant community. Black-market clients provide another sort of confirmation. Everyone seems to agree that with clients the use of at least some Hungarian is appropriate. The black-market transaction, while considered necessary by the bilingual community, is offically illegal and is risky. Use of Hungarian may well serve as a reminder by those rendering the service and a reassurance by the client that both are community members subscribing to community values, thereby implying that mutual trust, at least about the transaction, is warranted.

In sum, while style-shifting and conversational language-switching are used to convey indirectly the speaker's attitude toward various momentary aspects of the ongoing interaction, the invariable choice of German or Hungarian with an interlocutor is an expression of the social identity claimed by the speaker. Although this chapter has focused primarily on the variation within the language use of single speakers, this last issue, concerning the functions of invariable language choice, directs attention to the differences between people in their patterns of language choice and to the factors that can account for such differences.

CONCLUSION

Choice between German and Hungarian is of particular interest because it symbolizes the social and cultural contrasts between traditional peasant and modern worker, thus reflecting the economic and social changes now occurring in Oberwart. Within language choice there is variation between speakers as well as in one person's use with different interlocutors. The implicational relationships among language choices can be formally represented by arraying them in a matrix. The identity of the speaker and that of the interlocutor are sufficient to predict language choice in the majority of instances.

Displaying language choices as part of an implicational scale has several advantages. First, within such a predictive model, conversational language-switching can be seen as one type of linguistic variation within a larger framework of variation. Functionally, it corresponds to style-shifting and contrasts with invariable language choice. That is, while conversational language-switching, like style-shifting, is used for expressing momentary intents in an interaction, the invariable choice of one language conveys the speaker's claim to a social identity. Second, it is possible to demonstrate that there is a systematic relationship between the choices of any one speaker with a particular interlocutor and the pattern of the group as a whole. The ranking of interlocutors along a dimension of "peasant–Austrian urbanite" reveals the implicational relations among one person's choices: If Hungarian is used at all it is used with interlocutors listed toward the peasant end of the continuum. Similarly, to understand the variation between speakers in patterns of language choice, it is necessary to determine the principles by which speakers are ranked.

5

Social Networks

Given the current symbolic values of German and Hungarian, one could follow Oberwarters' own assessments of the linguistic situation and confidently predict that in the simplest terms, old peasants use more Hungarian and young workers use more German. Certainly people's habitual language choices are somehow related to their identities, to their positions on the social dimension of peasant-to-Austrian urbanite. But there are several ways of analyzing this relationship. Each mode of analysis carries with it a conception of the relationship between linguistic and social facts. The most common approach is to choose an aspect of the speaker's social status such as age, class, or, in this case, degree of "peasantness," and to devise a measure of it that can be correlated with linguistic patterns. Although in this strategy status is measured independently of social interaction through indices such as income, education, and occupation, it is implicitly taken to be the major determinant of speakers' linguistic behavior in interaction.

A second approach adds to the first by considering not the identity of the speaker, but the statuses of those people with whom the speaker most often interacts. This is a measure of social networks specifically tied to, rather than being independent of, the nature and frequency of the speaker's interaction with others. This view argues that speakers' linguistic behaviors are constrained and shaped by the sorts of social contacts they maintain and suggests that their speech influences other people's perception of their status.

Both measures can be used to rank informants along the peasant-to-urbanite continuum, and in Oberwart both are correlated with language choice. But the focus here is on social networks, because, in contrast to status measures alone, a consideration of people's networks allows an analysis of the processes through which speakers in interaction exercise control over each other's language choices and hence maintain linguistic diversity.

SOURCES OF EVIDENCE

Accounting for interinformant variation in language choice required determining how strongly people's positions on the dimensions of age and peasant-to-Austrian urbanite correlated with their patterns of language choice. Although in Oberwart age and peasantness generally are highly correlated—old people are more likely to be peasants—in this group of informants a careful attempt was made to include both old people who had never been peasants and young people who were full-time peasants, as well as the combinations in between. This was not a representative sample of a community, but a sample chosen to represent a range of points on these two dimensions to be able to judge the importance of each as a correlate of language choice.

The ranking of people according to their degree of peasantness was based on a variety of easily observable details that Oberwarters them-selves consider to be signs of commitment to peasant agriculture as opposed to wage labor. Most of these indicators—whether or not a household owned pigs and cows, whether or not they grew potatoes and grain, where the household members were employed—were matters of public information. As long as I did not inquire into the exact number of hectares of land and schillings of income, people talked eagerly about their own and their neighbors' business.

The information I needed to construct a scale of network types was different in this respect. People seemed uncomfortable about discussing with me, in a systematic way, their daily contacts with others. This was because people's social interactions and relations were of major interest to informants themselves and constituted valuable information for gossip. On the one hand, it was a matter of course for new acquaintances of mine to trace their relationship with people I already knew or lived with. This was necessary to identify ourselves to each other. On the other hand, informants treated with distaste the related task of providing lists of the people to whom they spoke during a particular day. They did not flatly refuse, but they gave such lists only reluctantly. Directly asking about social contacts was not the native method of finding out what everyone agreed was important to know. The usual way of gathering such information was to keep an eye on one's neighbors' yards and on the street, to see who talked to whom over the years.

In fact, an adjustment to this native method of data gathering was evident in the building of houses and the placement of windows and gates. Compromises had to be made between being able to see everybody and being seen by everybody. For instance, Oberwarters greatly value huge gates which block the neighbors' view of one's yard and therefore of what is going on in the yard and with whom. In the last century, those who could afford it often added such gates to their houses. However, when added to traditionally built houses, gates also blocked one's view of the street from the kitchen window. Today, new houses are usually built with the entrance on the side or the back of the house, out of sight from the street. But the kitchen is most often placed so that its window looks out toward the street, facilitating neighbor-watching.

The problems of collecting information on social networks were most serious at the beginning of my stay. At that time, many people were anxious to conceal black-market activities that they later did not feel were necessary to conceal. In addition, I had too few contacts of my own to be able to reciprocate by revealing my daily activities. Eventually, however, I was more able to reciprocate and informants became more willing to provide lists of their daily contacts. Some people waited until they saw that I already knew, as a result of living next door to them or by visiting them daily, who most of their usual contacts were. Even so, people doubtless failed to report some of their interactions; they probably forgot some and they probably lied about others. However, I have no reason to suppose that everyone forgot or deliberately suppressed information about the same kinds of contacts. As a result, it is difficult to say in what way the data on social networks were systematically affected.

My question to each informant was: "Who did you talk to or meet today?" Sometimes I asked, "What did you do today?" In the latter case I asked if the informant had done it alone or, "Who else was with you?" For most informants I asked these questions once a week for several weeks and would ask not only about "today" but also about the three previous days. Occasionally it was possible to check with someone every day for a week, but this did not seem to affect the number of people an informant recalled. The number of days for which an informant was asked to report his or her contacts was not the same for all informants. The range of number of days was 3 to 30; the average was 15 days, the median was 7 days. All informants were asked about those days that, from the point of view of social contacts, would necessarily differ from others: market day and Sunday.

For each person named as a network contact, I asked who the person was, at least for the first occurrence of the name. The answers were always some specification of the kin, acquaintance or business ties between the informant and the contact. If I did not already know the person, we discussed where the person lived and the person's age and occupation. This allowed me to find out later whether, or to what extent, the contact was involved in peasant agriculture. There were some people who were simply identified by the service they rendered: the *Verkäuferin* 'saleslady' at the store or the *irodás* 'clerk' at the social security office. These people were invariably monolinguals, the informants did not know them by name, and could tell me nothing more about them. In addition to these questions, I also asked about the occasion or purpose of the meeting between informant and contact. The answers took the forms: she came over as usual, we met in the street–market–store, I helped her pick potatoes, he came to get milk.

Speakers could differ in their frequencies of contact with peasants and could, therefore, be ranked according to the peasantness of their social networks. In order to correlate this with habitual language use, it also was necessary to rank speakers according to their positions on the implicational scales of language choice (Table 5.1). Because the interview responses comprised a more complete set of data than observations and were, at the same time, quite similar to the observations, the responses to the interview questions were taken to represent language-choice patterns generally. Of the 48 people who were interviewed, 32 also supplied information about their social networks: 14 men and 18 women. Because, for the purposes of this correlation, the language choices of men and women have been put into the same matrix, the one interlocutor category they did not share (salespeople) has been omitted from Table 5.1. When Spearman rank-difference correlations were computed between speakers' ranks on this scale, on measures of status and on social network, a group of informants was given identical ranks in language choice if choices were the same for all filled cells. So, for instance, speakers E1 and F1 were given the same rank because, even though the third category of interlocutor types was not applicable for E1, all other choices were identical. Some choices of some informants failed to fit the scale model, despite the attempt to attain maximum scalability. When ranks were assigned for correlations, cells which failed to fit the scale model were counted as empty cells.

TABLE 5.1[a]

Choice of Language in Oberwart
by Men and Women

Speakers	Age of speaker	1	2	3	4	5	6	7	8	9	10	11
					Interlocutors							
A	14	H	GH		G	G	G			G		G
B	15	H	GH		G	G	G			G		G
C	17	H	GH		G	G	G			G		G
D	25	H	GH	GH	GH	G	G	G	G	G		G
E	27	H	H		GH	G	G			G		G
F	25	H	H		GH	G	G			G		G
G	42		H		GH	G	G	G	G	G		G
H	17	H	H		H	GH	G			G		G
I	20	H	H	H	H	GH	G	G	G	G		G
J	39	H	H		H	GH	GH			G		G
K	22	H	H		H	GH	GH			G		G
L	23	H	H		H	GH	H		GH	G		G
M	40	H	H		H	GH		GH	G	G		G
N	52	H	H	H	GH	H		GH	G	G	G	G
O	62	H	H	H	H	H	H	GH	GH	GH	G	G
P	40	H	H	H	H	H	H	GH	GH	GH		G
Q	63	H	H		H	H	H	H		GH		G
R	64	H	H	H	H	H	H	H	GH	GH		G
S	43	H	H		H	H	H	H	G	H		G
T	35	H	H	H	H	H	H	H	GH	H		G
U	41	H	H	H	H	H	H	H	GH	H		H
V	61	H	H		H	H	H	H	GH	H		G
W	54	H	H		H	H	H	H	H	H		G
X	50	H	H	H	H	H	H	H	H	H		G
Y	63	H	H	H	H	H	H	H	H	H	GH	G
Z	61	H	H		H	H	H	H	H	G	GH	G
A1	74	H	H		H	H	H	H	H	H	GH	H
B1	54	H	H		H	H	H	H	H	H	GH	H
C1	63	H	H	H	H	H	H	H	H	H	GH	H
D1	58	G	H		H	H	H	H	H	H		H
E1	64	H	H		H	H	H	H	H	H	H	H
F1	59	H	H	H	H	H	H	H	H	H	H	H

[a] Data are from interviews. Spaces indicate inapplicable questions.
Interlocutors: (1) to God; (2) grandparents and their generation; (3) black-market client; (4) parents and their generation; (5) pals (*kolegák*), age-mate neighbors; (6) brothers and sisters; (7) spouse; (8) children and their generation; (9) government officials; (10) grandchildren and their generation; (11) doctor.
Scalability = 97%.
Number of Speakers = 32 (both men and women).

PEASANT STATUS

Among the various attributes of speakers it is neither their status as peasants nor the nature of their social networks that correlates most closely with language use. It is their ages. Informants listed at the top of Table 5.1 are much younger (A, B, C are under 20) and use more German than those toward the bottom who are much older (A1, C1 and E1 are over 60) and use more Hungarian. The correlation between the ranking of informants strictly by age and their ranking by language use is high: .82.[1] Although this relationship is extremely important and will be discussed in detail, it is clear that age does not account for all differences between speakers. Many older speakers in Table 5.1, for instance informants J and G, who are 39 and 42, are in the company of teenagers, while informant O, 62, is among speakers who are more than 10 years younger than he is. It was to account for this additional variability that I turned to a measure of peasant status.

A person's commitment to peasant agriculture can range from tending a kitchen garden and raising a few chickens to a full-scale farm run for subsistence and occasional profit. Similarly, a person's dependence on wages can vary from intermittent, agricultural day labor to a highly skilled professional or managerial position, which usually precludes agricultural work. In addition, farm labor and wage work can be combined. For at least a century there have been some Oberwarters who were partially peasants and partially wage earners, and, since World War II, there have been many bilinguals who do no peasant work at all. Nevertheless it is common for people who are workers to do some agricultural work for themselves, so as not to have to buy all of their food.

Oberwarters themselves take the type and number of animals owned by a household as an indication of the household's commitment to agriculture. Only those households with several cows can be called *naccs paraszt* 'big peasant'. Owning cows implies a large farm, because those who have cows usually also have other animals. In addition, it is the requirements of the animals that mainly determine the amount, if any, of grain, potatoes and cattle turnip needed and, thus, the amount of time and capital invested in agriculture. However, there are further distinctions to be made. Households that own pigs are viewed differently from those which own only chickens. Even people who do not have any animals may grow potatoes and some grain for their own use or sale. Whether or not they own animals,

---

[1] This and all further references to correlations are to Spearman rank-difference correlation coefficients.

some members of a household may hold regular nonagricultural jobs that are informally ranked in a hierarchy based primarily on the pay earned and the education required.

All of these factors, and several more, were taken as measures of a person's degree of peasantness. There were eleven criteria in all, each of which could have two values, one indicating more peasantness and the other indicating less. Each value indicating more peasantness was counted as one, while each indicating less peasantness counted as zero, so that the higher the total for all criteria the greater the degree of peasantness. A person who ran a peasant farm and also held a job would score about five or six.

The criteria were applied to individuals and their activities, although some required a judgment to be made about the entire household. For instance, cows are said to belong to the household, but it is also true that each member is involved in the task of maintaining them. Feeding and cleaning cows is the work of the men, whereas milking is usually the work of the women and children. Because households were sometimes involved in the criteria, it was necessary to decide what constituted separate as opposed to joint households. The usual and preferred arrangement is a household consisting of one nuclear family. However, there are also a few stem households, which include parents and a married son with his wife and children. In addition, it is common, when a son or daughter marries, for the parents to contribute money to build an apartment for the new couple either on top of, or next to, their own house. This makes for a close relationship and a certain amount of sharing of housework and utensils. However, such arrangements were counted as separate households as long as the two couples cooked and ate separately.

The first five criteria concerned agriculture. Did the individual live in a household that owned (*1*) cows, (*2*) pigs, (*3*) chickens, and that grew (*4*) grain and (*5*) potatoes? The next three criteria were ones considered by Oberwarters to be physical symbols of peasantness. Did the individual's household use: (*6*) an outhouse or a flush toilet; (*7*) did the oldest woman of this individual's household bake bread or buy it at a store; (*8*) did the individual wear, during workdays, an apron (for men) or a kerchief (for women) both indoors and outdoors regardless of the weather? Toilets and bathrooms were a powerful symbol of urbanness. They were always the first improvement to be added when young worker families moved into older structures. At the same time, some big peasant families installed neither a toilet nor a bathroom when building an addition to their house.

The final three criteria concerned the individual's employment and educational preparation for it. Did the individual do (*9*) only agricultural

Taking bread to be baked in the *Felszeg*.

work as distinct from a regular job outside of agriculture? These two kinds of work contrasted sufficiently in the eyes of Oberwarters to require two separate expressions: *dolog* meaning 'farm or household labor' and *munka* 'work at a job', although the words, both meaning 'work', are not differentiated in this way by standard speakers. Black-market occupations, such as running an unlicensed barber shop or electric-repair business, were considered equivalent to legal employment for wages in shops, factories, and offices. Students were rated as having such a job. Did the individual (*10*) attend only the eight mandatory years of school in contrast to additional training in academic, craft, or commercial schools? The distinction between a person who is trained in a craft and someone who is qualified only for unskilled labor is important. Men who do unskilled labor because it pays better than the craft they learned, or because they could not find a job in that trade, always point out that they are skilled. In referring to them, others also make the distinction by saying, for instance, he's working on a roadbuilding gang now, but he's a mechanic. And the final distinction was (*11*) did the individual stop school after commercial or craft training, or go on to university or higher technical schools. Those who did continue often became the teachers, the engineers, and the government administrators in Oberwart.[2]

The correlation between ranking of informants according to their degree of peasantness and their ranking according to language choice was .67. This correlation is not due to the influence of informants' ages since age and peasantness do not correlate at all for this group (.45, not statistically significant). In addition, an attempt was made to include in the peasantness measure criteria (toilet, apron, kerchief, bread) which are unrelated to social interaction, but still influence the way a person is socially categorized.

The drawback in correlating language use with social status measured independently of interaction is not simply that the correlation is relatively low. No doubt different measures of peasant status could be devised, which, though equally *ad hoc,* would correlate better with language choice. But, even if language choice could then be predicted with greater

[2] A score of $\frac{1}{2}$ was given when both yes and no were equally true, as when one woman sometimes baked her own bread but equally often bought it. This occurred in only three instances. One-half was also given on criterion (9), a regular job, to those women who did not have jobs but whose husbands worked in regular jobs. This was done because they had to be distinguished from women who held regular jobs, and were therefore more urban, and from women whose husbands did not hold jobs. Retired people were scored on the basis of what they had done in the five years before retirement. The one child (informant A, aged 14) who was under 15 and had not yet taken the entrance exams for trade school, which she wished to attend, was scored on the basis of this aspiration and her good grades in school, as if she had entered that school.

accuracy, it would still be necessary to explain why social status affects language choice at all. In other words, a hypothesis is required that would outline how the status of speakers influences the genesis and maintenance of differences in language choice.

The process that has been put forward, sometimes implicitly, to relate social status to speech is that of presentation of self or impression management. Most simply, each person fits a certain status category or point on a scale and, by speaking in a way that symbolically represents that category, asserts that he or she either is a member of it or wants to claim membership. However, this formulation doesn't explain the language choices of many Oberwart speakers. Hungarian, and the peasant status that it represents, are stigmatized, especially by workers who often want to deny all association with it. This makes it difficult to understand why an informant such as J, a full-time worker who ranked very low on peasantness (4.5 out of 32, Appendix 2), would still present herself as a peasant in almost half of the cases summarized in Table 5.1. It is true that in-group linguistic variants, such as Hungarian, which are stigmatized by the majority culture, are often supported by in-group values, which themselves contradict majority values. However, even this is not helpful since the positive in-group values associated with Hungarian (hard work, land) are specifically those rejected by such workers as informant J.

Another example will illustrate the difficulty of applying to the Oberwart data a theory that views language choice primarily as a symbolic representation of status. János Vonatos (informant G) and Sándor Ács (informant U) are both workers at the foreman level. Because neither man is much of a peasant they both rank low and close to each other on that scale (8.5 and 12, Appendix 2). Yet their patterns of language use are very different. Mr. Vonatos uses virtually no Hungarian while Mr. Ács uses hardly any German. These two men, though quite similar in status, nevertheless differ substantially in linguistic presentation of self.

THE EFFECTS OF SOCIAL NETWORKS

Building on the initial understanding that status and speech are linked in the process of impression management, it is possible to show that speakers' social networks can act as powerful constraints on their linguistic presentations of self and, hence, their language choices.

Social network was defined as all of the people an informant spoke to during a unit of time. Each network contact was assigned to one of two categories: (*a*) those whose households owned either cows or pigs or both, and (*b*) those whose households owned neither cows nor pigs. This was a very rough measure of the contact's peasant status. In all cases, German monolingual contacts unfamiliar to the informant were counted in the nonpeasant (b) category, and an informant's school-age children, regardless of how many, counted as one person. For each informant the percentage of all meetings with contacts in category (a) was taken as a measure of the peasantness of that informant's social network. Because this measure was sensitive not only to the status of contacts, but also to the frequency with which an individual interacted with contacts of different statuses, and because not all informants saw their household members equally often, it was important to include the members of informants' households as part of their networks. For instance, those men who were commuters, working in Vienna during the week and coming home only for weekends, may have had in their households people who were in the same status category as the people in the households of men who work in Oberwart. However, the commuter necessarily has a somewhat different relationship with his household than the noncommuter and the frequency of interaction is part of this difference. The same applies, though to a lesser extent, to those who worked night shifts on the railroad and to students who did not come home daily from trade school or university. In contrast to the scale of peasant status which provided an indication of an individual's commitment to peasant life, this network scale reflected the extent of a person's social involvement with others who were peasants.

The correlation of language choice with social network was .78. The statuses of the speaker's social contacts predicted language choice at least as powerfully as the speaker's own status. This was the case despite the marked difference in elaborateness of the two measures. The index for determining peasant status was a complicated emic measure distinguishing gradations between peasant, peasant–worker and worker. Yet it did not predict language choice better than the rough dichotomy between peasant and nonpeasant network contacts. In addition, for 21 out of 32 informants, including J, János Vonatos, and Sándor Ács (whose usage seemed anomalous), the ranking by networks came closer to predicting language choice than did peasant status (Appendix 2). For most informants the more peasants there were in their social networks, the more they used Hungarian, and the fewer peasants there were in their networks, the less they used Hungarian. Linguistic presentation of self appears to depend at least in part on the expectations of those with whom one habitually interacts.

Participants constrain each other's language choices if only because choices are subject to interpretations. For instance, one man explained that if he ever spoke German to his aunt, with whom he had always spoken Hungarian, she surely would get very angry or think he was crazy. Whether or not he was right, this man was displaying his knowledge about the force of imputations concerning one's character and identity that are made on the basis of language choice.

But in Oberwart, more direct social control of speech is also common. Recall, for instance, that use of standard in everyday Hungarian conversations among natives is often ridiculed. In addition, people can influence not only the way an individual speaks when he or she is interacting with them, but also how that person speaks when interacting with others. Oberwarters are no doubt constrained by the knowledge that their speech can affect their reputations, as in the case of the woman who was labeled pretentious after she was overheard pronouncing her name in a standard way. I once witnessed what sounded like the beginning phase of such a process. An old man, preparing to play cards, recounted to his friends how insolent a young bilingual salesman at the local grocery store had been to him: *A kis dög nimetü válaszot* 'The little creep answered me in German.' Such cases of people who have apparently violated the constraints show what the constraints are and give some indication of how they are enforced.

German monolingual women who have married bilingual Oberwarters provide an extreme example of some ways in which speech can be controlled. There have been a few such women in Oberwart at least since the turn of the century and many more since World War II. Some of them have learned to speak Hungarian and others have not. I interviewed all the women who had married into one section of the *Felszeg* to find out which ones had learned Hungarian and what their language-learning experiences had been. In the case of each woman there was a rough neighborhood consensus about whether she had learned Hungarian. This was based on whether she spoke it to certain of the old peasant women of the neighborhood to whom everyone else spoke Hungarian. It was agreed that of the 12 women I interviewed six had learned Hungarian by this criterion. I divided the women into prewar (5) and postwar (7) brides for purposes of comparison. For each group a range of factors that influence language learning was thereby held constant. For instance, the number of years each woman had spent as an Oberwart wife was roughly comparable within each group. In addition, community attitudes toward the two languages and the absolute number of monolinguals living in Oberwart changed drastically after World War II, making the early experiences of the prewar brides quite different from that of the postwar brides, but relatively constant within each group. Of the prewar brides, four learned Hungarian. Of the seven postwar brides, two learned Hungarian. In both groups all of those who married into peasant households and lived with

their parents-in-law for several years learned Hungarian. In both groups those who established their own household with a working husband did not learn Hungarian.

All of the women who learned Hungarian told similar stories about their early years of marriage and language learning. Each said that there was hardly anyone who would speak German to her. The members of the family she lived with spoke Hungarian to each other, and the young wife worked with them all day. Before the war, the neighbors and friends who helped with the farm labor also spoke Hungarian to each other and to the family members even when the new bride was present. Usually only the husband of the woman would speak German to her, and during the day they were rarely together. Whereas he worked with his father, she worked mostly with her mother-in-law. Although in each case the family members knew how to speak German while the bride spoke no Hungarian at all, the family implicitly demanded that she learn Hungarian, and thereby express respect and solidarity toward them. They refused to adapt to her; she felt she had little choice but to adapt to them.

Those wives who did wage work or whose husbands worked, had very different experiences. Contacts at work were willing to use German with them. In the case of postwar wives, including those in peasant households, there were monolingual and bilingual neighbors and friends who were also willing to use German. Relatives could not exercise the same kind of sanctions against the worker wife as against the peasant wife. With an independent source of income, little interest in inheriting land, and a supply of acquaintances from work or elsewhere, it mattered little, these women said, if the older peasants refused to help or considered them haughty.

If the confluence of social pressures and inducements from family, neighbors and acquaintances, all in the direction of using Hungarian, could have the effect that women marrying into peasant families learned a new language, it is evident that the same sort of pressure from social contacts could influence a bilingual individual's pattern of language choice.

To unambiguously illustrate how this process works among bilinguals, one would have to find cases in which social networks affect language choice while all other factors remain the same. One way of accomplishing this is to select pairs of speakers who are matched in age and peasant status, but whose networks differ greatly in peasantness. There are few such pairs of speakers, however, because peasant status and peasantness of network are themselves closely related (.90), as are age and peasantness of network (.62). Although such cases are rare, they are nevertheless important sources of information. By separating the effects of the three variables, they isolate and highlight the role of social networks. It is possible, with such pairs of informants, to contrast their networks for detailed ethnographic evidence of the process by which networks influence language choice: For each informant, what is the purpose of interactions with different contacts? How does each informant want to influence contacts? What do the contacts expect of the informant regarding linguistic behavior? What sanctions and inducements are available to different contacts for influencing the informant's language choices? Do many of each informant's contacts know each other, and do they all expect the same kind of linguistic behavior from the informant?

The contrast between János Vonatos and Sándor Ács provides such an example. They are men of the same age, they are very similar to each other in peasant status (the difference in their ranks is 3.5), but they differ quite a bit in the peasantness of their networks (difference in rank, 10.5). This large difference between their networks corresponds to a large difference between their patterns of language use (difference in rank, 13.5). While János Vonatos used Hungarian exclusively with his grandparents, Sándor Ács used Hungarian to everyone except his children, and even with them he did not always choose German.

János Vonatos worked for the national railroad at the Oberwart station, in a secure, well-paying job. He switched tracks, hooked up trains and took charge of the ticket office on his night shifts. Sándor Ács was trained as a carpenter and worked as the foreman of a group of laborers at the county's water-control department. He and his workers built sewers, strengthened the embankments of rivers, and participated in a variety of other water-related building projects. Both men considered themselves skilled and quite above the ordinary laborer. Each trained several years for his job: Mr. Vonatos in the railroad's apprenticeship program, Mr. Ács in a trade school and as a carpenter's apprentice in a nearby town. Each man was in his early forties and married: the Vonatos family had two children, the Ács family had four. Neither wife was employed, both raised chickens, but only Mrs. Ács planted potatoes and corn for their own use. Otherwise neither family engaged in agriculture. Mr. Vonatos owned a car while Mr. Ács owned only a motorcycle, and this difference neatly counterbalanced the fact that the Vonatos house was much older than the Ács's. In short, the level of wealth of the two men, gauged by such indirect measures as these, was as similar as their worker status.

János Vonatos worked mainly with Oberwart monolinguals and even spoke exclusively in German to his favorite *kolega*, 'pal', a bilingual fellow worker at the railroad. He was proud of his job and liked it well enough to want his son to enter a railroad apprenticeship just as he had done. He also liked his fellow workers well enough to spend his leisure hours in the inn at the railroad station, talking to the railroadmen who were still on duty or drinking and playing cards with those who were off and with the other, primarily monolingual, patrons such as police officers from the nearby headquarters or clerks from neighboring offices.

Like his favorite *kolega*, János lived in a section of town which, despite its large bilingual population, was traditionally considered German and Lutheran. As a result there were no full-time peasants living on his street, only workers and a few worker–peasants. Among the workers were János's uncle and his niece, who lived across the street. His other consanguineal relatives—two brothers in Vienna, and a first cousin in a neighboring village—were also workers. Although they all saw each other at regular intervals, they did not ordinarily rely on each other for any financial assistance. In contrast to these relatives, the parents of János's wife had been peasants before they retired, but they lived on the other end of the *Felszeg* section of town and he saw them only once a week. They and some of their neighbors were perhaps the only peasants he had regular contact with. Although his in-laws were acquainted with his other relatives, they saw each other only rarely, and, with the exception of his favorite *kolega*, János's fellow workers at the station did not know any of his relatives or neighbors.

Staying abreast of the news, not only about his own part of town, but also about those in the central *Hauptplatz*, helped János maintain his self-image as a worldly and knowing citizen, well informed about everyone's business. When my German monolingual assistant interviewed János and his wife Ilse, she had never met them before. The assistant lived in the *Hauptplatz*, was about to start at the university in Vienna, and had only one bilingual friend. During the first minutes of the taped interview the assistant and the Vonatos couple attempted to identify each other by finding mutual acquaintances. It is indicative of the range of János's network ties that they not only were able to do this very quickly without using my assistant's bilingual friend as a link between them, but János was able to provide my assistant with some choice bits of gossip she had not heard before about the marriage plans of some of her own monolingual student friends. Ilse Vonatos was similarly familiar with people in various parts of town. On the one hand she kept in touch with the *Felszeg* through her parents. At the same time, she always bought her groceries in the stores on the mainstreet where she even stopped, every once in a while, and joined some monolingual acquaintances for an expresso in the nearest café.

In sum, for János the only possible source of pressure to conform to peasant norms in language choice, despite his status, came from his in-laws, who were relatively far away and who, having long ago given

their land to their daughter, were relatively powerless to influence him, at least through material inducements. Any pressure from other kin, work mates, and even neighbors would not have been toward peasant norms. These people had little reason to want or expect János to act in ways other than the worker they knew him to be, to use anything but German in most interactions.

Sándor Ács also worked only with monolinguals, but most of them were not Oberwarters and most of his work took him to other towns and villages. Moreover, none of his work mates frequented the inn where Sándor spent his leisure hours. He lived in the center of the *Felszeg* and his favorite inn was the local one that was also preferred by the peasants and peasant–workers of the neighborhood. Although there were workers living on his street, there was also a full-time peasant next door and another one across the street. Sándor had several neighbors and *kolegák* with whom he enjoyed talking and drinking when they met at the inn. One was a full-time peasant, another an unskilled laborer who raised pigs, and a third was a fellow carpenter with whom he often shared black-market building jobs. All of these men had been born in this section of the *Felszeg* and had been his pals since grade school.

One of Sándor's brothers and his mother were peasants; his other brother had a job, but also raised pigs, as did his wife's parents. All of these relatives lived within a few blocks of each other in the *Felszeg* and visited daily. More important, they all participated with the Ács family and some neighbors in a system of labor exchange (*összesegités*) which enabled each household to accomplish essential agricultural tasks despite the small number of household members and the lack of machinery. For instance, Sándor's mother, wife, and mother-in-law regularly relied on each other for help in potato picking, duck plucking, corn husking, and various other tasks. Sándor himself was sometimes called on to aid his mother in the heavy work of cutting wood, usually receiving food in return. In fact, some kinds of food rarely had to be bought by the Ács family because Sándor's wife, Juli, often did farm work for her closest acquaintance, a full-time peasant wife, in return for eggs and milk. Most other food Juli bought at the *Felszeg* grocery store, as she hardly ever shopped in the center of town, except on market days. But even then she visited only the market stalls and not the grocery and specialty shops. In fact, Juli's trip to the appliance shop to buy a coffee pot for a neighbor's wedding present was unusual enough to be an exciting event for her.

Not only did Sándor participate in mutual-help arrangements with his neighbors, kin and *kolegák*, he was also involved with them in technically illegal activities. That is, although he was not licensed as a builder, he, like many other Oberwarters, often worked for acquaintances and

neighbors who needed to have a gate fixed, a cement floor poured, or a shed built. Because of the prohibitive expense of hiring a licensed contractor, such black market labor was for people in the *Felszeg* the only reasonable way to get things done. This kind of work increased Sándor's income, although he was not always paid in money, but sometimes in food and in returned services.

His regular job with monolingual laborers apparently did not bring Sándor into much contact with the monolinguals of Oberwart. For instance, when my assistant first interviewed him and his wife, she had never met them before. They soon found that the assistant's one bilingual friend was a distant relative of theirs, but, with this one exception, they could not, in the course of an hour-long interview, think of any one else they all knew, or any friends of friends they had in common.

So, although the carpenter was a worker, the majority of his contacts away from work were with peasants and peasant–workers who knew each other. They lived in the same neighborhood, depended on each other for help and drank together. The symbol of solidarity and trust for these people was Hungarian, especially in black market transactions. If for some reason the carpenter had rejected this linguistic symbol, which most of his contacts expected of him, I suspect they would have interpreted it as a rejection of them and of their values. Had they collectively labeled him untrustworthy, pretentious, or unsociable, he would have been left nearly alone socially. In addition, from the point of view of the carpenter, winning the favor and trust of his pals, neighbors, and kin was part of the way in which he assured his household's participation in *összesegités*, maintained his black-market business and extra income. The relationship between Sándor Ács and his black-market contacts was therefore of a different quality, involving more mutual dependence in a variety of spheres, than any of the work contacts of János Vonatos.

A comparison of the details of these men's lives shows how the social network contacts of one allowed him to present himself as the worker he was. Most of his peasant and peasant–worker contacts had only minimal sanctions with which to control his linguistic behavior and were geographically and socially dispersed, making collective sanctions difficult to apply. Moreover, those people with whom he interacted most and identified were themselves workers. The effect of whatever influence they wielded over him was to encourage and support him in claiming a worker's status by speaking mostly German. For the other man, though he was equally a worker, linguistically presenting himself as such was not encouraged by his network contacts. The variety of social and economic bonds that linked him to his neighbors, kin, and *kolegák*, and that linked many of them to each other, made them a powerful influence on his life. And, being mostly peasants and peasant–workers, these contacts demanded of him the use of Hungarian, a linguistic affirmation of solidarity with them.

In sum, the analysis of social networks illustrates the ways in which speakers exercise control over each other's linguistic presentations of self and thereby contributes to explaining the variation between informants in their patterns of language choice. The status that a person can symbolically claim in speech depends as much on the nature of the speaker's social network as on factors tapped by traditional status indices.

6

The Process of
Language Shift

So far I have been discussing language choice and its social correlates at a single point in time. These synchronic patterns, along with historical evidence, provide the basis for an account of how diachronic change in language choice has occurred. The present differences in language choice between speakers of different ages are a reflection of change over time—of language shift in progress. And language shift shares the characteristics of other kinds of linguistic change: it arises out of synchronic heterogeneity; it is quantitative before it becomes categorical; and it is closely linked to broad social changes through the changing self-identification of speakers and through the changing association of some linguistic forms with prestigious and others with stigmatized social groups. Finally, an additional link with social change constitutes the crucial step in the process— the redistribution of communicative forms over functions in everyday interaction, so that the invariant forms, which at first were exclusively affirmations of the speaker's identity, come to be used variably and metaphorically as expressions of momentary intent.

Although in the simplest cases of linguistic change, the younger the speakers the more frequently they use new forms, most detailed studies of ongoing phonological and syntactic change have found that the difference between generations is complicated by differences within generations that reveal the social motivation of the change. Similarly, my conclusions about language shift are based both on the correlation of language choice with age and its correlation with the peasantness of speakers' social networks. This is because each new generation, by observing the socially differentiated use of its elders, reinterprets the relationship between linguistic forms and social groups and consequently reevaluates the prestige and meaning of linguistic forms. The reevaluation affects the new generation's own use leading to further change.

To describe the process of language shift and to identify it as an instance of socially determined linguistic change, the following questions will be discussed in turn: (*1*) How can it be demonstrated that age-related differences in language choice reflect changes due to the passage of time, rather than to changes in the life cycle of individuals? (*2*) By what steps does an earlier pattern of language choice evolve into a later one? (*3*) How do social differences within generations affect the course of the change? (*4*) Why is this language change occurring at this historical moment? Or, how does the pre-World War II symbolic significance of each language contrast with that current after the war? (*5*) How do the changed connotations of the two languages affect everyday verbal interactions? Specifically, how does the complementary relationship between style-shifting and language choice change as the community undergoes language shift?

AGE AND HISTORICAL CHANGE

Synchronic linguistic differences between speakers of different ages can come about in two ways. Either speakers regularly change their patterns of language choice as they age, so that in each generation young people use more German and then switch progressively to using more Hungarian as they grow older, or, a secular change in language use is occurring in the community. In the latter case, people within a generation retain their patterns relatively unchanged throughout life, but each generation systematically differs from the preceding ones, so that old people's choices constitute a historically older pattern that is being replaced, as the older generations die, by the newer patterns of the young. The simplest way to ascertain which of these is the accurate characterization of a particular community is to compare the patterns of two generations. To assure that age differences are not confounded with generational differences, the two generations must be of the same age when each is observed. Thus, historical evidence is necessary. For instance, a report on the language choices of 15-year old Oberwarters in 1930 could be compared to the observations reported here of 15-year olds in 1974. If a series of such comparisons shows generational differences, but little or no change during the life cycles of individuals, then it can be concluded that the synchronic differences constitute evidence of historical change in language choice. Furthermore, the range of speakers' ages can then be taken as "apparent time" and synchronic differences between speakers of different ages can be considered an adequate analogue for the repeated sampling, over many years, of the same age group in a series of generations (Labov 1965:94–95).

Fortunately, there is historical information about language use in Oberwart that makes possible the comparisons necessary to establish generational differences. There have probably been bilinguals in Oberwart since the 1500s, although the present pattern of community-wide bilingualism did not develop until more recently. Imre, in a retrospective judgment of the quality of bilingualism in Oberwart, notes that while his own grandfathers, both peasants born before 1870, only spoke German well enough to get by at markets in neighboring villages, the knowledge of German of his parents and his uncles and aunts (born before 1890) was much more intensive (1973:129). Wallner (1926), in a contemporary estimate of the number of bilinguals, notes that 57% of Hungarian Oberwarters spoke German by 1910.

These and other reports further suggest that the pattern of language use was very different in the past from what it is today. In the nineteenth century and well into the twentieth, most peasants in Oberwart behaved like Imre's grandfathers and used German only with outsiders from neighboring villages. Evidence for this is provided by a report on turn-of-the-century Oberwart that is most noteworthy for what it fails to mention. Varga (1903) was a Hungarian linguist concerned with maintaining the ethnic purity of the region's inhabitants. His article lamented the loss of local customs and argued that the ethnically Hungarian traditional life of the town was dying. He noted that along with the corruption of native rituals, "[T]he folk dialect, which is the main reflection of the spiritual and intellectual life of the people, is quickly losing its genuineness, its local flavor, its local metaphors and its dialect words (quoted in Kovács 1942:74, my translation)." Surely a Hungarian linguist concerned with linguistic authenticity and careful enough to notice the loss of dialect words would have reported the use of German within the native Hungarian community if he had observed any. His failure to mention it even though it would have greatly strengthened his argument suggests that he did not observe such use. The same logic can be applied to another comment by Imre (1941), about the state of the local Hungarian dialect before the 1930's. Imre was concerned then with the great number of

German loan words and considered them a threat to the local language. He went as far as to say: "[I]f the Magyars of Felsőőr do not awaken to this danger facing them, then not only the pureness of the language, but its very existence will be endangered (1941:3, my translation)." Despite his concern with German linguistic influences on the local community he makes no mention of the occurrence of German conversations, among the peasant families whose speech he is discussing. In his writings since 1969 Imre carefully notes this phenomenon, so his failure to mention it earlier again suggests that German was not, at that time, used very much among peasants.

The earliest reported pattern then, was the use of German with outsiders and strangers, and Hungarian among locals. There is further information, gleaned mostly from informants' memories, which allows comparisons between the language use of older and younger generations with particular interlocutor types. Today, for children under 15, the use of German between age mates is quite common. In contrast, Imre reports, as do many older Oberwarters, that in the 1920s children spoke only Hungarian to each other. In fact, they knew only as much German as they learned in school, which was "hardly more than nothing (Imre 1973:129)." Only after finishing school, when German was needed for work outside the community or for higher education, did young people learn it. Similarly, one peasant woman noted that, although her eldest son, now aged 35, always used to speak to his pals in Hungarian during his bachelor days about 15 years ago, she now hears her youngest son, still a bachelor at 22, using both German and Hungarian to his pals when they visit.

There is also evidence of generational differences for another interlocutor pair, parents and children. The use of GH and German is common today between young parents and children. However, if the rich peasants of the 1900s and 1910s had spoken German to their children at home, there would have been little need to send them to German villages with the expressed purpose of learning German. Therefore, at least until 1921 when child trading ceased, it is unlikely that Oberwart parents and children spoke German to each other.

Some indirect information also exists on earlier language use in schools and business interactions. Until World War II, the Calvinist school, attended by almost all of the Calvinist children, was conducted in Hungarian, with German taught as a foreign language. Today all schools are conducted in German, with Hungarian as an optional foreign language in the higher grades. And, in business transactions, it is noteworthy that German tradesmen and craftsmen who moved into Oberwart in the 1920s usually learned to speak Hungarian relatively well. They say they learned

Hungarian because it was a considerable help in their business. This suggests that in contrast to today, business interactions in the 1920s and 1930s were, at least part of the time, conducted in Hungarian (cf. Imre 1973a:124).

Although language choice in the last 70 years cannot be reconstructed in detail from such historical sources, these comparisons between speakers of the same age but different generations show that language use in the community has indeed changed. At the same time, the language choices of individuals remain relatively stable over their lives. For instance, informant Al, who was traded for a year to a neighboring village in order to learn German, presumably did not speak German to his mother then and, as she was still alive in 1974, I can report that he still does not speak German to her. Informant Z, who could well have been among the children Samu Imre played with in the 1920s and 1930s, still uses only Hungarian to his age-mate pals. The few changes in use that do occur in the lives of individuals tend to be concentrated at particular times, usually when social networks and status change significantly. For instance, in recent years, preschool children often use Hungarian with their parents or grandparents, but change to GH after they have started school. Marriage is another point at which, under particular circumstances, changes sometimes occur. For example, informant D, a woman whose parents were both workers with relatively nonpeasant networks, reported that she had always used German with her parents until she married and went to live with her husband's parents. The marriage was somewhat unusual because the husband's was a peasant family, but the young man himself had begun doing wage labor before his marriage. The woman reported that after her marriage she began to use both German and Hungarian to her parents as well as to her in-laws. But, in contrast to this young woman, most married couples report that they are still adhering to whatever pattern they used while courting. Age-mate pals also report little change in language use since the pattern was established, usually in childhood. Thus, despite limited changes in habitual usage within people's life times, the striking difference in language choice between the younger people and those born near the turn of the century is not a life-cycle change but a generational shift from older to newer patterns.

The oldest people, who today use German only to strangers and German-speaking outsiders, are preserving an old pattern, which, perhaps in the first few decades of this century, and before, was common to everyone. Each subsequent generation has introduced more and more German into its speech. Because the correlation of age with ranking by language choice can be viewed as change in apparent time, the implicational scales of language use can be interpreted, reading from bottom to top, as the history of language choice in Oberwart. When informants are divided into 10-year age groups, as in Fig 6.1, and the proportion of German used ([G + GH]/[G + GH + H] for each informant in Table 5.1, p. 135) is plotted against apparent time, it becomes clear that the older the language choice pattern the less German and GH it includes.

Not only has the use of German increased in the last 70 years or so, but it also has done so systematically, being introduced in an ordered series of situations. German was used with interlocutor types who were perceived as Austrian and urban before it was used with interlocutors who were seen as peasants. Looking at each interlocutor type separately, by reading up the columns, it is evident that before German was used by anyone with a particular interlocutor, GH was used with that interlocutor in an earlier pattern and Hungarian was used in an even earlier pattern. Furthermore, the use with any one interlocutor was usually categorical for the old form (H) before it became variable (GH). And it was variable before it became categorical for the new form (G). This corresponds to Bailey's (1970) findings that such a sequence of categorical, variable, categorical is typical for linguistic changes in each new environment to which they spread.

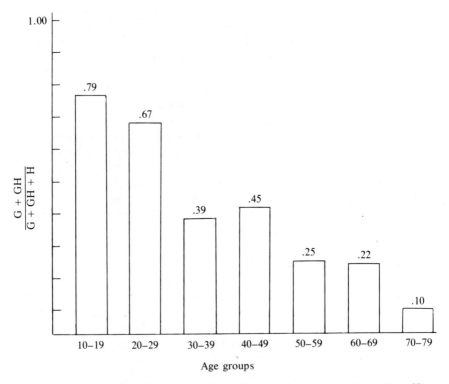

Figure 6.1. Proportion of German used by informants in seven age groups. ($n = 32$)

SOCIAL DETERMINANTS

This systematic increase in the use of German did not equally affect all bilingual Oberwarters in the last 50 to 70 years. Rather, the change followed social divisions in the community. The differential adoption of the new patterns by some speakers and their rejection by others, in the same generation, highlights the social motivation of the change.

In each generation, the use of German was greatest among those with nonpeasant networks. This can be illustrated by comparing speakers in three age groups (Figure 6.2). The groups correspond to generational breaks among informants, so that the parents of many of the speakers in the youngest group are in the middle and the parents of those in the middle are in the oldest group. The proportion of German used by each speaker ([G + GH]/[G + GH + H]) was calculated and in each generation informants were grouped according to the peasantness of their networks. Those

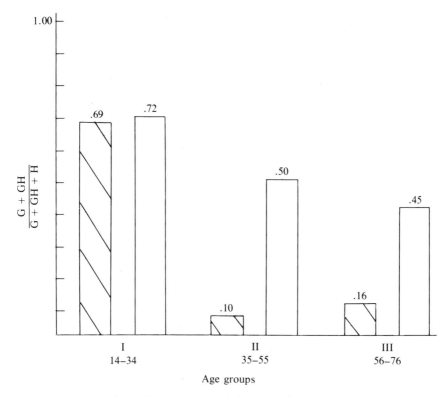

Figure 6.2. Proportion of German used by informants with peasant and nonpeasant networks in three age groups. ⟨ ⟩ = informants with peasant networks. ☐ = informants with nonpeasant networks. ($n = 32$)

with scores at or above the median in peasantness of network were considered to have "peasant networks" and those with scores below the median were considered to have "nonpeasant networks". Viewed diachronically this indicates that in each generation during the last 70 years, those with nonpeasant networks have adopted the newer pattern—speaking German with progressively more interlocutors—to a greater extent than did people with heavily peasant networks.

In the century before World War II, as Oberwart grew into a city, some bilingual Oberwarters took nonagricultural jobs and their social networks expanded to include other social classes, local German-speaking merchants, workers from other villages and many monolinguals. In contrast, the social networks of other bilinguals remained limited to local peasants. These differences in experience and identity can account for the regular differences in language choice within each of the prewar generations. Those with nonpeasant networks in the middle generation, observing that a relatively greater use of German was characteristic of those in the previous generation who were in contact with the wider world, increased their own use of German to identify themselves similarly. At the same time, people with peasant networks continued to use primarily Hungarian, identifying with, and being constrained by, their counterparts in the previous generation.

While the contrast between those with peasant networks and those with nonpeasant networks is apparent in the youngest age group, as in the older ones, it is slighter than for older speakers and is overshadowed by the marked increase in use of German by all younger speakers regardless of their networks. For this youngest group, born during and after World War II, the effect of social networks on language choice is complicated by the further influence of sex-role differences. However, before these can be understood it is important to explore the more general reasons for the difference between the youngest group and their elders: the postwar generation's rejection of peasant life and, just as important, the consequent reinterpretation—by those with peasant networks as much as by those with nonpeasant ones—of what it means to choose German as opposed to Hungarian.

Following the postwar Soviet occupation of the Burgenland, industrialization proceeded rapidly. Recall that by the boom years of the 1960s, employment in commerce, industry, and bureaucracy became available to the children of peasant families. Such employment was much more lucrative than the traditional subsistence agriculture to which Oberwart's peasants were restricted by the limited capitalization of farms and the small size of holdings. Young people were drawn to wage work in large numbers. With the newly available money, Oberwarters became socially mobile. Workers turned away from land accumulation as a subsistence strategy and participated instead in Austria's growing consumer economy. Acquisition of cars, houses, appliances, and furniture replaced land as the route to higher social standing. Since these items were out of reach for peasant farmers perennially low on cash, the prestige of the traditionally respected peasant landowner dropped, while the previously disdained status of worker gained prestige in the eyes of young people in the 1960s. But this reversal adversely affected the use of Hungarian only after a second change had occurred: a shift in the connotations and evaluations of German and Hungarian.

The present connotations of the two languages, described in detail earlier, contrast sharply with prewar conceptions. Before the 1940s, Hungarian and German represented, to peasant Oberwarters, parallel and coordinate social groups: each language included much-admired forms that had their own quite separate sources of prestige. Despite the fact that German was the language of elite groups in Oberwart and in the entire region, the two languages were not ranked with respect to each other within the peasant community. In fact, although German was economically useful for most bilinguals, it remained external to their own peasant prestige hierarchy. It was merely the language of outsiders: merchants, bureaucrats, and other villages.

The sources of prestige for Hungarian included its position as the national language up to 1921 and the presence, in Oberwart, of a nationalistic Hungarian bureaucratic elite. During Magyarization around the turn of the century, Hungarian was also considered the language of the intellectuals and upper classes. Even after the annexation of Burgenland by Austria, Hungarian books, newspapers and magazines were available in Oberwart. Hungarian was the language of instruction in the Calvinist school; the Hungarian Reading Circle was in full operation, and the present Hungarian library of the Calvinist church dates from those years. Oberwarters continued to send children to Hungary for higher education. Since Catholics could choose between a German and a Hungarian school, both run by the church, the popularity of the Hungarian school, even when the region belonged to Austria, indicates the high regard in which the language was held.

Even local Hungarian, as identified by its stereotyped features, did not lack positive evaluations. It represented the local peasant community whose values were then respected by the peasants themselves. In addition, it was the language of the *üöri* 'native Felsőőri', regardless of status. This contrasted with *vidiki* 'outsider, stranger', people who most often spoke German, and *dzsütmënt,* nonnative Oberwarters living in town who, after 1921, were also native German speakers. By this tripartite division of the world, native-speaker-of-Hungarian and native-of-Oberwart were nearly equivalent. In fact, for older Oberwarters, the label *üöri* implies Hungarian speaker, so that no word has ever existed, nor was one needed, to identify native Oberwarters who did not speak Hungarian. Today there are a great many such people, but in the 1920s and 1930s the three categories, *üöri, vidiki* and *dzsütmënt* were not only adequate to classify everyone but in most cases to simultaneously identify one native language with each category.

On the other hand, German also had prestige, but deriving from very different sources. Recall that a local elite of Lutheran merchants conducted their school and church in German and published a newspaper well before German became the national language and the language of the bureaucracy, courts, and higher education in 1921.

Only after World War II, as wage work and its related values started to predominate among the children of peasants, were the two languages brought within one conceptual system and ranked with respect to each other, thereby producing the evaluations current today. After the war, for peasants and former peasants, Hungarian and German came to represent not mutually exclusive ethnic and class groups but rather differing statuses, all available to bilinguals, but ranked by them in terms of income and prestige. More specifically, by the postwar years the connotations of Hungarian had been drastically limited. Of its prestigious associations only one, the Calvinist church, remains today. The church is respected and retains its link to the use of Hungarian through its Hungarian services and the popular annual play. However, even the church is adapting to the linguistic consequences of socioeconomic changes: For several years there have been monthly services in German, mainly for families with monolingual members, and confirmation class, while continuing to teach Hungarian hymns and prayers, is now conducted in both German and Hungarian. More generally, after the war, the association of Hungarian with prestigious intellectual circles was forgotten and its value as a symbol of local identity was neutralized by the increasing number of German monolinguals native to Oberwart. What remained was its association with a single status, peasant, which, during those years, was becoming a stigmatized identity. For bilinguals, the connotations of German were simultaneously expanding to include the newly available identities of worker, bureaucrat, and consumer, in addition to local merchant and artisan. I want to focus here on two important illustrations of these reinterpretations and how they influenced the youngest generation's language choices.

The demise of the Hungarian school in Oberwart was both a sign and a cause of the newly limited associations evoked by Hungarian after the war. The Calvinist and Catholic churches had provided elementary education in Hungarian until 1938–1945, when non-German schooling was suspended. In the postwar years a Hungarian school was again estab-

Felszegi funeral.

lished, this time unaffiliated with any church, but supported by the Austrian government's guarantee of minority rights. However, the school did not last long. By the 1955–1956 school year there was no Hungarian first grade. By 1956–1957, the school was discontinued. And, most importantly, this was done on the orders of the bilingual community, which voted to close the school. Despite the Austrian government's official support, the bilinguals of Oberwart did not want their children to attend a Hungarian language school.

Even before the final closedown, there was a steady decrease in enrollment at the Hungarian school as each year more and more Hungarian mother-tongued children were transferred by their parents to German classes. Because a shortage of teachers meant that some of the same teachers taught both the Hungarian and the German classes, and because, under initial postwar conditions, both sets of classes lacked basic equipment and good housing, it is unlikely that either the quality of the instruction or of the physical environment had anything to do with these switches. Rather, as informants' interview responses indicated, it was the language which motivated switches to the German school. Parents who had transferred their children said they did it because Hungarian was useless, and the children needed to learn German to get ahead, to find jobs. I pointed out that the previous generation had learned German without a German school. Many parents and their now grown children answered that by the 1950s one could not learn anything in the Hungarian school, because no one but children from backward peasant homes went there; those who were capable of nothing more than peasant work. The implication was that since so many had transferred out there remained only peasants and the school was, therefore, inferior.

In light of such memories and judgments it is interesting that postwar school records show not an increase in the percentage of children from peasant homes enrolled in the Hungarian school, but rather a decrease by almost half (69% in 1950–1951 to 38% in 1956–1957). If anything, the Hungarian school had a smaller percentage of peasants in it than ever before. Evidently, by the 1950s Hungarian was so strongly identified as the peasant language that Oberwarters perceived the Hungarian school to be a peasant school even though the actual percentage of peasant children attending was small. In short, the language was being stripped of its sources of prestige. The one association that it still evoked was that of newly devalued, even stigmatized, peasant status. As for most of the children attending school then and later, this was all they ever learned about the social meaning of the Hungarian language.[1]

[1] It is important that such re-evaluations can continue to occur, in response to changing circumstances. This is now happening for some speakers who are far removed from peasant status. For instance, in 1974, one young bilingual woman who had attended all-German

The second example of prewar–postwar contrasts provides a good illustration of the way in which for bilinguals, German and Hungarian came to be ranked with respect to each other in one conceptual scheme, instead of continuing to represent separate social spheres. It concerns the etiquette of switching to German in the presence of German monolinguals. Today, almost all bilingual Oberwarters follow this practice, explaining it as a form of politeness meant to assure monolinguals that they are not being discussed or excluded. Older informants, however, report that bilinguals did not always do this. In addition, I observed several exceptions to the rule, which shed light on its development.

The present-day exceptions are all peasant men and women in their sixties and seventies who apparently do not consider it impolite, but merely normal, to speak Hungarian in the presence of German monolinguals. For instance, I heard a man of 32 reprimanding his old peasant father for speaking Hungarian when monolinguals as well as bilinguals had come to visit at their house. Although the son was very upset at this breech of good manners, the father merely shrugged. In another incident a monolingual German neighbor was invited by an old peasant couple to help with a pigkilling. Although instructions during the pigkilling were shouted to the monolingual in German, the rest of the conversation during the three or four hours of work and subsequent eating was all in Hungarian. I assume that the couple was not trying to be impolite to the monolingual since he had helped them, they had invited him, and were feeding him with expected good-will and generosity. Other exceptions include peasant parents who refused, even after World War II, to speak German to monolingual daughters-in-law who came to live with them.

These exceptions constitute the maintenance of the older no-switch pattern. Just as in the past, when it conveyed pride in local peasant identity and values represented by Hungarian, the occurence of the no-switch pattern today appears to have a similar function, as evidenced by its restriction to aged peasants who still voice respect for peasant traditions, and to activities related to the peasant homestead.

A further example will clarify the changes implicit in the new etiquette. Men who worked on road gangs and in factories in the 1920s and 1930s recounted that at that time, if bilinguals worked together, they usually spoke Hungarian to each other even in the presence of monolinguals. Noting the contrast with current custom, they added that although the

---

schools, including a commercial secondary school, and who had a prestigious clerical job in a travel agency and a monolingual husband, was sending her 4-year-old child to Hungarian camp for the summer so he could learn standard Hungarian because, as she said, a foreign language can be very useful.

monolinguals did not like this, and asked them to stop, the bilinguals did not care and continued to do so if they wanted to.

A similar incident that occurred in 1974 in a crowded *Felszeg* inn provides a comparison. Several monolingual construction workers, strangers to Oberwart, had been repairing the street in front of the inn. At lunch time they entered and sat down near the table of four bilinguals who were conversing in Hungarian. The monolinguals jokingly but insistently told the bilinguals to stop. "Let us hear what you are saying. We live in Austria. We are all Austrians. Don't you know how to talk German?" were among the comments made. The bilinguals switched to German. Apparently the use of Hungarian in this incident, as in the 1930s, was taken by German monolinguals as a somewhat hostile act even though, in this case, it was apparently done inadvertently.

Whereas in the 1920s and 1930s the problem of monolingual demands was encountered only in certain work situations, it has now entered the neighborhood inn and, when bilinguals marry monolinguals, even the home. But the presence of monolinguals in local inns and homes did not, it itself, revise linguistic etiquette. What has changed since the 1920s is not so much the pressure exerted by German monolinguals as the responses and conceptions of the bilinguals. They now acknowledge rather than resist the right of monolinguals to demand use of German in their presence. The earlier pattern implicitly defined those who use only German and those who use Hungarian to be separate, so that the demands of monolinguals were irrelevant to talk among bilinguals. In contrast, the present pattern allows that there is only one social sphere and in it German can, if necessary, legitimately replace Hungarian. Unlike older peasants, young Oberwarters do not have to be asked to switch to German: In this respect they have already joined the monolingual world by adapting, on their own, to its expectations.[2]

Although the peasant–worker contrast remains most important in explaining differences within a single generation, for the youngest age group language choice is also related to sex-role differences, accentuating the contrast with previous generations. It is not that young men and women in Oberwart have basically different language-choice patterns. Rather, age, network and language choice interact differently in the case of women

---

[2] No doubt contributing to this change is the lack of unity among Burgenland's small number of Hungarian-speakers (approx. 5000). In contrast to the much more numerous Croatian-speakers of Burgenland and to ethnic-linguistic minorities elsewhere (e.g. Cole and Wolf 1974:270-3), among the Hungarian-speakers there are no political, folk-cultural, or youth organizations nor symbolic links that override both intervillage antagonisms and the population's tripartite religious division.

than men, because women in the youngest generation perceive and evaluate the life possibilities represented by each language differently than do the men.

Although the correlation of language choice with peasantness of social network is similar for both men and women (men: .78, women: .74), the correlation of language choice with age (men: .69, women: .93) is significantly higher (p < .05) for women than for men. This difference is illustrated by comparing the proportion of German used by men and women of three generations and with peasant as opposed to nonpeasant networks (Figure 6.3). Among men more German is used by those with nonpeasant networks and there is a steadily increasing use of German over time by those with nonpeasant networks. Women, however, differ. First, in the oldest generation there were no women in this sample who could be categorized as having nonpeasant networks, reflecting the fact that there were very few women over 56 in Oberwart who had such networks. It is the youngest generation of women that is noteworthy. All of the youngest women use more German than any of the youngest men. These young women do not show the difference in use between those with different kinds of social networks that is apparent for the men of all three generations and the women of the middle generation. Whereas even the youngest men who have peasant networks are constrained to use more Hungarian, young women with peasant networks do not choose differently from those with nonpeasant networks.

This greater rejection of Hungarian by young women can be seen as the linguistic expression of their greater rejection of peasant life. Although there are some young men who, despite the general preference for industrial and commercial employment, take over family farms, young women since World War II have consistently refused to do this when the choice has been open to them. Because a woman's life possibilities usually depend on whom she marries, many mothers warn their daughters not to marry peasant men. Young women themselves not only express disdain for "dirty" farm work, but also reject peasant men as husbands. The effects of this have been dramatic. Whereas before the war most peasant men married within the bilingual community with higher frequency than nonpeasant men, in recent years the situation has reversed: Peasant men have had to marry exogamously and they have done this with greater frequency than nonpeasants, indicating that local young women have acted on their expressed preferences (Table 2.4, p. 53). This rejection of peasant men extends to opposition of the sort of arrangement, common elsewhere in Europe and the smaller villages of Burgenland, in which the wife runs the peasant farm while the husband takes wage work

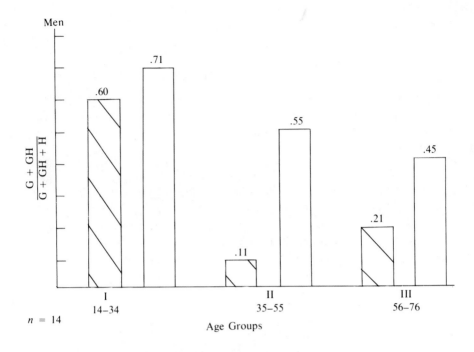

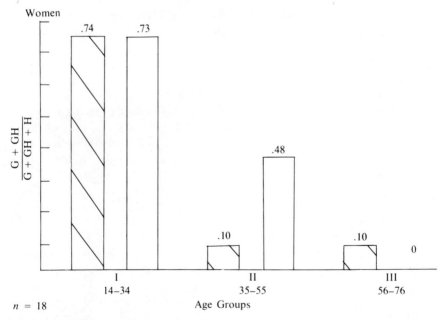

Figure 6.3. Proportion of German used by men and women with peasant and nonpeasant networks in three age groups. ⬜⬜ = informants with peasant networks. ⬜⬜ = informants with nonpeasant networks.

Wedding in the Reformed Church.

(Lockwood 1973; Sozan 1976). Accordingly, there are no such arrangements among the youngest generation.

Young women opposed peasant life more than young men partly because, while men's farm work has been largely mechanized and is considered to be no more difficult (though perhaps more time-consuming) than unskilled employment in industry, peasant women's work has not been eased by machines. Young women, when discussing life choices, usually emphasize the heaviness of peasant work. The combines, tractors and hay gatherers, with which men do farm work, are common in peasant households. But silos, potato planters and washing machines, which could lighten the peasant wife's work are the last to be bought, if they are bought at all. In this, Oberwart exemplifies the pattern in central Europe, where peasant women work many more hours than their husbands (Franklin 1969:37–44; Minge-Kalman 1978). Further, for men there is at least the appearance of much-valued independence in peasant life. Young peasant men often contrast their freedom of movement with a worker's schedule, which is imposed by others. But peasant wives must often live and work in the household of their in-laws and for them life is seen to offer little of this independence. Several women said, in discussing marriage: *Im bizo nëm mënëk e napám alá* 'You can be sure I won't go (to live) under my mother-in-law'.

In contrast to the peasant wife, the worker's wife is engaged primarily in household, child-care, and garden tasks. Workers' wives often hold jobs as maids, salespersons or clerks, although sometimes these are part-time. Workers' wives are more likely to have a household separate from their in-laws, and access to money means they can look forward to a new house, as well as to washing machines and electric ranges—status-enhancing, labor-saving appliances bought only by worker families.

In comparing male and female life and work, young women believe that they have more to gain than men by embracing upward mobility in the form of nonagricultural employment. They voice this in discussions about their future plans and act on it in their choices of husbands. They do not want to be peasants and, whether they have peasant or nonpeasant social networks, they are equally adamant in their linguistic rejection of this status (Gal 1978). As a result, language choices of young women contribute importantly to the increased use of German by the youngest generation.

In sum, to understand the linguistic behavior of the postwar generation as a whole, it is necessary to look at the association of statuses and languages as that generation came to conceive of them in their formative years. Cut off from knowledge about Hungarian speakers outside Oberwart, the younger people based their evaluation of the languages and their interpretation of the connotations of each on experience with local speakers of older generations, both bilingual and monolingual. As a result, German remained, as always, the language of the local elite and of wage work, while Hungarian lost its prestigious connotations and was linked primarily with peasant status. This, occurring at the time that peasant status was being stigmatized not only by the German-speaking upper classes of Oberwart, but by bilingual workers themselves, created the current evaluations of each language and thereby contributed to the newest patterns of language use.

LANGUAGE CHOICE AND STYLE CHOICE

From the point of view of the bilingual individual engaged in verbal interaction, the introduction of German into conversations that, for previous generations, were conducted exclusively in Hungarian, has meant an increase in the linguistic means available for expressing social meaning. Today, just as in previous generations, the range of functions to be expressed linguistically remains unchanged: People still want to present themselves as individuals with particular social statuses; they still want to indirectly convey a variety of meanings such as anger, respect, intimacy, authority, and formality; and they still want to accomplish interactional goals such as winning an argument or impressing others. But, whereas near the turn of the century, despite widespread bilingualism, only Hungarian was used within the community, today the tools available for expressing these meanings among bilinguals include not only styles of Hungarian but also use of German.

The expression of one's social status, the display of solidarity with members of a social category, is separate from all other functions. It is clear from the connotations of each language, from the choice of language in black-market transactions, from the correlation of language choice patterns with peasantness, and from many other ethnographic details that in Oberwart it is choice of language that, in most interactions, expresses the speaker's claim to a social status. Language choice implicitly relates the interactants to the social groups associated with each language. One need not be the member of a social category, such as peasant, to claim that identity; those with heavily peasant networks do so as much as those who qualify as peasants by other measures. But whatever reasons individuals have for presenting themselves as members of a social category, it is choice of language that symbolizes such membership in verbal interaction. All other functions are served by style-shifting within the invariably chosen language. So, when only one language is chosen for a particular interaction, variation within that language remains as a resource for conveying a variety of meanings separate from social status. The variation in the Hungarian speech of the old peasant couple, Anna néni and Miska báccsi, as well as in the German speech of the two adolescent girls, demonstrated some of the functions of intralanguage variation. They illustrated the fact that choice of language and stylistic shifting can fulfill complementary functions.

Oberwart speakers are not unique in using one invariant set of linguistic alternates for the symbolization of social status while the expression of what may be called rhetorical or interactional functions is accomplished by another, a varying set. For example, Labov (1965), in his studies of phonological variation in monolingual communities, found a similar dichotomy between values of linguistic variables that were always used by members of a group, and therefore were identified with the group (indicators), and other variables that showed rhetorical, or in his terms, stylistic variation (markers). Other studies have found similar synchronic differences between phonological variables (Laberge and Chiasson-Lavoie 1971; Sankoff 1974).

This separation of linguistic means according to functions is characteristic of Oberwart today, as it was 70 years ago. But although choice of language still conveys one's social status, some bilinguals even among themselves currently claim the status represented by German and not that represented by Hungarian. Most important, for a certain set of bilingual speakers, neither status is claimed all of the time and neither language is used invariably. It is for these speakers that a breakdown occurs in the usual separation of linguistic means according to functions.

For those bilinguals whose status, way of life and values have not changed from what was general in the community 50 to 70 years ago—for the oldest generation with peasant networks—choice of language is invariably Hungarian with almost all interlocutors. Their pattern of choice has not changed and continues to serve the function of asserting peasant status. For them this choice still carries connotations of prestige and local pride. For those whose status, way of life and values are most different from what was general in the community 50 years ago—those in the youngest generation with nonpeasant networks—choice of language is just as invariant with most interlocutors, but the choice is German, not Hungarian. For them German has connotations that include prestige and pride in their social mobility and in their worker status. For both these sets of people, when variable choice of language does occur (GH), it tends to be unreciprocal use with someone far from them in age, usually grandparents or grandchildren. For both these sets of people, stylistic shifting within the invariably chosen language functions to express social meanings other than the peasant–nonpeasant distinction. Neither of these groups experiences the immediate conflict of values, attitudes and loyalties that are often the ideological accompaniments of social change.

It is the people in the middle who form the notable contrast to this: Neither totally peasants nor solidly workers, neither heavily involved in peasant networks nor disengaged altogether, they are usually also in the middle by age. In nonlinguistic as well as linguistic ways they do not always express the same social status. Their values and loyalties with regard to the peasant–worker distinction are problematic, undecided, manipulable. It is these people in the middle who most often engage in variable choice of language (GH) with more than one interlocutor, sometimes with as many as four out of ten interlocutor types (e.g., Table 4.1, p. 102, informant 18). For them, in conversations with those interlocutor types who are themselves in the middle on the peasant–urbanite continuum, choice of language expresses not only their varying claims concerning social status, but also interactional functions. Only in these interactions does conversational language-switching occur. For such people, and those interlocutors, the linguistic means are not segregated by function, and choice of language is often used to express the communicative intent of the speaker.

The distribution of conversational language-switching among Oberwart bilinguals shows that it is not characteristic of all speakers nor of all the interactions of any one speaker. Rather, it is historically and contextually limited. This, in fact, is part of its importance. Viewed not in isolation but as part of the community-wide process of language shift, conversational language-switching can be explained as the middle and variable step in the process by which the language choice patterns of the community change from categorical use of one language to categorical use of the other. It occurs in contexts where the old form is no longer invariably used, and the new form is not yet invariably used. Further, if the functions of conversational language-switching are examined in relation to those of other kinds of linguistic variation simultaneously present in the community, it becomes clear that during language shift there is a redistribution of communicative functions among the available linguistic means. Linguistic forms, in this case languages, previously used invariably and restricted to functioning as indicators of social status are used metaphorically to express rhetorical meanings as well and are thus variable for some interactions between certain speakers.

Just as the categorical–variable–categorical sequence by which German is introduced into each social situation corresponds to the sequence by which new forms enter linguistic contexts during phonological, syntactic and lexical change, so the expansion in the function of language choice in Oberwart corresponds to the expansion in function of indicator variables during the process of phonological change. In particular, when phonological changes are a result of speakers' conscious attempts to alter their speech in the direction of a prestige form—as is the case in Oberwart—then, in the course of phonological change: "The linguistic variable . . . shows regular stylistic stratification as well as social stratification (Labov 1965:535)." In short, here too, expression of social identity and expression of other communicative functions are accomplished by the same variable linguistic means. In these respects the social mechanism of change between two languages is the same as the mechanism of change within a single language.

But conversational language-switching, while being a step in language change, is, at the same time, also an instrument of the social change that language shift reflects. In conversational language-switching, the opposing values and differential prestige of the peasant and the urban ways of life are symbolically juxtaposed; the social contrast is thereby implicitly equated with some interpersonal contrast in the immediate conversation. For instance, when in the midst of a disagreement conducted in Hungarian, one speaker switches to German, the effect is to imply that the German statement should win in the interpersonal conflict just as the way of life it symbolizes dominates in the social sphere. The clout, the prestige, and the authority that the urban worker life and values carry in the minds of many bilinguals is invoked on behalf of the views expressed by the speaker who has switched. In light of this it is noteworthy that much of conversational language-switching in Oberwart, as elsewhere (Gumperz 1976b), takes place in arguments or in persuasion. Further, as in some of the examples of conversational language-switching provided earlier, the issues in such disagreements often concern the conflict of values current in the community: which should be followed, the urban or the peasant rules about raising children and relations with local merchants. As a result, conversational language-switching contributes to the argument and persuasion through which people's loyalties and opinions about these values can be articulated and changes in them expressed. But not everyone is sensitive to such change. Although the social distinctions that exist in Oberwart are obvious to all, the dilemma of choosing between contrasting values does not touch everyone equally. In fact, only a limited set of speakers use conversational language-switching: This social conflict is a potent symbol for interactional conflict only to those in the middle, those who are ambivalent regarding social allegiances and self-identification.

In sum, speakers allude to the large scale social changes occurring in Oberwart when they engage in conversational language-switching. Although language shift may roughly correlate with industrialization and urbanization, it is only indirectly, through changes in social networks and in the connotations of linguistic variants, that the social changes that speakers experience are linked to their strategies for the use of old and new forms during verbal interaction. In language shift, as in other sorts of linguistic change, alternation between old and new forms characterizes the spread of change to new speakers and new environments. The moving force behind the expansion is provided by the social meanings that the alternate forms come to convey and the expressive use of these connotations in everyday interaction.

Appendix 1

Language Usage Interview

The following list of questions was asked in the context of an interview. I wrote down informants' answers. For each informant the names of relatives, friends and neighbors were used in questions about those categories of people. Informants were allowed to give lengthy and detailed responses if they wished. In some cases I probed further, and asked in more detail than the questions below indicate, about particular interactions. The order of questions within each broad category (e.g., Church, Work) was not always strictly adhered to. Questions were asked in whichever language was customary between the informant and me. No special attention was given to keeping the form of the questions identical for everyone. However, care was taken to ask each question of all informants.

CHURCH

1. Which language do you prefer to hear in church?
2. Which service do you go to? H? or G?
3. Why do you go to that particular service?
4. What way do you talk to the minister when paying taxes?
5. In what language were you confirmed?

OFFICIAL BUSINESS—DOCTOR

6. What way do you talk at the town hall to the head notary; to the messenger; to the secretary?
7. To the woman who records births and deaths?
8. Which doctor do you go to for general trouble or check ups? What way do you talk to him?
9. Did you use a midwife? Which one? What way did you talk to her then? (This for women only.)
10. Have you ever been to the hospital? When? Which doctors did you talk to then? What way did you talk to them?

WORK

11. Are there any people on your job who speak H? What way do you talk to them? (Children: school.)
12. Give an example of when you have talked H to them.
13. What did the G monolinguals say when that happened?
14. What part of the day or week do you work?
15. Have you ever worked away from Oberwart? How many years? Where? Commuting worker or permanently away?
16. Do you have the kind of job where you are in contact with the public? When clients come to talk to you what way do you talk to them?
17. Do you ever work for other people away from your job? For your own private income? Give an example of when that happened. Who are some people you have worked for? How did you talk to them?
18. Do you and your family ever exchange labor with another family during potato picking, harvesting, or other times when lots of people are needed? (*Összesegités* 'helping together') What way did you talk to those people? Who did you do that with? When?
19. Have you ever hired anyone to do a job for you when that person was not licensed? Who? For what? What way did you talk to them when arranging it?
20. Do you ever go to the local dairy (e.g., to deliver milk or to buy it)? If so who do you talk to there? What way do you talk to them?

SHOPPING

21. What way do you talk if you meet friend (name) at the Wednesday market?

22. What way do you talk to Mr. (name) who sells the frankfurters at the market?
23. What way do you talk to the sales people at (name) store? Which salespeople do you usually talk to? How do you talk to Mrs. (name) when you shop there?
24. Where do you buy your groceries? Which sales clerk do you usually talk to there? What way do you talk to her–him?
25. Where do you buy your milk? Which family member goes to get it? Who do you talk to if you go to get it? What way do you talk?
26. When you go to (name) drug store, who do you talk to and what way?
27. When you go to (name) hardware store, who do you talk to and what way?
28. When you go to (name) department store outside of town, who do you talk to and what way?
29. Do you ever go to the post office? Who, of the clerks, do you usually talk to there? What way do you talk?
30. Do you ever go to the cafe? (List cafes and ask which one usually.) How do you talk to the waitress there? Do you ever go to cafe (name)? When there how do you talk to (waitress' name)?

SCHOOL

31. When did you start school? How many years did you go?
32. In what language was the instruction conducted? Why H school; why G school? Which kind did you send your children to?
33. Who were your teachers? How did you talk to them in school? Outside of school?

KIN

34. What way did you (do you) talk to your parents?
35. What way did you (do you) talk to your grandparents?
36. Did you ever live with your in-laws? How long?
37. Did you ever do farm work with your in-laws? Did you ever do mutual help (*összesegités*) with your in-laws or with brothers and sisters?
38. What way do you talk with your in-laws?
39. With brothers and sisters? Spouses of brothers and sisters? (name siblings)
40. What way do you talk to your brothers and sisters if you go to market with them? (name each sibling)

41. What way do you talk to your cousins (name)? Older cousins (name) younger cousins (name)?
42. To your own children (name each one)?
43. To your children before they went to school? (name each one).
44. To your spouse (name) when you were courting? Before you got married?
45. To your spouse now?
46. Did you have other boyfriends–girlfriends before you got married? How did you talk to them?
47. Do you visit your spouse's relatives? Where do they live? What way do you talk to them? (ask for more relatives)
48. What way do you talk to your grandchildren?
49. To your daughter- or son-in-law? Do they live in your house?
50. Did you ever get letters from America? Who is in America in your family? What way do they write letters to you? G? H?

NEIGHBORS

51. Who are your present neighbors? (If the person leaves out any immediate neighbors on any side of the house then ask about those by name) Do you ever talk to your neighbors? When usually? What way? (ask about each one separately and by name)
52. Did you ever live in a different house than this one? Who were your neighbors then? What way did you talk to them? Where was the house?
53. Which of your neighbors help if you need someone for a favor? What way do you talk to them?
54. Is there a bench in your neighborhood where people sit outside in the summer time? Where is it? Who sits there? Do you ever go there to sit? What way do you talk there? Where do you go to sit in the summer if you don't go there?

PALS (KOLEGÁK)

55. Do you have a close pal? Who? How do you talk to him–her?
56. Did you have a close pal in school? Before marriage? Did you have a whole bunch, a gang? How did you all talk? What way do you talk to these people now if you see them?
57. Who do you go with when you go to the inn? What way do you

talk? Who do you usually meet at the inn? If you go shopping do you ever ask anyone to go with you? Who? What way do you talk? Does anyone ever come over to watch TV with you? How do you talk? Do you ever go over to watch TV at someone else's house?

58. Did you ever go on a trip with other people? Where? By bus or by car? How did you all talk?

59. When you meet your close pal on the street, or at the market how do you usually talk? When was the last time you met? How did you talk then?

ENTERTAINMENT

60. Which inn do you usually go to? Why?

61. Who do you meet there usually? How do you talk to them?

62. What do you do on Sunday afternoons? (pursue this)

63. Have you ever been to Hungary?

64. When you were in Hungary did you talk Hungarian? (Pursue this and ask about experiences.) If you didn't talk H in Hungary then why not?

65. Do you have a TV? Do you have a Hungarian TV? (i.e., attachment that allows you to watch Hungarian TV programs)

66. Do you have a radio? Do you ever listen to Hungarian radio programs? When? What programs?

GENERAL ATTITUDES

67. Do you have any monolingual friends or acquaintances who speak only German? Do you have any who speak only Hungarian?

68. Which language do you find is most comfortable for you?

69. Which language do you prefer? Do you have a favorite? Which sounds better?

70. Are there some things that sound better in German? Are there some things that just sound better in Hungarian? Like what? Give an example.

71. Do you find that one language is easier for you to express yourself in? Can you bring out your thoughts better in one language? Which one?

72. Do you read newspapers, magazines? Which ones? Any Hungarian ones? Any books?

SELF RANKING

a. If you had to describe how well you speak Hungarian which would
   you say:

   1 = Perfect Felsőőr Hungarian, as well as any native in Oberwart
   2 = Very well but not perfect
   3 = Moderately well
   4 = Not so good
   5 = Hardly at all

b. If you had to describe how well you speak German which would
   you say:

   1 = Perfect everyday Oberwart German
   2 = Very well but not perfect
   3 = Moderately well
   4 = Not so good
   5 = Hardly at all

Appendix 2

Language Choice, Peasantness and Social Network

Comparison of Absolute Rank Differences Between Peasantness and Language Choice and Between Social Network and Language Choice for All Speakers

Speaker	Language choice rank[a]	Peasant rank[a]	Peasantness of Network rank[a]	Absolute rank difference between peasant and language	Absolute rank difference between network and language	Language choice predicted better[b] N = Network P = Peasant
A	1.5	4.5	2	3	.5	N
B	1.5	8.5	1	7	.5	N
C	3	4.5	3.5	1.5	.5	N
D	4	18.5	19	14.5	15	P
E	6	4.5	10.5	1.5	4.5	P
F	6	1	8	5	2	N
G	6	8.5	6	2.5	0	N
H	8.5	22.5	20	14	11.5	N
I	8.5	27.5	23	19	14.5	N
J	10.5	4.5	7	6	3.5	N
K	10.5	20.5	13	10	2.5	N
L	12	14	12	2	0	N
M	13	11	3.5	2	9.5	P
N	14	4.5	9	9.5	5	N
O	15.5	4.5	14.5	11	1	N
P	15.5	13	10.5	2.5	5	P

Appendix 2 (cont.)

Speaker	Language choice rank[a]	Peasant rank[a]	Peasantness of network rank[a]	Absolute rank difference between peasant and language	Absolute rank difference between network and language	Language choice predicted better[b] N = Network P = Peasant
Q	19.5	24	27	4.5	7.5	P
R	19.5	16	18	3.5	1.5	N
S	19.5	10	5	9.5	14.5	P
T	19.5	16	14.5	3.5	5	P
U	19.5	12	16.5	7.5	3	N
V	19.5	20.5	16.5	1	3	P
W	23.5	32	26	8.5	2.5	N
X	23.5	27.5	25	4	1.5	N
Y	25.5	22.5	29	3	3.5	P
Z	25.5	18.5	21	7	4.5	N
A1	28	27.5	28	.5	0	N
B1	28	31	32	3	4	P
C1	28	27.5	23	.5	5	P
D1	31	27.5	31	3.5	0	N
E1	31	27.5	30	3.5	1	N
F1	31	16	23	15	8	N

NOTE: Speakers appearing here are the same as those in Table 5.1. Their ranks with respect to language choice are based on interview data as shown in Table 5.1. Chapter 5 describes the way in which speakers were ranked with respect to peasantness and with respect to the peasantness of their social networks.

[a] When two or more speakers were tied in their ordered position the average of the ranks was assigned to the tied speakers.

[b] A smaller absolute rank difference is a better prediction of speakers' rank with respect to language choice.

Total predicted better by peasantness rank: 11.

Total predicted better by network rank: 21.

References

Agar, M.
   1973   *Ripping and running: A formal ethnography of urban heroin addicts.* New York: Academic.
Albert, E.
   1972   Cultural patterning of speech behavior in Burundi. In Gumperz and Hymes (Eds.), *Directions in sociolinguistics.* New York: Holt, Rinehart & Winston. 72–105.
Bader, W. B.
   1966   *Austria between East and West, 1945–1955.* Stanford: Stanford University Press.
Bailey, C.-J. N.
   1970   Building Rate into a Dynamic Theory of Linguistic Description. *Working Papers in Linguistics* (University of Hawaii), 2(9):161–233.
   1974   *Variation and linguistic theory.* Washington, D.C.: Georgetown University Press.
Bárczi, G., Benkő L., and Berrár, J.
   1967   *A Magyar Nyelv Története [History of the Hungarian language].* Budapest: Tankönyvkiadó.
Barnes, J. A.
   1974   *Social networks.* Reading Mass.: Addison-Wesley Modular Pub. Addison-Wesley.
Barth, F.
   1969   Introduction. In F. Barth (ed.) *Ethnic groups and boundaries.* Boston: Little, Brown. Pp. 1–8.
Bauman, R. and Scherzer, J.
   1974   Introduction. In *Explorations in the ethnography of speaking.* London: Cambridge University Press. Pp. 6–12.
Bedi, R.
   1912   *A soproni Hiene nyelvjárás hangtana [The phonetics of the Hienc, German dialect of Sopron].* Sopron: Romwalter Nyomda.

Benkő, L.

1967a *Magyar nyelvjárástörténet* [*Hungarian dialect history*]. *Magyar Nyelvészeti Füzetek* [*Hungarian Linguistics Monographs*]. Budapest: Tankönyvkiadó.

1967b (Ed.) *Magyar nylev történeti etimológiai szótára* [*Etymological dictionary of Hungarian*] Vols. I and II. Budapest: Akadémiai Kiadó.

Benyon, E. D.

1939 Migrations of Hungarian peasants. *Geographical Review* 27:214–228.

Bickerton, D.

1973 The nature of a Creole continuum. *Language* 49(3):640.

1975 *Dynamics of a Creole system.* London: Cambridge University Press.

Blom, J.-P., and Gumperz, J. J.

1972 Social meaning in linguistic structures: Code switching in Norway. In J. Gumperz and D. Hymes (Eds.) *Directions in sociolinguistics.* New York: Holt, Rinehart, & Winston. Pp. 407–434.

Bloch, M.

1975 Introduction. In M. Bloch (Ed.) *Political language and oratory in traditional society.* London: Academic.

Bloomfield, L.

1933 *Language.* New York: Holt, Rinehart & Winston.

Bott, E.

1971 *Family and social network.* 2nd ed. New York: Free Press.

Breu, J.

1970 *Die Kroatensiedlung im Burgenland und in den anschliessenden Gebieten.* Vienna.

Brosnahan, L. F.

1963 Some historical Cases of language imposition. In J. Spencer (Ed.), *Language in Africa.* Cambridge: Cambridge Univ. Press. Pp. 7–24.

Brown, R., and Gilman, A.

1960 The pronouns of power and solidarity. In T. Sebeok (Ed.), *Style in language.* Cambridge, Mass.: MIT Press. Pp. 253–76.

Brudner, L.

1972 The maintenance of bilingualism in Southern Austria. *Ethnology XI*:39–54.

Bundesamt für Statistik

1928 *Statistisches Handbuch für die Republik Österreich.* Vienna.

1937 *Statistisches Handbuch für die Republic Österreich.* Vienna.

Bundesministerium für Landesverteidegung

1972 *Das Burgenland: Eine Wurdigung anlässich seines 50 jahrigen Bestehens als Bundesland der Republik Österreich.* Vienna.

Burghardt, A.

1962 *Borderland: A historical and geographical study of Burgenland.* Madison, Wis.: University of Wisconsin Press.

1972 Reply to Zimmerman. *Austrian History Yearbook VII:*89–96.

Burke, K.

1935 *Permanence and change: An anatomy of purpose.* New York: New Republic.

Carden, G.

1973 Disambiguation, favored readings and variable rules. In C.-J. Bailey and R. Shuy (Eds.) *New ways of analyzing variation in English.* Washington, D.C.: Georgetown University Press. Pp. 171–182.

Cedergren, H.

1973 On the nature of variable constraints. In C.-J. N. Bailey and R. W. Shuy (Eds.) *New ways of analyzing variation in English.* Washington, D.C.: Georgetown University Press. Pp. 13–22.

Cedergren, H., and Sankoff, D.
1974 Variable rules: Performance as a statistical reflection of competence. *Language* *50*:333–55.

Chaianov, A. V.
1931 The socio-economic nature of peasant farm economy. In P. A. Sorokin, C. C. Zimmerman, and C. J. Galpin (Eds.), *A systematic sourcebook in rural sociology.* Minnesota: University of Minnesota Press. Pp. 144–145.

Chen, M.
1972 The time dimension: Contribution toward a theory of sound change. *Foundations of Language 8*:457–498.

Chomsky, N.
1965 *Aspects of the theory of syntax.* Cambridge, Mass.: MIT Press.

Cole, J. W.
1973 Social process in the Italian Alps. *American Anthropologist 75*:765–786.

Cole, J.,and Wolf,E.
1974 *The hidden frontier.* New York: Academic.

Cooper, R. L., and Horvath, R. J.
1973 Language, migration and urbanization in Ethiopia. *Anthropological Linguistics 15*:5:221.

DeCamp, D.
1971 Implicational scales and sociolinguistic linearity. *Linguistics 73*:30–43.

Deutsch, K. W.
1942 The trend of European nationalism: The language aspect. *American Political Science Review 36*:533–541.

Dougherty, J.
1977 Color categorization in West Futunese: Variability and change. In M. Sanches and B. Blount (Eds.) *Sociocultural dimensions of language change.* Academic. Pp. 103–188.

Dovring, F.
1965 *Land and labour in Europe, 1900–1950.* The Hague: Martinus Nijhoff.

Éhen, G.
1905 *Vasvármegye Közgazdasági Leírása* [*Economic description of Vas Province*]. Budapest.

Elliott, D., Legum, S., and Thompson, S. A.
1969 Syntactic variation as linguistic data. In R. Binnick *et al.* (Eds.) *Papers from the 5th Regional Meeting of the Chicago Linguistic Society.* Chicago: University of Chicago Press. Pp. 52–9.

Erdei, F.
1938 *Parasztok* [*Peasants*]. Budapest: Adadémiai Kiadó.

Ervin-Tripp, S.
1972 On sociolinguistic rules: Alternation and co-occurrence. In J. Gumperz and D. Hymes (Eds.) *Directions in sociolinguistics.* New York: Holt, Rinehart & Winston. Pp. 213–250.

Fasold, R. W.
1970 Two models of socially significant linguistic variation. *Language 46*(2):551.

Fél, E., and Hofer, T.
1969 *Proper peasants.* Chicago: Aldine.

Ferguson, C.
1964 Diglossia. In D. Hymes (Ed.) *Language in culture and society.* New York: Harper and Row. Pp. 429–437.

188 REFERENCES

Fishman, J.
1964 Language maintenance and language shift as fields of inquiry. *Linguistics 9*:32–70.
1965 Language maintenance and language shift: The American immigrant case within a general theoretical perspective. *Sociologus XVI*:19–38.
1966 *Language loyalty in the United States.* The Hague:Mouton.
1968 Sociolinguistic perspective on the study of bilingualism. *Linguistics 39*:21–49.
1971 The relationship between micro- and macro-sociolinguistics. In J. Fishman *et al.* (eds.) *Bilingualism in the Barrio.* Bloomington, Indiana: Indiana University and Mouton. Pp. 583–604. (Reprinted in J. Gumperz and D. Hymes (eds.), *Directions in sociolinguistics.* New York: Holt Rinehart and Winston 1972).
Franklin, S. H.
1969 *The European peasantry.* London: Metheun.
Frake, C.
1964 How to ask for a drink in Subanun. In J. Gumperz and D. Hymes (Eds.) *The ethnography of communication, American Anthropologist 66*(6:II)127–132.
1972 "Struck by speech": The Yakan concept of litigation. In J. Gumperz and D. Hymes (Eds.) *Directions in sociolinguistics.* New York: Holt, Rinehart & Winston. Pp. 106–129.
Friedl, J.
1972 Changing economic emphasis in an Alpine village. *Anthropological Quarterly 45*(3):145.
Friedrich, P.
1972 Social context and semantic feature: The Russian pronominal usage. In J. Gumperz and D. Hymes (Eds.) *Directions in sociolinguistics.* New York: Holt, Rinehart & Winston. Pp. 270–300.
Gaál, K.
1966 Gemeinschaft, Sänger und Lieder. In *Spinnstubenlieder–Lieder der Fraugemeinschaften in den Magyarischen Sprachinseln im Burgenland.* München–Zürich: Verlag Schnell und Steiner. Pp. 11–33.
Gaál, K.
1969 *Zum bäuelichen Gerätestand im 19, und 29, Jahrhundert.* Vienna: Hermann Böhlaus.
Gal, S.
1974 Közelkép egy nyelvszigetről: A magyar nyelv helyzete Felsőőrben [A speech island close-up: Hungarian language maintenance in Felsőőr, Austria]. In Hofer Tamás, Kisbán Eszter, Kaposvári Gyula (Eds.), *Faluk (villages).* Szolnok: Magyar Néprajz Társaság. Pp. 169–134.
1977 *Der Gebrauch der deutschen und ungarischen Sprache in Oberwart.* In L. Triber (Ed.) *Die Obere Wart.* Oberwart.
1978 Peasant men can't get wives: Language change and sex roles in a bilingual community. *Language in Society 7*:1–16.
Garfinkel, H.
1967 *Studies in ethnomethodology.* Englewood Cliffs, N.J.: Prentice-Hall.
Geoghegan, W.
1969 The use of marking rules in semantic systems. *Working Paper #26, Language Behavior Research Laboratory,* University of California, Berkeley.
1971 Information processing systems in culture. In P. Kay (Ed.) *Explorations in mathematical anthropology.* Cambridge, Mass.: MIT Press. Pp. 4–35.
Goffman, E.
1959 *The presentation of self in everyday life.* New York: Doubleday.
1967 On face-work. In *Interaction ritual.* New York: Anchor.
Golde, G.
1975 *Catholics and Protestants: Agricultural modernization in two German villages.* New York: Academic.

Gräftner, P.
1966   *Lautlehre der Ortsmundarten von Apetlon, Gols, Weiden, im burgenlandischen Seewinkel.* Unpublished Ph.D. dissertation, University of Vienna, Vienna.

Gumperz, J. J.
1958   Dialect differences and social stratification in a North Indian village. *American Anthropologist 60*:668–682.
1964   Linguistic and social interaction in two communities. In J. Gumperz and D. Hymes (Eds.) *The ethnography of communication. American Anthropologist 66*(6:II):137–154.
1968   Types of linguistic communities. In J. Fishman (Ed.) *The sociology of language.* The Hague:Mouton. Pp. 460–470.
1969   Communication in multilingual societies. In S. Tyler (Ed.) *Cognitive anthropology.* New York: Holt, Rinehart and Winston. Pp. 435–48.
1970   Verbal strategies in multilingual communication. *Working Paper #36, Language Behavior Research Laboratory,* University of California, Berkeley.
1972   Introduction. In J. Gumperz and D. Hymes (Eds.) *Directions in sociolinguistics.* New York: Holt, Rinehart & Winston. Pp. 1–25.
1974   The sociolinguistics of interpersonal communication. Ms.
1976a. The sociolinguistic significance of conversational code-switching. *Working Paper #46, Language Behavior Research Laboratory,* University of California, Berkeley.
1976b Social networks and language shift. *Working Paper #46, Language Behavior Research Laboratory,* University of California, Berkeley.

Gumperz, J. J., and Bennett, A.
in   Language and society. In I. Rossi (Ed.) *Man in culture.* New York: Praeger. Pp.
press. 1–38 in manuscript.

Gumperz, J. J., and Hernandez, E.
1971   *Bilingualism, bidialectalism and classroom interaction.* In *Language in social groups: Essays by J. J. Gumperz.* Palo Alto: Stanford University Press. Pp. 311–339.

Gumperz, J. J., and Wilson, R.
1971   Convergence and creolization: A case from the Indo-Aryan/Dravidian border in India. In D. Hymes (Ed.) *Pidginization and Creolization of languages.* London: Cambridge University Press. Pp. 151–167.

Guttman, L.
1944   A basis for scaling quantitative data. *American Sociological Review 9*(2):140–150.

Gyenge, I.
1973   *200 Jahre reformierte Kirche in Oberwart–200 éves a felsőőri református templom.* Oberwart.

Harmaan, H.
1975   *Soziologie und Politik der Sprachen Europas.* München: Deutscher Taschenbuch Verlag.

Hechter, M.
1975   *Internal colonialism: The Celtic fringe in British national development, 1536–1966.* Berkeley, Calif.: Univ. of California Press.

Hoffman, G. W.
1967   The political–geographic basis of the Austrian national problem. *Austrian History Yearbook 3*(1):122.

Honigmann, J. J.
1963   Bauer and Arbeiter in a rural Austrian community *SWJA 19*:40–53.

Hornung, M., and Roitinger, F.
1950   Burgenland. In *Unsere Mundarten* Vienna. Pp. 47–55.

Hymes, D.
1962 The ethnography of speaking. In T. Gladwin and William C. Sturtevant (Eds), *Anthropology and human behavior*. Washington, D.C.: Anthropology Society of Washington. Pp. 13–53.
1968 Linguistic problems in defining the concept of 'tribe'. In June Helm (Ed.) *Essays on the problem of tribe*. Seattle: University of Washington Press.
1972 Models of the interaction of language and social life. In J. Gumperz and D. Hymes (Eds.) *Directions in sociolinguistics*. New York: Holt, Rinehart & Winston. Pp. 35–71.

Imre, S.
1940 Felsőőr helynevei [*Place names in Felsőőr*]. *Magyar Nyelv II:*47–80.
1941 A *felsőőri földmŭvelés* [*Felsőőr agriculture*]. *Dolgozatok a Magyar Királyi Ferenc József Tudományegyetem Nyelvtudományi Intézetéből #3* [*Papers of the Franz Joseph Royal Hungarian University's Linguistic Institute*]. Kolozsvár.
1942 Az é hangok állapota a felsőőri nép nyelvében [The 'e' Sounds in the Folk Dialect of Felsőőr]. *Magyar Nyelv II:*115–29.
1943 Német kölcsönszók a felsőőri magyarság nyelvében [German loan words in the Hungarian dialect of Felsőőr]. *Magyar Nyelv IV:*183–95.
1971a A *mai magyar nyelvjárások rendszere* [*The structure of today's Hungarian dialects*]. Budapest: Akadémiai Kiadó.
1971b A *Felsőőri nyelvjárás* [*The Felsőőr dialect*]. *Nyelvtudományi Értékezések #72* [*Linguistic Monographs #72*]. Budapest: Akadémiai Kiadó.
1973a Az ausztriai (Burgenland) magyar szorványok [The Hungarian Ethnic Groups in Austria]. In *Népi kultura népi társadalom* [*Folk culture, folk society–Yearbook VII of the Ethnography Group of the Hungarian Academy of Sciences*]. Budapest: Akadémiai Kiadó.
1973b *Felsőőri Tájszotár* [*Felsőőr dialect dictionary*]. Budapest: Akadémiai Kiadó.
1977 Der ungarische Dialect der Oberen Wart. In L. Triber (Ed.), *Die Obere Wart* Oberwart. Pp. 301–308.

Irvine, J.
1974 Strategies and status manipulation in the Wolof greeting. In R. Bauman and J. Scherzer (Eds.), *Explorations in the ethnography of speaking*. London: Cambridge University Press. Pp. 167–191.

Jakobson, R.
1960 Concluding statement: Linguistics and poetics. In T. Sebeok (Ed.), *Style in language*, Cambridge, Mass.: Harvard U. Press. Pp. 350–377.

Jászi, O.
1929 *The dissolution of the Habsburg monarchy*. Chicago: University of Chicago Press.

Karner, H.
1930 *Lautlehre der hienzischen Mundart von Rechnitz und Umgebung*. Unpublished Ph.D. dissertation, University of Vienna, Vienna.

Kay, P.
1975 Synchronic variability and diachronic change in basic color lexicon. *Language in Society 4*(3):257–270.
1978 Variable rules, community grammar and linguistic change. In D. Sankoff (Ed.) *Linguistic variation: Models and methods*. New York: Academic.

Keenan, E.
1974 Norm-makers, norm-breakers: Uses of speech by men and women in a Malagasy community. In Richard Bauman and Joel Scherzen (Eds.), *Explorations in the ethnography of speaking*. London: Cambridge University Press. Pp. 125–143.

Keller, R. E.
1961 Upper Austrian. In *German dialects: Phonology and morphology*. Manchester: Manchester University Press. Pp. 200–247.

Khera, S.
1972a An Austrian peasant village under rural industrialization. *Behavior Science Notes* *1*:29–36.
1972b Kin ties and social interaction in an Austrian peasant village with divided land inheritance. *Behavior Science Notes 4*:349–365.
1973 Social stratification and land inheritance among Austrian peasants. *American Anthropologist 75*:814–823.

Kniezsa, I.
1938 Magyarország népei a XI században [Hungary's people in the XI century]. In *Emlékkönyv Szt. István halálanak 900-ik evfordulójára [Essays on the Occasion of the 900th Anniversary of the Death of St. Stephan]*. Budapest.

Kovács, M.
1942 A *felsőőri magyar népsziget [The Felsőőr Hungarian folk island]. Települési és nepiségtörténeti értekezések #6 [Settlement and Ethnic History Monographs #6]*. Budapest: Sylvester Nyomda.

Kranzmayer, E.
1955 Hochsprache und Mundarten in den österreichischen Landschaften. *Wirkendes Wort VI*:262–9.
1956 *Historische Lautgeographie des gesamtbairischen Dialektraumes*. Graz-Köln: Hermann Böhlaus.
1972 *Die burgenländische Siedlungsnamengebung innerhalb des Rahmens der zwei, Sprachländer im Lichte der strengen Gruppenforschung. In Internationales kulturhistorisches Symposium 1969: Österreich und die Türken*. Mogersdorf.

Laberge, S., and Chiasson-Lavoie, M.
1971 Attitudes face au Francais parlé à Montréal et degrès de conscience de variables linguistique. In R. Darnell (Ed.) *Linguistic Diversity in Canadian Society*. Edmonton. Pp. 89–126.

Labov, W.
1963 On the social motivation of a sound change. *Word 19*:273–309.
1964 Phonological correlates of social stratification. In J. Gumperz and D. Hymes (Eds.), *The ethnography of communication. American Anthropologist* 66(6:II):164–175.
1965 On the mechanism of linguistic change. Charles W. Kreidler (Ed.), *Georgetown University Monograph Series on Languages and Linguistics, No. 18*. Pp.: 91–114; 131–132. (Reprinted in J. Gumperz and D. Hymes, Eds., *Directions in sociolinguistics*, 1972, pp. 512–538.)
1969 Contraction, deletion and inherent variability in the copula. *Language 45*(4):715–762.
1970 The study of language in its social context. *Studium Generale 23*:30–87.
1972 *Sociolinguistic patterns*. Philadelphia: University of Pennsylvania Press.
1973 On the linguistic consequences of being a lame. *Language in Society 2*:81–115.

Labov, S., and Waletzky, J.
1967 Narrative analysis: Oral versions of personal experience. In *Essays on the verbal and visual arts. Proceedings of 1966 Meeting of American Ethnological Society*. Seattle: University of Washington Press.

Laky, A.
1937 *Lautlehre der Mundart des Pinkatales*. Unpublished Ph.D. dissertation, University of Vienna. Vienna.

192   REFERENCES

Lieberson, S.
1970   *Language and ethnic relations in Canada.* New York: J. Wiley.
Lockwood, W.
1973   The peasant worker in Yugoslavia. *SES 1*:91–110.
Lyons, J.
1971   *Introduction to theoretical linguistics.* London: Cambridge University Press.
Ma, R., and Herasimchuk, E.
1971   The linguistic dimensions of a bilingual neighborhood. In Joshua Fishman (Ed.), *Bilingualism in the Barrio. Final Report on OECD 1-7-062817.* Washington, D.C.: Office of Education.
Macartney, C. A.
1937   Hungary and her successors: The treaty of Trianon and its consequences, 1919–1937. London: Oxford Univ. Press.
Magyar Statisztikai Közlemények [Hungarian Statistical Reports].
1910   Budapest.
Mead, G. H.
1934   *Mind, self and society.* Chicago: University of Chicago Press.
Mills, C. W.
1940   Situated actions and vocabularies of motive. *American Sociological Review V*:904–913.
Miller, W.
1971   The death of a language or serendipity among the Shoshoni. *Anthropological Linguistics 13*(3):114.
Minge-Kalman, W.
1978   A theory of the European household economy during the peasant worker transition: With an empirical test from the Swiss Alpine village. *Ethnology* (April).
Mitchell, J. C.
1971   The concept and use of social networks. In J. C. Mitchell (Ed.), *Social networks in urban situations.* Manchester: Manchester University Press.
Moór, E.
1936   *Westungarn im Mittelalter im Spiegel der Ortsnamen.* Szeged.
Nagy, I.
1937   *Nyugatmagyarorsrá Ausztriában.* Pérf.
Österreichisches Statistisches Zentralamt
1964   *Die Zusammensetzung der Wohnbevolkerung Österreichs nach allgemeinen demographischen und kulturellen Merkmalen, 1951, 1961.* Vienna.
1971   *Statistisches Zentralamt Volkszählungs Ergebnisse*, 1951, 1961, 1971. Vienna.
1972a   *Statistisches Jahrbuch österreichischer Städte, 1971.* Vienna.
1972b   *Statistisches Jahrbuch für die Republik Österreich.* Vienna.
Pfalz, A.
1951   Mundart des Landes. In *Burgenland Landeskunde.* Vienna: Burgenlandische Landesregierung. Pp. 380–385.
Puhr, F.
1925   *Pörgölény község és környéke hienc nyelvjárásńak hangtana [Phonetics of the German dialect of Pörgölény and vicinity].* Unpublished Ph.D. dissertation, University of Budapest, Budapest.
Rauchbauer, P.
1932   *Die deutschen Mundarten im nördlichen Burgenlande.* Unpublished Ph.D. dissertation, University of Vienna, Vienna.
Rubin, J.
1968   Bilingual usage in Paraguay. In Joshua Fishman (Ed.), *Readings in the sociology of language.* The Hague: Mouton. Pp. 512–530.

Ryan, A., ed.
1973 *The philosophy of social explanation.* London: Oxford University Press.
Sacks, H.
1972 On the analyzability of stories by children. In J. Gumperz and D. Hymes (Eds.), *Directions in sociolinguistics.* New York: Holt, Rinehart & Winston. Pp. 325–345.
Sankoff, D., and Laberge, S.
1978 The linguistic market and the statistical explanation of variability. In D. Sankoff (Ed.), *Linguistic variation: Models and methods.* New York: Academic.
Sankoff, G.
1971 Quantitative analysis of sharing and variability in a cognitive model. *Ethnology* X(4):389–408.
1972 Language use in multilingual societies: Some alternate approaches. In J. Pride and J. Holmes (Eds.), *Readings in sociolinguistics.* London: Penguin.
1974 A quantitative paradigm for the study of communicative competence. In R. Bauman and J. Scherzer (Eds.), *Explorations in the ethnography of speaking.* London: Cambridge University Press. Pp. 18–49.
1976 Political power and linguistic inequality in Papua, New Guinea. In William O'Barr (Ed.), *Politics and language.* New York: Academic.
1977 Creolization and syntactic change in New Guinea Tok Pisin. In M. Sanches and B. Blount (Eds.), *Sociocultural dimensions of language change.* New York: Academic.
Sankoff, G., and Cedergren, H.
1971 Some results of a sociolinguistic study of Montreal French. In R. Darnell (Ed.), *Linguistic diversity in Canadian society.* Edmonton. Pp. 61–87.
Saussure, F. de.
1959 *Course in general linguistics* (Translated by Wade Baskin). New York: McGraw Hill.
Seidelmann, E.
1957 *Lautlehre der Mundart vom Morbisch am Neusiedlersee.* Unpublished Ph.D. dissertation, University of Vienna, Vienna.
Shanin, T.
1973 The nature and logic of the peasant economy. *Journal of Peasant Studies* 1:1:63–80.
Shuy, R., Wolfram, W., and Riley, W. K.
1967 *A study of social dialects in Detroit. Final Report, Project 6-1347.* Washington, D.C.: Office of Education.
Simić, A.
1973 *The peasant urbanites: A study of rural-urban mobility in Serbia.* New York: Seminar Press.
Somogyi, L.
1966 *Die burgenlandischen Maygaren in geographischer Sicht.* Unpublished Ph.D. dissertation, University of Graz, Graz.
Soós, K.
1971 *Burgenland az europai politikában 1918–1921* [*Burgenland in European Politics 1918–1921*]. Budapest: Akadémiai Kiadó.
Sozán, M.
1974 Alsóőr 1974-ben: Szociál-antropológiai helyzetkép egy burgenlandi faluról [Alsóőr in 1974: Portrait of a Burgenland village]. In Hofer Tamás, Kisbán Eszter, Kaposvári Gyula (Eds.), *Faluk* [*Villages*]. Szolnok Magyar Néprajz Társaság. Pp. 159–168.
1976 Sociocultural transformation in East Central Europe: The case of the Hungarian peasant-workers in Burgenland. *East Central Europe* 2:195–209.

Stadler, K.
1971 *Austria.* New York: Praeger.
Sudnow, D. (Ed.)
1972 *Studies in social interaction.* New York: Macmillan.
Tabournet-Keller, A.
1968 Social factors of language maintenance and language shift: A methodological approach based on European and African examples. In J. Fishman, C. Ferguson and J. Das Gupta (Eds.), *Language problems in developing nations.* New York: John Wiley.
Tagányi, B.
1913 Gyepű és Gyepűelve [*the Gyepű System*]. *Magyar Nyelv IX*:97–266.
Timm, L. A.
1973 Modernization and language shift: The case of Brittany. *Anthropological Linguistics 15*(6):281.
Tóth, J.
1971 *Az Őrségek népi épitészete* [*Folk architecture of the Őrség region*]. Műszaki Könyvkiadó.
Trudgill, P.
1972 Sex, covert prestige and linguistic change in the urban British English of Norwich. *Language in Society* 1:179–195.
Tucker, R. G., and Lambert, W. E.
1969 White and negro listeners' reactions to various American-English dialects. *Social Forces 47*:4.
Varga, I.
1903 A Felsőőrvidék népe és nyelve [The people and language of Felsőőr and vicinity]. *Nyelvészeti Füzetek IX.*
Végh, J.
1959 *Őrségi és Hetési nyelvatlasz* [*Dialect atlas of Őrség and Hetés countries*]. Budapest: Akadémiai Kiadó.
Wall, M.
1969 The decline of the Irish language. In Brian Ó. Cuív (ed.), *A view of the Irish language.* Dublin.
Wallace, A. F. C.
1961 *Culture and personality.* 2nd ed. New York: Random House.
Wallner, E.
1926 A Felsőőrvidéki Magyarság települése [The settlement pattern of the Hungarians of Felsőőr and Vicinity]. *Földrajzi Közlemények 54*(i–iv):1–36.
Wambaugh, S.
1933 *Plebiscites since the World War.* Washington, D.C.
Wang, W., S.-Y.
1969 Competing changes as a cause of residue. *Language 45*:9–25.
Waterman, J. T.
1976 A history of the German language. rev. ed. Seattle: U. of Washington Press.
Weinreich, U.
1953 *Languages in contact.* New York: Columbia University Press.
Weinreich, U., Labov, W., and Herzog, M.
1968 Empirical foundations for a theory of language change. In W. Lehmann (Ed.) *Proceedings of the Texas Conference on Historical Linguistics.* Austin, Texas: University of Texas Press. Pp. 97–195.

Wenger, C.
 1977   *Welsh language and nationalism.* Unpublished doctoral dissertation. University of
        California, Berkeley.
Wiesinger, P.
 1967   Mundart und Geschichte in der Steiermark: ein Beitrag zur Dialektgeographie eines
        österreichischen Bundeslandes. In L. E. Schmitt (Ed.) *Beitrag zur oberdeutschen
        Dialektologie. Deutsche Dialektgeographie (Marburg) 51*:81–184.
Wolf, E.
 1966   *Peasants.* Englewood Cliffs. N.J.: Prentice-Hall.
Wolfram, W.
 1972   Linguistic assimilation in the children of immigrants. *The Linguistic Reporter
        14*(1):1.
Wolfson, N.
 1976   Speech events and natural speech: Some implications for sociolinguistic methodol-
        ogy. *Language in Society 5*:189–209.
Zimányi, V.
 1972   Comments on Zimmermann. *Austria History Yearbook VIII*:80–83.
Zimmermann, F.
 1972   The role of Burgenland in the history of the Habsburg monarchy. *Austrian History
        Yearbook VIII*:7–38.

Subject Index

LANGUAGE, THOUGHT, AND CULTURE: *Advances in the Study of Cognition*

Under the Editorship of: E. A. HAMMEL

DEPARTMENT OF ANTHROPOLOGY
UNIVERSITY OF CALIFORNIA
BERKELEY

Stephen A. Tyler, The Said and the Unsaid: Mind, Meaning, and Culture

Susan Gal, Language Shift: Social Determinants of Linguistic Change in Bilingual Austria

In preparation

Ronald Scollon and Suzanne B. K. Scollon, Linguistic Convergence: An Ethnography of Speaking at Fort Chipewyan, Alberta

Elizabeth Bates, The Emergence of Symbols: Cognition and Communication in Infancy